MOUNTAINS
A PASSION FOR CLIMBING
IN MY HEART

MOUNTAINS
A PASSION FOR CLIMBING
IN MY HEART

GERLINDE KALTENBRUNNER

WITH KARIN STEINBACH TARNUTZER | TRANSLATION BY BILLI BIERLING

MOUNTAINEERS
BOOKS

Mountaineers Books is the nonprofit publishing division of The Mountaineers, an organization founded in 1906 and dedicated to the exploration, preservation, and enjoyment of outdoor and wilderness areas.

MOUNTAINEERS BOOKS

1001 SW Klickitat Way, Suite 201 • Seattle, WA 98134
800.553.4453 • www.mountaineersbooks.org

Original German-language edition, *Ganz bei Mir*, © 2009 by Piper Verlag GmbH, Munich. Chapter 16 © 2013 by Piper Verlag GmbH, Munich
Translation copyright © 2014 by Billi Bierling

Quote on page 6: Herbert Tichy, *Land der namenlosen Berge*, revised and updated edition, Edition Sonnenaufgang, Vienna 2009.

Printed in the United States of America
17 16 15 14   1 2 3 4 5

Copy Editor: Carol Poole
Design and Layout: Heidi Smets Graphic Design, heidismets.com
All photographs © the author unless credited otherwise
Front cover photograph: *Gerlinde Kaltenbrunner with Central Rongbuk Glacier and the north face of Everest in the background* © Ralf Dujmovits
Back cover photograph: *Gerlinde Kaltenbrunner on Gasherbrum I* © Ralf Dujmovits

A catalog record for this book is available at the Library of Congress

♻ Printed on recycled paper
ISBN (paperback): 978-1-59485-856-7
ISBN (ebook): 978-1-59485- 857-4

CONTENTS

I believe that some things in this world are complete and impossible to outshine; things that are perfect in shape, sound or spirituality. It could be a statue from ancient Greece, one of Beethoven's symphonies or a passage from the Sermon on the Mount. Just as complete and perfect as these things are, are some of the mountains in the world.

—Herbert Tichy

ACKNOWLEDGMENTS

When the idea for this book was born, I didn't know that I would embark on a long and exhausting expedition with a lot of bad weather and other crises. First of all, I would like to thank the team of the original German-language publisher, Malik Publishing House, for having such great patience with me.

My special thanks go to: My sponsors and partners for their continuous support, without which I wouldn't have been able to go to the high mountains and achieve my dreams. My gratitude goes to OMV, Banner, VKB Bank, Schöffel, and Lowa as well as to Adidas Eyewear, Ökofen, the Upper Austria Tourism Board, Deuter, Komperdell, and the Friends of Nature of Austria.

My family, who has always given me support and strength in difficult times, despite our geographical distance.

My husband Ralf, with whom I have shared a lot of happy but also difficult moments within a very short period of time; who has supported me in achieving my dreams; and with whom I feel a very profound bond of love.

My friends, who are always in my thoughts and who show me understanding, even though I am often not there for them.

Father Erich Tischler, who introduced me to the world of nature and mountains by taking me on many beautiful hikes and climbs.

My climbing partners in the Alps and on numerous expeditions.

The Nepalese, Pakistanis, and Tibetans, who have allowed me to gain insight into their lives, who have supported me in many ways, and have accompanied me on many of my treks to the base camps of the 8000-meter peaks.

All those who follow my expeditions and presentations and give me strength and energy with their good wishes.

And last but not least, my co-author, Karin Steinbach Tarnutzer, who has done a wonderful job putting my tales into words.

This is why I climb 8000-meter peaks: Watching the sun rise over the twin peaks of Annapurna I after an acclimatization night at Camp 2 on Dhaulagiri. *(Photo by David Göttler)*

SHADOWS AND LIGHT

The crisp pink of dawn is making way for a brighter light toward the east. Day is slowly breaking, and a beautiful glow is spreading across the horizon beyond the mountains. A single ray of light is moving up higher, slowly changing the color of the sky to a pure, fresh blue. The light is getting more intense, and the sun is gradually coming up from behind the snow-covered peaks. Beginning as a mere crescent, it moves higher, its warm orange rays seeming to caress the mountain tops.

It is 5:00 a.m. and freezing cold. I am still wearing my warm wool hat with its huge earflaps. I probably still look sleepy, but my senses are wide awake. I am watching the sun rise behind the nameless 6000-meter peaks left of the Annapurnas. The sun's first rays are gently touching the twin peaks of Annapurna I, and the wide snow flank is glistening. I can hardly believe that I stood on one of its summits four years ago. Watching the day unfold above me at 6750 meters is a unique and moving experience.

Yesterday, David and I came up here from Dhaulagiri's Camp 1 and pitched our tent to spend an acclimatization night. Both of us slept well. There are a few other expeditions on the mountain, but they are currently at base camp or Camp 1.

We are alone, enjoying the peace and quiet. Later, we will go down to base camp to get some rest before we start our summit attempt.

Last year, I endured a few terrifying hours at Dhaulagiri's Camp 2, only 150 meters below where we are now. An avalanche buried my tent and my Spanish friends' tent as well. I was lucky that I managed to dig myself out of the snow. But my help came too late for Ricardo and Santi; when I reached them with my shovel, they were already dead. I often wondered why I survived and they did not. Now I have returned to the mountain that nearly took my life in May 2007. Of course, the memories of this tragic event are omnipresent, but the feeling of being surrounded by the beauty of the mountains and the intensity of the moment is a lot stronger. How is it possible that life and death, desperation and happiness, are so close together?

I sit in the snow next to our backpacks, absorbing the view, gazing in awe at the beauty around me. I see a bit of haze on the horizon, but otherwise the skies are completely clear. I live and climb 8000-meter peaks for these moments. Whenever I tell other people about my expeditions, I can sense that they only see the inconveniences of such an undertaking: the cold, the storms, and the dangers. Only a handful of people can relate to the intensely beautiful moments which are the reason why I keep coming back to the Himalaya. I seek these highlights: the overwhelming impressions of beauty, the intense sensation of being alive and being my pure self.

Up here, I am free; I can leave all responsibilities behind. I don't have to please anyone else. Far away from everything down there, I can be at one with myself. Whenever I succumb to the world of the high mountains I feel content, even-keeled, and filled with joy. When I climb I am determined; I feel independent and competent. I make my own clear decisions. In the mountains, I feel very differently than I do down in the valley. I am in my true element.

Just below Camp 3, with a few nameless 6000-meter and 7000-meter peaks in the background
(Photo by Ralf Dujmovits)

Using a makeshift "cable car" to cross an estuary of the Braldu River on our approach to Broad Peak. There were no bridges back then.

CHAPTER 1

CURIOSITY

W hen I reached the summit of my first 8000-meter peak, on July 2, 1994, I didn't feel as elated and happy as I had expected to feel. Of course, I was euphoric to have made it, but I was also very exhausted and worried about the descent. The feeling of sheer joy and contentment only overcame me once I was back at base camp. When I stood on the false (or fore) summit of Broad Peak at 8011 meters I couldn't quite believe it. Had I really made it up here? I had just wanted to have a go at an 8000-meter peak. I had wanted to find out whether I would be able to cope with the extreme cold everyone talked about. I wanted to know how it would feel to climb in thin air, or in the death zone, as altitudes above 7000 meters are called.

The ascent of 900 meters to the summit from our high camp was extremely exhausting. To this day I find high-altitude mountaineering very tiring, but I definitely reached my absolute limit on that first expedition. I guess my body was not used to it. I had never been higher than 4800 meters before, and compared to today, my body was not used to making all the adjustments to the low oxygen and the heavy breathing. I was twenty-three years old, and everything was new to me, from acclimatizing to melting snow for drinking water at high altitudes. Things I now do automatically took a lot of effort then; I had to concentrate hard to do everything right and not forget anything. Too busy focusing on myself, I was unable to pay much attention to the beautiful surroundings.

It was cold, the wind was freezing, and it was overcast. Base camp had vanished in the fog, and K2 was slowly disappearing, its summit just peeking out of the clouds but covered in thick mist lower down. We didn't even discuss whether we should continue to Broad Peak's true summit, which had completely disappeared. This was our summit, and this was where we would stop. Siegfried, Ernst, and I hugged each other, and a few tears rolled down my cheeks. I was thinking about my parents and my siblings, wondering whether they could possibly imagine what I was experiencing at that very moment. I had been thinking about my family over the course of the expedition, and they were still on my mind when I finally reached my goal. On Broad Peak in 1994, we didn't have a satellite phone; we used mail runners, not emails. I felt very far away from my family.

On July 2, 1994, the three of us were the only people on the summit. None of us had ever been so high. I had climbed many mountains with Siegfried, but this experience was very special. We first met when I was taking my final written exams to become a qualified nurse. I had actually noticed him earlier, but I had been only sixteen years old. A mountain guide from Windischgarsten, he gave a slide presentation about K2 in my home village of Spital am Pyhrn. He was a member of an Austrian expedition to K2 in the summer of 1986, when thirteen people died on the mountain. I had previously seen Willi Bauer's presentation about it—a truly dramatic story, especially because Fredl Imitzer, who was from Spital am Pyhrn, didn't come back. I asked my father whether he would let me go and see it. He gave me a hundred Austrian shillings and said, "Well, if you must!" He couldn't quite understand why I was interested in mountains. During his presentation, Siegfried talked less about the tragedy—he had not joined the summit attempt due to unstable weather—but more about the mountain range, the Karakorum. He showed pictures of the trek to base camp, the porters, Concordia, and the point where the glaciers meet. I was absolutely fascinated by this imposing mountain scenery. I knew that I wanted to go there one day!

By chance, Siegfried and I met again in the summer of 1990 at the annual beer festival in Spital am Pyhrn. He had shaved off his wild beard and looked so different that at first I didn't recognize him. We had a drink and our conversation immediately turned to climbing. I only discovered who he was after we had already made arrangements to go climbing together.

Luck was definitely on my side! I was a passionate climber, and now the experienced mountaineer Siegfried Wasserbauer was taking me climbing!

I didn't really climb difficult routes then. I had been on my first hikes with the Youth Club of the Catholic Church when I was eight. Every Friday, we would meet up to play, do handicrafts, sing, or rehearse for a play. One of the highlights of the Youth Club was the summer camp organized by Erich Tischler, the priest from Spital am Pyhrn who had christened me. Only children from the age of six were allowed to go, but because I begged relentlessly and my older sister Manuela was also there I was allowed to go, even though I was only five. The nine- to twelve-year-olds looked after me and another "little sister" Eva. We were especially attached to the "Youth Club Granny," Hermine Schwaighofer, who had been cooking for the club for eighteen years and was extremely popular. We went to Lake Almsee in Grünau in Upper Austria, and one day we visited the fairy-tale park, Schindlbach. Our priest—I affectionately called him "Father Tischler" up until my wedding day, when he suggested I address him by his first name—took a photo of Eva and me standing next to the mountain giant, Rübezahl. Looking at the picture today makes me smile; we were so short next to the giant that we only reached up to his knees. On the same outing, Eva, Mrs Schwaighofer, and I also visited the Hansel and Gretel scene, and when I saw the cat on the witch's shoulder, I cried out, "Grandma, is this the muscle cat?" I must have heard this expression somewhere without actually knowing what it meant. *(Translator's note: A "muscle cat" is the German expression for sore and stiff muscles after exercising.)*

From that year on, I was part of the summer camp team. While our days were filled with playing games, going on treasure hunts, or competing in the camp Olympics, we spent the evenings sitting around the campfire singing along to Father Tischler's guitar or accordion. I really enjoyed the jovial company of the other children. We had a lot of fun in the dormitory at night, shared the kitchen duty with different children, and were generally taught to develop a good sense of team spirit. The summer camp was the highlight of my year; its positive effects stayed with me for a long time afterward, but at the same time my impatient suffering caught up with me when I had to wait for months on end for the next camp. The word "home-sickness" never entered my vocabulary in those days.

Father Tischler was also a keen hiker who climbed at least one mountain with us during our time at the camp. I was not allowed to go on the hike on my first trip, but once I was old enough I enthusiastically joined them. Father Tischler later told me that I was one of the most eager and daring hikers in the group. I wanted to do everything; nothing seemed too much for me. I was always keen to go for a second summit; I could never get enough. These hikes were the crowning moments at summer camp for me. After a hearty breakfast in the morning, we would spend the whole day outside in the fresh air, devouring our snacks during the long rests, and listening carefully when Father Tischler talked of one of his mountain adventures.

From my very first day of school I went to children's service on Friday. I liked religious studies, and became an altar girl when I was twelve. Whenever I was on church duty I got up very early, snuck out of the house, and arrived at church at 6:45 a.m. In winter, it was still pitch black when I left home. The morning service started at 7:00 a.m., and afterward Father Tischler and I would walk back to school, where he had to teach religious studies and I had to attend my lessons. He could probably tell from my discipline that I was very good at pursuing my goals, and so he offered to take me and a few other altar girls hiking after Sunday mass. He didn't have to ask me twice. I eagerly joined these hikes, which took place at least once a fortnight. Because of his morning service, we could never set out before 11:30 a.m., so we usually climbed mountains in the surrounding area, such as the Großen Hengsten in the Niederen Tauern. On these hikes, Father Tischler taught us a lot of useful things, such as that a good mountaineer should always concentrate on every step; a group of climbers should adjust to the pace of the slowest; and you should always stay together and wait for one another. He also taught us that the best way to walk uphill was to use the whole foot and not only the toes, making it easier to put your heel on a rock on steep ground and keep the foot relatively flat. I still apply this technique today when I am trekking. Another one of Father Tischler's keen interests was hunting, and so he pointed out animal tracks and told us about wildlife. Those Sunday outings were a very enriching experience for all of us.

When I was thirteen a few other altar girls and I wanted to have a go at rock climbing, so Father Tischler took us on an easy route on the Sturzhahn in the Toten Range. Being roped up, touching the warm rock with my hands, and making airy steps on an exposed face absolutely fascinated me. I was over the moon when the Spital Alpine Club offered a climbing course at the summer camp the following year. On this course we learned how to tie knots and set up belays. In winter we went ski touring, and in spring Father Tischler rented mini skis from the mountain rescue team and whizzed down the valley with us.

One day, Father Tischler took my friend Isabella and me up Schafdach Mountain in the Sölk Valley. It was around the end of May or beginning of June when we embarked on this tour with our mini skis. As usual, Father Tischler went ahead; he always wanted to set the pace and never allowed us to go in front. Isabella and I didn't notice the dark clouds accumulating in the south, but we did notice that suddenly something weird was going on with Father Tischler's hair. It was standing on end. His hair being short and thin, it looked very funny and made us laugh. We were a bit surprised by his new static-electricity hairdo, but we enjoyed it, giggling like geese. Father Tischler never turned around. He just said, "You have to concentrate, girls. The weather is seriously deteriorating. We have to get to the summit quickly, so stop giggling!"

But when we saw that Isabelle's hair, which was shorter than mine, was also standing on end we were in stitches. My long hair was tied into a ponytail and didn't show any sign of static. Father Tischler turned around, and when he saw the state of Isabelle's hair, he looked absolutely terrified. He shouted at us to descend as fast as we could, even though we were only about 150 feet or less below the summit. Keeping a good safety distance between us, we skied down without having reached the summit. Back in the valley, he explained that the electricity of the approaching thunderstorm, which is extremely dangerous in the mountains, had caused our hair to stand on end. We'd had no idea that we could have been struck by lightning at any moment.

The next time I was faced with the perils of the mountains was when Father Tischler took my friend Silvia and me to the Dreistecken Ridge, which is a long ridge between the Großen Bösenstein and the Dreistecken Mountains in Austria. From the Edelraute Hut we climbed up toward the Bösenstein, but when a thunderstorm moved in we had to descend rapidly to get away from the ridge. The route to the summit was fixed with steel cables, which would have been far too dangerous to use in the thunderstorm. Father Tischler then led us through a narrow snow-packed couloir. Silvia slipped on the hard snow and hit a rock so badly that she needed sutures. Fortunately, this was the only mountain accident I witnessed in my younger years, and Silvia got off pretty lightly.

Erich Tischler often took children and teenagers on outings; the community trusted him. It was never a concern for my parents that I went climbing with him. At most, my parents were surprised by my enthusiasm for the mountains. We children considered ourselves lucky that we had this opportunity; he laughed a lot and knew how to make the days interesting for us. Once on the summit, we proudly signed the summit book and eagerly listened to Father Tischler naming the surrounding mountains. Sometimes, though, it was impossible to give him our undivided attention. There were too many other things distracting us, such as looking down the valley or throwing down rocks, which was completely forbidden.

Unfortunately, the hikes with Father Tischler stopped when I turned fifteen. That year I enrolled in the Social Services School in Rottenmann in Styria, a boarding school where I lived for two years, during which I had no time to join the Sunday outings. Over the years, Father Tischler and I kept in touch, and whenever we met I would tell him about the little adventures I was now doing independently. He always showed great interest and often knew the mountains I had climbed. Later, when I was an adult, he would follow my expeditions. Whenever I go back home to Spital, I visit him to express my gratitude and give him something back for what he taught me in my younger years. It was he who kindled my passion for the mountains.

Ever since the climb on the Sturzhahn, I had dreamed of climbing properly, using ropes, carabiners, and everything that goes along with them. Unfortunately, I had never had the opportunity to do so. So I was even more excited when I arranged to see Siegfried again in 1990. We went to a climbing wall in Styria called Pürgg, where we were climbed some grade V routes. We finished off by climbing a multi-pitch route on the 650-foot wall. I was very happy that evening; I had never felt so much enthusiasm about anything before. Siegfried and I got on very well and obviously liked each other—so much, in fact, that we quickly arranged another meeting. Of course, all of this was done in secret as Siegfried was fourteen years my senior, a fact which would have triggered endless discussions at home.

Soon afterward, we arranged to do a climb in the mountains. We decided upon the Kalbling south ridge in the Gesäuse Range. It was sunny the day we set out, and we climbed on solid rock. I was in high spirits. I climbed second, and every time I reached Siegfried at the belay I had a big smile on my face because I was so happy. I learned a lot that day: how to choose the right equipment, find the approach route, climb a multi-pitch route on a ridge, reach the summit, and descend. Altogether I had entered a fascinating new world. I loved moving on rock, and when I came home that night I was filled with pride and a lot of new emotions. The best thing about it was that rather than climbing on my own, as I had often done before, I was now sharing the climb with someone I really liked!

Once during this time Siegfried visited me in Vienna, where I was doing my internship until my oral exams in September. I picked him up from the station. As soon as we sat down in a café near my boarding school we immediately talked about climbing. Even though I am anything but a night owl, we talked until two o'clock in the morning. Siegfried told me about his expeditions and his plan to climb Mount Everest one day. I listened enthusiastically to every word he said, and finally I put into words what I had been thinking for a long time: "I also want to climb an 8000-meter peak one day."

Had I said this to anyone else, they probably would have thought I was insane, but Siegfried understood and simply said, "Yes, why not?"

By now, we had fallen in love. It wasn't long before we spent our first weekend together in the Dachstein Mountains. We intended to go to the Bischofsmütze and climb the southwest ridge of Hochkesselkopf, staying the night at the Hofpürgl Hut. As usual, Siegfried was leading the climb on Hochkesselkopf, when suddenly I heard a loud bang. I looked up and saw a huge boulder tumbling down toward me. I was lucky that it didn't hit me. I didn't think very much of it, but when I saw how pale Siegfried was when I reached him at the belay I realized how dangerous the situation must have been. The rope had loosened some of the rocks, and Siegfried couldn't see whether or not I or the other climbing teams were in the line of fire.

Siegfried and I did a lot of alpine climbing together. During that time, I learned a great deal and was soon able to do more difficult routes. We often climbed on Kalbling Mountain going whenever we had a day off together. I now worked for the district hospital in Rottenmann in Styria, which meant that I was financially independent and able to rent my own flat in Spital. With a cash advance from my dad, I bought a small car so I could drive to work through the Bosruck Tunnel. It was a Fiat Panda with four-wheel drive, which I needed to get to the mountains for ski mountaineering. I had not even applied for a job at Kirchdorf Hospital where my elder sister Brigitte was working. It was too far away from the mountains, and it was often foggy there. In Rottenmann the mountains were literally on my doorstep, which was important: Climbing had become a very big part of my life. Everything else revolved around it. It was in the mountains where I found happiness and contentment. When I stood on top of a peak gazing into the big wide world, I felt blissfully happy and free; here I was able to leave everything else behind and feel good in body and mind.

Siegfried trained me to climb safely on alpine terrain. He taught me everything I needed to know for alpine climbing: how to check hand- and footholds; place nuts, Flexible Friends, and slings; and set up a belay point on an unbolted route. I trusted him completely and felt safe when I was climbing with him. I totally relied on him until I became an independent alpinist myself. It didn't take very long until I started leading, which was important to me, and Siegfried encouraged me to do so. He introduced me to extreme mountaineering. We spent seven very intense years together and traveled a lot. In spring and fall we often went to Arco at Lake Garda in Italy, which gave us the opportunity to extend our climbing season. We also went to the Dolomites where we did a different route every day, often exploring the surrounding area on our mountain bikes in the afternoons. We shared the same passion and that was the basis of our relationship.

About a year after we started seeing each other, I moved in with Siegfried. He lived next to his parents' farm in a very modest hut, a short distance above the village of Windischgarsten. There was no bathroom, only a toilet and a sink, and the shower was in a corner in the kitchen. The big tiled stove in the kitchen, an that was fueled by firewood, was the only source of heating in the whole house; the water pipes often froze in the winter. Later, we made the house a bit warmer and cozier by connecting another fireplace to the chimney in the living room and converting one of the two rooms on the first floor into our bedroom.

Our little house was nestled in a beautiful setting. On one side we looked across lush meadows and a forest, and on the other side we could see the Pyhrgas and Bosruck mountains as well as the Stoder Valley. At dusk, deer came out of the forest to feed; in fall, we could hear the stags roaring in the evenings. The sunbaked grazing meadows around the house attracted many cows—it almost felt like living in an alpine pasture. I got along very well with Siegfried's parents as well as his brother and his family, who looked after the farm. I would sometimes help them in the cow stable or go next door to get fresh milk, which made my coffee even more delicious. This basic lifestyle really suited me even though it was not always easy. There was no access road to the hut, and the dirt road ended at the farm. My Panda sometimes got stuck in the snow despite its four-wheel drive, and I was always happy when Siegfried's brother pulled me out of the snow with his tractor.

We climbed intensely in the summer and went on many ski tours in the winter. Soon we added ice climbing to our repertoire. Siegfried was not that keen on it, but I absolutely loved it. I bought my own ice tools. One day I drove up the Hengst Pass to climb a route that was easy enough for me to solo. The steep sections of about fifteen to twenty feet in the ice gullies all flattened out on top, making them suitable for a solo ascent. I went on these outings on my days off, which were often during the week when everyone else had to work. A few times I went climbing in the frozen Vogelgesang Gorge, which was essentially a winter hike with a few steep sections. The only place where I felt a bit uncomfortable was the first steep section. I could hear the water gushing underneath the ice, which made me worry about drowning if the ice broke.

I loved ice climbing. No matter where I placed my tools, I could always tell by the sound of the metal hitting the ice whether the placement was solid or not. I filed my crampons with enthusiasm, making them grip much better. I practiced placing ice screws and constructing Abalakov anchors, a technique invented by the Soviet climber Vitaly Abalakov for putting protection in the ice. With an ice screw you drill two holes in the ice, making sure they interconnect at the end to form a V-like channel. You then take a cord, thread it through the holes, make a solid knot, and loop your rope through in order to rappel down. The quality of the ice always varied, depending on the temperature. (When placing ice screws it is important to assess the conditions first because the screws only offer solid protection in stable ice.) Frozen waterfalls fascinated me: They disappear in spring and newly form every winter. I also liked the fact that all safety gear is usually taken out of the ice without leaving any traces, at least on the classic ice routes, which were my favorites. I was not that keen on mixed climbing, which involves both rock and ice climbing.

Ice climbing requires a lot of strength and energy as well as concentration. Just as with rock climbing, I was completely focused on my moves and felt at one with myself. No matter whether it was on rock or ice, climbing gave me so much. I had found something that made me very happy.

Siegfried and I joined the Friends of Nature Association. While the Austrian Alpine Club was the main alpinists organization in Tyrol, the Friends of Nature was more active for the alpinists in eastern Austria. Unlike the Alpine Club, the Friends of Nature didn't concentrate only on local hiking and climbing groups, but also offered trips abroad. Siegfried and I regularly went climbing with some of the members of the association. It must have been around the beginning of 1993 that the group came up with the idea of organizing an expedition, something Siegfried and I had been thinking about for a long time. At one point we talked about

Pakistan, and I got very excited; at that time, I didn't know much about Nepal. Finally, I would be able to go to the Karakorum! We were looking for a mountain that was not too busy, not too technically difficult, and not too high, and so we came up with Broad Peak. Despite being one of the easiest 8000-meter peaks, the route is relentlessly steep. All eight members of our expedition were good technical climbers, but only two—Siegfried, and Nik Rafanovic—had experience on 8000-meter peaks. Everyone else would have to wait and see how they would cope with the altitude. I was eager to find out how it would feel up high, and how far I would get. I didn't even dream of climbing other 8000-meter peaks at the time. I knew from the outset that I wanted to climb with my own strength and without supplemental oxygen. Up until then, Mont Blanc had been my highest summit. I had not seen much of the world yet, so the run-up to the expedition was an extremely exciting time for me.

We started preparing for the trip about a year in advance. The first step was to apply for the relevant permits. We didn't use a local agency to arrange the trip for us, which was still possible at the time. Instead, we organized everything for ourselves, from applying for visas in Vienna to acquiring gear and money, and much more. In the winter, we usually met on the weekends not only to discuss the important matters but also to go ski mountaineering to get fit. We also sought some financial support from sponsors but only found private funding. We sold Broad Peak T-shirts to our friends and collected addresses for a greeting card campaign.

When it came to gear sponsors, we were more successful. Producers and retailers equipped us with clothes and food, including bacon and sausages, fruit juice, and about 120 cans of pineapple, so our food supply was pretty well covered. Being an importer of sports gear, Nik had good connections with transport companies and managed to get one of them to finance our material transport to Pakistan. This saved us a lot of money and meant that we didn't have to be overly selective about how much equipment to take. We worked out that we would need sixty to seventy porters. Nik and Siegfried got in touch with Alika, whom they knew from previous expeditions in Pakistan, told him how many porters we needed, and asked him whether he would like to be employed as our cook.

I am captivated every time I see Ama Dablam—this magnificent 6000-meter peak in the Solu Khumbu. I reached its summit together with six friends in autumn 1997. *(Photo by Ralf Dujmovits)*

In order to be well prepared for this expedition, I trained intensely. In the summer of 1993 I biked to work as often as the weather allowed. The leg from Windischgarsten to Rottenmann was twenty-five miles and included the Phyrn pass which I biked twice a day. In order to arrive at the hospital at 6:15 a.m. I had to leave home at 3:30 a.m. I actually love sleeping, but during this time I was so motivated that getting up early was not a problem. I would leave in the dark and cycle into the sunrise. I saw hardly any cars, but I heard the birds sing and watched the deer leap out of the forest. I enjoyed the peaceful atmosphere, feeling totally aware of what was going on around me. I knew which families had already switched on their lights and were up at this ungodly hour. After a quick shower at the hospital, I felt as fresh as a daisy during the handover procedures. Even though I could feel my legs, I was fully energized and in high spirits all day. In the evenings I would bike back home, have a shower, eat dinner, and collapse into bed. There was no time for anything else during my work week. And whenever we had a day off, Siegfried and I went out climbing anyway.

Even though we were organizing the expedition without using a local agent, which kept the cost down, it was still a huge financial burden for me. In order to come up with the funds, I worked as many night shifts as possible, six per month, which was very tiring, especially when I biked back home the following morning. Frequently I was caught in the pouring rain, but my motivation to get fit for Broad Peak never diminished.

I also wanted to get used to the cold. We slept with the window open, so in the mornings when the fire in the oven had gone out the whole house was freezing. We didn't shy from the cold in the winter: Cuddled up under two duvets, we slept with the windows wide open and woke up with cold, red noses. The end of our bed was near the window, so the wind sometimes blew snow into our bedroom, and we would wake to find it thinly covering our duvets. I was so obsessed with climbing an 8000-meter peak that none of this seemed excessive or absurd to me as ways to get properly prepared.

Finally, the big day arrived. On May 19, 1994, we flew to Islamabad, where our organizational frenzy continued. We had to look after all our documents, hire the liaison officers, and buy socks, sunglasses, and cigarettes at the bazaar for the porters. Logistics were time-consuming, and I would not want to do it again, but I am happy that I had the chance to experience the process. We stayed at Flashman's Hotel, which was frequently used by mountaineers despite its dilapidated state. Six days later, when everything was done, we hopped on a bus to Skardu and then took a jeep for the scary and bumpy ride along the narrow road to Askole, which lies at an altitude of 3000 meters and is the start of the trek to base camp.

When we distributed the loads to the porters—back then, the Pakistani porters carried 66 pounds each, whereas they now carry 55 pounds as they do in Nepal—we had a rude awakening. We needed 108 porters for all our food, 4 for the canned pineapple alone! After we had sorted it all out, more than one hundred heavily loaded men were marching eastward in a neat line along the Braldu River. On our first day we gained about 200 meters of altitude, and on the second day we reached Paiju at almost 3500 meters, where we had a rest day before we continued on to the Baltoro Glacier. We slowly gained altitude and notched our way up, first to 4000 meters, then to 4300, then 4600, until we finally reached our base camp at 5000 meters. As the altitude gain on the approach trek across the Baltoro Glacier is very slow, the body acclimatizes easily. I had read about the acclimatizing process in books, and I took Siegfried's experienced advice to heart: "Take your time, go slowly, and drink plenty of fluids."

Everything was new and exciting for me. In Paiju, the porters killed a goat and I was horrified when they offered us fresh goat brain for dinner that evening. Our expedition doctor, Karin, and I were lucky, however, and managed to avoid the "feast"; a member of a Korean expedition had a growth on his hand which needed to be removed. After Karin and I had operated on it, the Koreans kindly invited us to stay for dinner, which saved us from having to eat goat brain!

When we reached Concordia at 4800 meters, I set my eyes on K2 for the first time in my life. I had heard so much about that mountain and had been longing to see it one day. Only to see it! Its pyramid shape was so incredibly beautiful that I was at a loss for words. We spent another night at Concordia while a Czech group, also trekking in, pressed on to base camp. The expedition doctor of the young Czechs was a veterinarian, and on most days the group was moving faster than our team. I asked Siegfried why we were not carrying on to base camp as well.

"It's only a few hundred feet higher," I said. "It would take us only two and a half hours, and we are all feeling great."

"That's exactly the problem," he replied. "We are staying another night to acclimatize better. You will see—the Czechs will feel pretty unwell at base camp. They are racing each other, vying to be the first to arrive at camp. Take your time and just ignore them."

In the evening, I sat on a rock writing in my diary. The light was almost ethereal and everything around me was dipped in a beautiful glow. I felt extremely happy.

During our first night at base camp one of the Czechs came running to our tents, calling for a doctor. A member of his group was suffering from pulmonary edema. Karin and I ran to the Czech camp, which was about twenty minutes farther down the hill. Karin immediately sent me back to get the necessary drugs and infusions. After I had brought her what she needed, I returned to our camp while Karin spent the whole night with the patient. We also had a portable hyperbaric chamber bag that is pumped up to increase the air pressure to simulate a lower altitude. The following morning, we put the Czech climber into the bag, but he felt so claustrophobic that he was unable to stay in there, though Karin had given him drugs to calm him. His teammates then started to carry him down, but sadly he died just below base camp at an altitude of less than 5000 meters.

I was deeply shocked. Of course, I had heard about the possibility of getting pulmonary edema, but I had never expected to experience it so close to me, or actually see someone die from it. Was high-altitude climbing really so dangerous that you could just die without warning? Could this tragedy have been avoided if the Czech team had ascended more slowly? During the long days at base camp, we discussed this incident intensely, which seemed to help us come to terms with it.

As we were climbing alpine style, we set up the high camps ourselves, without help from high-altitude porters. We carried our gear to Camp 1, pitched it, and descended again to base camp to recover. Unfortunately the weather then turned and we were stuck at base camp for six days, but that was actually quite good for our acclimatization. In good weather, it is very tempting to leave base camp too soon without being properly acclimatized to the altitude.

There was another expedition at Broad Peak base camp: an International Army Expedition consisting of Pakistani, French, and North American soldiers. One day their expedition doctor showed up at our camp asking for Gerlinde. My heart sank; what did he want from me? When I stepped out of my tent, he handed me a bundle of wet letters. Apologizing, he told me that the mail runner had fallen into the river and the letters were in an undeliverable state. All the letters I had written to my family and friends were completely soaked, and the addresses were blurred and illegible. I guess that of the eight of us I had written the most letters, and that was why they were able to decipher my name.

Hanging out with international mountaineers was fascinating. It was a shame that my English was not better, and I vowed that I would work on it for future expeditions. After the army expedition had arrived, our liaison officer spent most of his time in their camp. We didn't mind at all; his absence made it less likely that we would get into trouble for our little secret. One of our sponsors, who had given us orange and apple juice, had filled some lemonade cans with beer so we could get around the alcohol prohibition in Pakistan. Our bootlegging certainly led to a few surprises when we gave our non-Islamic guests a "soft drink" which foamed unambiguously when they opened the can.

Once the weather improved we climbed to Camp 1, where we spent our first night on the mountain. The view of K2 was incredible. I marveled at the amazing evening: the sky had just cleared after heavy snowfall, and everything was glowing in a mystic light. I listened to my body to make sure there were no signs of altitude sickness. Nothing, I didn't even have a headache; I was feeling great. I had been climbing slowly and had drunk as much as I could. I also kept in mind Siegfried's advice not to sit or lie down immediately after getting to camp, but to keep moving and do the necessary jobs, such as melting snow and cooking.

TOP: In the gully leading up to the "Buhl" bivouac at about 5500 meters
BOTTOM: With Siegfried Wasserbauer on top of the false summit of Broad Peak at 8027 meters

On our ascent the following day we were able to catch a few glimpses of Nanga Parbat. Once again I was speechless. So many famous, magnificent mountains! We set up Camp 2 and stayed another night at 6250 meters.

I fell asleep thinking that I had never been so high in my life.

In the meantime, the expedition leader of the Czech group had gone back to Skardu to deal with all the formalities related to the death. The team had decided to continue the expedition, but was instructed to stay at base camp and wait for her return before setting up the high camps. But the weather was too good to wait and the Czech team continued to work on the mountain and set up their high camps. We met them on our descent to base camp after we had done a carry to our Camp 3.

On our trek to base camp, we had met the South Tyrolean climbers Hans Kammerlander and Hans Mutschlechner. I was very excited to meet Hans Kammerlander personally as I had heard a lot about him. "Hans & Hans," as we called them, were already acclimatized and on their summit attempt. From base camp we watched them with our binoculars and were excited to see Hans Kammerlander become the first person to reach the summit that season and ski down from Camp 3. Hans Mutschlechner didn't have skis and turned back just below the saddle at about 7800 meters due to very cold toes.

Hans Kammerlander briefly stopped at Camp 2, where the Czech team was at the time. He talked to someone and maybe had a drink before he continued to ski down. At base camp we were excited to watch him do his turns. Suddenly I saw someone fall down across the rocks.

"It must have been a Czech," I thought, then shouted out loud: "That's impossible, this can't be true." The person was wearing a turquoise anorak, which got stuck on a rock at one point. After a few seconds, it was over. Was this real? Had it really happened? A dead body was lying at the foot of the north face.

I was shaken, completely disturbed by this second death. It made me feel very insecure. Was I risking too much? What had happened up there? Why had the climber lost his footing? That evening the entry in my diary read, "It cannot be true that happiness, contentment, and death are so close together."

We later found out that the Czech climber had only been wearing his inner boots when he slipped and fell down the mountain. Camp 2 was precariously close to the edge of the face, which was too steep for him to stop such a fall. Even though it was a tragic event, it certainly didn't happen because of the perils of the mountain; irresponsible behavior and human error led to the accident.

A day after this horrific incident we continued our climb. We spent one night at Camp 2 and set up our Camp 3 at 7100 meters. I was so nervous that I couldn't fall asleep that night. "Tomorrow is the day; tomorrow we start our summit attempt," I kept thinking. My head was spinning. Would I be able to reach the top or would I have to turn back?

I turned back. When we were getting ready at 2:00 a.m., the thermometer had dropped to −22 degrees Fahrenheit. After climbing for about an hour, I had lost all feeling in the toes of my right foot. My plastic boots had good insulation, but with no gaiters my feet were just not warm enough. The only person who continued was Martina Bauer, who had borrowed neoprene gaiters from the Spanish team. My toes were definitely more important than the summit, and so I turned back. Siegfried had also lost all feeling in his toes and followed me.

After we had rested at base camp for a few days, we crawled out of our sleeping bags at Camp 3 exactly one week later for our second summit attempt. I was now the proud owner of Martina's neoprene gaiters; she had stayed at base camp with Nik and didn't need them. In order not to spend too much time fiddling with my gear in the dark, I had attached the gaiters and crampons to my outer boots the previous evening. We headed out between 3:00 and 3:30 a.m. There were three of us in a tent too small for all of us to get ready at the same time. Since it was too cold to wait around, Siegfried and I set off a bit earlier. From the face to the saddle we had to climb over a big bergschrund, strenuously digging through the deep snow and breaking trail to the saddle. Whenever I broke trail Siegfried still sunk in, so neither of us really benefitted from me going in front. For this reason, we took a very long time to climb this section.

We saw Ernst Weseßlintner climbing up toward us when we stopped for a drink on the saddle; the others must have turned back. Siegfried took a sip and immediately vomited. I was frightened. Being a nurse, I thought that vomiting meant being sick. What I didn't know was that it was almost normal for mountaineers to throw up at altitude. Siegfried's stomach was very sensitive to the altitude and he was unable to take anything in. On our first summit attempt, he had been stunned to see Martina and me gobble down our spaghetti with tomato sauce at Camp 3 at 7100 meters, something I can no longer do at such a high altitude.

The ridge continued on mixed ground. We waited for a while at yet another ledge where Ernst caught up with us, and we carried on together. And then, in the early afternoon of July 2, 1994, we reached the top of the false summit of Broad Peak. We had done it! We had crossed the magical line of 8000 meters! We would have had to climb another forty minutes or so to reach the main summit, but we had abandoned that idea a long time ago. We were in a very similar situation to that of the first successful expedition of 1957. They also stopped at the false summit, but Fritz Wintersteller, Marcus Schmuck—whose book I had read prior to this expedition—Kurt Diemberger, and Hermann Buhl went back up eleven days later and stood on the real summit.

The fact that we didn't reach the real summit only sunk in when we got back to base camp, but it didn't spoil the wonderful experience. I was not disappointed and didn't deem our climb a failure. Having reached higher than 8000 meters was a great achievement. It was only later that this difference became important to me, which made me go back to the real summit in 2007. In 1994, I was simply happy: This expedition had become the absolute highlight of my climbing career so far.

When we reached base camp I was so exhausted and dehydrated that I drank the glacial water running through the gully across the rocks. On the way down, I kept on thinking about the pineapple. I was dying to eat a whole can and drink the delicious juice. I was lucky that that we still had about fifteen cans of pineapple per head. After this delicious refreshment I crawled into my sleeping bag. My whole body ached, and I fell into a deep sleep for sixteen hours, after which I was finally able to digest the events of the day.

When we packed up base camp, I caught myself thinking about the next expedition. I had no idea where I wanted to climb next, but I hoped I would soon be able to go on another high climb. I had the feeling that I was good at this, technically and physically. In hindsight, I have to admit that I climbed Broad Peak with too little high-altitude experience. I would now recommend that a climber get used to high altitude much more slowly and start with a 6000- or 7000-meter peak. Then, however, I was obsessed with the thought of coming back and couldn't let it go. I had made up my mind: I definitely wanted to return to this magical place.

Looking at the glorious evening sky from high above the clouds at Cho Oyu's high camp

CHAPTER 2
DESIRE

I don't think I had ever been as struck by the opulence of the western world as I was when I landed in Vienna after my first expedition to Broad Peak. Being in the midst of all the trendy people running around like crazy was a true culture shock. I had just come back from a country where the main priorities were finding food, staying warm, and simply surviving. Beauty was not important; in Pakistan, it was all about basic needs.

It was hard for me to adjust back to my old world. My family and friends picked me up at the airport, and there was so much going on around me that I had no time to think. Of course, I was happy to be back home, but I was soon overwhelmed by a feeling of emptiness. We had been preparing for Broad Peak for such a long time, and suddenly I was left without perspective. I could no longer relate to people's striving for wealth and status. A glance into my wardrobe made me realize how much I owned and how little I actually needed. My life became even simpler; after the expedition I rarely bought new clothes, and I had never really been a fan of going out in the evenings.

I went back to my job in Rottenmann. One day I had a stroke of genius and found the solution to my problem: I would go to Pakistan and work there as a nurse! At the end of our Broad Peak expedition, we had given all our leftover medical drugs to the hospital in Skardu, where I was shocked to see how basic their medical equipment was and how limited their supplies. I would be able to help the people as well as live in the country I was longing to go to. I immediately got in touch with our liaison officer, who was in the military, and told him about my idea. He sent me a very nice reply telling me that it would be difficult for a woman to work in Pakistan, especially if I were coming on my own. So he was not sure whether he could be of any help. We stayed in touch by writing letters and sending each other photos of our expedition, but all of a sudden he stopped writing. After a while, I received a letter from a doctor, one of his colleagues, who told me that it was strictly forbidden for a member of the army to be in contact with a foreigner, especially a woman. He said corresponding with me would endanger his friend, so I should stop writing to him. Back then, I knew very little about the life of Pakistani women.

This was obviously not the right way for me to get to Pakistan. I then sought advice from the Pakistani embassy in Vienna, expecting to find support there. I wrote a letter and then called the embassy directly, talking to a secretary for a long time. She told me very clearly to forget my plan; I would not stand a chance fending for myself as a woman in Pakistan. My dream was shattered in a flash. I was completely focused on Pakistan because I could relate to the country and it was obvious to me that I was needed there. Now I had no other choice but to settle down in Austria again. I threw myself into my work, which I loved and that fulfilled me, but I couldn't stop thinking about going away again. It didn't necessarily have to be an 8000-meter peak, but I knew that I wanted to go abroad for climbing. The problem was that my next expedition couldn't be in the foreseeable future; I knew that, like Broad Peak, my next high-altitude climb would cost a lot of money and effort, and I needed an opportunity to go.

I shared my dreams with Siegfried, but he had other plans. He wanted to go to Everest in 1995, and it was too high for me to come along. Apart from the logistics and the money, there was another obstacle: vacation time. As a nurse I had five weeks vacation per year. For my expedition to Broad Peak, which took eight weeks, I had saved my days off, worked overtime, and gotten some additional days off in lieu. If it had not been for my boss, Sister Anni, who understood my yearnings, the Broad Peak climb would not have been possible. But it was not really feasible to take so much vacation every year: Sister Anni would have to justify her decision to the other nurses, and even though I couldn't have asked for better colleagues, it would have been difficult. They were very interested in my mountaineering, though, and were always willing to swap shifts whenever I wanted to get a chunk of time off.

Finally in late fall I saw a light at the end of the tunnel. Siegfried and I went climbing in the Dolomites and visited a few South Tyrolean climbers we had met during our expedition to Broad Peak. They had been on the mountain at the same time, but had left a little earlier. We had stayed in touch and now Hermann Tauber, who had led the expedition in spring 1995, asked me whether I was interested in joining his expedition to Mustagh Ata in China. Of course I was interested, especially as Mustagh Ata could be skied and I loved backcountry skiing. The so-called "Father of the Ice Mountains" stands at 7456 meters at the edge of the Taklamakan Desert. We would travel to China via Pakistan, which sounded very exciting, and then trek to base camp with camels, sleep in yurts, and meet new people in a completely unfamiliar environment.

After having sorted out my vacation days at the hospital, I signed up and, with this new focus in mind, immediately felt 100 percent better. Sixty thousand Austrian shillings was a lot of money, but I could be very frugal when I had set my mind on something, and I really wanted to go on this expedition. The prize money I received for winning a few mountain bike races was a welcome cash injection. I loved biking and had started racing as a nonprofessional through the Mountain Bike Association of Windischgarsten. I later added dual slalom to my repertoire, becoming Vice National Champion in the Windischgarten Championships, and soon the question arose whether I should race in the Austrian Cup Rating. I gradually realized that competing against time and other competitors was not really my thing. As in my early ski racing days, I refused to succumb to external pressure and eventually stopped competing.

In May 1995, six of our twelve-member team started our summit attempt on Mustagh Ata. Many of us had also been on the 1994 South Tyrolean Broad Peak expedition. I was very happy to see Martina, with whom I had a lot of fun, again in the group. Due to heavy snowfall, setting up the two high camps and depositing gear at Camp 3 was fairly tough, but descending in beautiful powder snow definitely made the effort worth it. The climb was technically easy. There were a few short icy sections where we had to take off our skis, strap them to our backpacks, and climb on a fixed rope with our crampons on. The weather was generally pretty bad with a lot of snowfall making the slopes avalanche prone.

On one occasion, we traversed a slope between Camp 2 and the deposit site for Camp 3. At about 30 degrees, the slope was gradual and the avalanche risk acceptable. Suddenly an avalanche thundered down, and even though we had kept a good safety distance between us, six of us were in the middle of the traverse when the avalanche struck. Though it was only the snow's top layer that slid down, it was still powerful enough to bury the four climbers in the center, including Martina and me. This was the first time I had been caught in an avalanche. Fortunately I managed to keep my head out of the snow, which enabled Hans to quickly pull me out. Martina was completely covered. When we finally got her out she was fine, but we still decided to abandon the expedition. We were in a state of shock, aware that we had been very lucky. There was simply too much snow on the mountain, and we were running out of time.

The deposit camp was gone and so were my spare pair of inner gloves and my camera, but the most important thing was that nobody got hurt. And even though we had only reached 6750 meters, our climb didn't seem like a failure. On the return journey we stopped in Kashgar, where I left the expedition behind and enjoyed the colorful hustle and bustle of the Sunday market. The only thing weighing heavily on my mind was not having enough money or vacation time to go on an expedition the following year.

Siegfried led a trek to Concordia in 1996 and asked me whether I would like to join him. Even though I would have preferred climbing, I decided to go trekking with him in the Karakorum, as it would take me back to that beautiful place. I was able to get four weeks off, so we hiked the same trek I had already done in 1994, crossing the Baltoro Glacier to Concordia, then continuing across the 5650-meter Gondogoro Pass to Hushe and back through the lush green Hushe Valley. I was delighted to be back in Pakistan and to see the wild mountains: the Trango Towers, the Gasherbrums, and K2. But I had underestimated my urge to climb a high peak. Trekking, I missed the climax of summiting, and when we met an Italian expedition to Broad Peak I realized how much I wanted to join them. I couldn't take my eyes off K2, even though at the time I would not have dared climb it due to its technical difficulties and hidden dangers. Maybe one day—but I kept this secret thought to myself.

In September, a long time after we had come back home from our trip to the Karakorum, Hermann Tauber called me. "Gerlinde, would you like to climb Ama Dablam?"

"Ama Dablam?" I asked. "Really? When?"

"In October 1997," he said.

I had only known this mountain from pictures. It was a magnificent, steep, and technically challenging 6000-meter peak. I was excited. Without thinking a great deal about it, I said, "Hermann, you can count on me."

I didn't even talk to Siegfried about it, which was probably in part due to our going through a rocky period which finally led to us breaking up in the spring of 1997.

The Ama Dablam expedition was the highlight of my early climbing career. The South Tyroleans had become good friends; I really enjoyed spending time with them. There was not a day when the team was not in great spirits, and there was not an evening when we didn't get together and sing. I was finally climbing in Nepal, a country that absolutely captivated and overwhelmed me with its colorful sights. Kathmandu was incredible: the traffic, the hooting, the holy cows leisurely wandering down the streets, the crowds of people in the tourist quarter of Thamel, the variety of shops, bars, and international restaurants, the loud music coming from the CD shops . . . and last but not least the poverty, which was right in your face, especially outside Thamel. I had been prepared for a third-world country, but compared to Pakistan this felt worse. Had Hermann not stopped me, in my naïveté I would have handed out my Nepalese rupees generously and the street beggars would never have left my side.

We visited the most important sights in Kathmandu, including the two Buddhist temples Boudnath and Swayambunath (Monkey Temple), and the holy Hindu site of Pashupatinath with its temple and pyres situated at the holy Bagmati River. I was fascinated by the exotic rituals and the

Nepali people, whom I found more open-minded than the Pakistanis. Religion must make a difference there.

One of the highlights of this trip was meeting Miss Elizabeth Hawley, who is still an essential part of most expeditions to Nepal. In 1960, this American lady moved to Kathmandu as a Reuter's correspondent. Along with writing articles she made it her life's work to collect data from all mountaineers attempting an expedition peak in Nepal. When I first met her in 1997, I was surprised by her attention to detail; she wanted to know every trivial fact, such as where we were going to set up our high camps. Miss Hawley, who is now in her nineties, has become the undisputed authority for the verification of summit successes in Nepal.

Finally we started our expedition to Ama Dablam. The flight from Kathmandu to Lukla offered a breathtaking view of the Himalaya. The landing was nerve-racking. It felt as if the plane was going to crash straight into the mountain before it touched down on the landing strip, which was still only gravel back then. It was all very exciting, a big adventure. On the trek to the Sherpa capital of Namche Bazaar we stayed in teahouses where I shared a room with the two other women of the expedition: Martina and Gabi Hofer from Vipiteno in South Tyrol. We also visited the monastery in Pangboche, where I first set eyes on Ama Dablam. What a beautiful mountain! It looked so steep that I was not quite sure where the route would go. To this day, the impressive panorama takes my breath away every time I trek through the Everest region.

Ama Dablam has become famous for its beauty and gets quite busy during the climbing season. Back then, it was not as popular as it is today, and we met only a few other climbers. Our base camp was situated in a magical spot on a meadow with flowers growing around our tents. There was a small winding creek where we could have a proper wash. The most amazing thing was that the mountain towered directly above us and we could see the whole route. In the evenings, the setting sun dipped Ama Dablam in a reddish light and gave her a surreal touch. The lower part was a rock climb with big snowy slabs on the bottom, looking pretty precarious. The upper part on the southwest ridge was covered in fluted snowy ribs with icy patches.

The terrain was so steep that we skipped Camp 2, which was at a very exposed place on the ridge. We would have had to put each other on belay to leave the tent. Nowadays, it is only used as a deposit camp. Camp 1 is also tiny and we had to split our team of eleven people into two groups, as there would not have been enough space for all of us. We climbed either roped up to each other or clipped onto the fixed rope that was set by us and another group. The route was interesting, and the higher I got the more excited I felt. During the ascent, we enjoyed a magnificent view of the surrounding valley. When I reached the summit at 6814 meters, I was at a loss for words as I gazed at the neighboring peaks. I enjoyed every fantastic moment up there.

Back in Austria, I sang Nepal's praises to my friend Birgit. In comparison, Pakistan now seemed very barren; the Nepalese landscape was greener, with settlements up to 4500 meters. I fondly remembered the colorful tin roofs, the arduously installed rice terraces, and the lovely people. And, of course, the mountains! Birgit was already used to my wordy, emotional outbursts, but up until then it had all been about Pakistan; she had shared my excitement during the preparations for Broad Peak. Though she had never been on an expedition herself, she was an alpinist and shared my enthusiasm.

I met Birgit Ertl on my very first day at the Rottenmann Hospital, where she also worked as a nurse on the same ward. While we were making the beds we started talking about mountaineering, which immediately created a connection between us. She spent a lot of time in the mountains and understood my passion, while other people often shook their heads when I told them about my mountaineering. For her, combining climbing with family was not always easy. She felt extremely responsible for her children and didn't want to take too many risks. Every once in a while, depending on our work schedules, we managed to go ice climbing or do a ski tour together. Even on smaller mountains, Birgit could relate to the feeling I experienced higher up. She understood the exhaustion, the motion of putting one foot in front of the other, the joy of having made it to the summit, and the feeling of freedom. She also understood the desire that drew me so powerfully to the next mountain. With her, I felt understood and supported.

Birgit and I worked well together in the hospital. We were alike in many ways, and had similar ambitions. We have never lost touch even though we have had long periods of being far away from each other. Sometimes we don't see each other for months, but whenever we meet it is as if we never parted. To this day, I try to go back to Austria to say goodbye to my friends and family before I go on an expedition, and it is always a sad moment with Birgit. She never forgets to give me something—a lucky charm, or some music she has recorded. We use email when I am on expedition, and I try to get in touch with her and my sister Brigitte before a summit attempt. After coming back from an expedition I have often sat with Birgit in her garden, telling her every little detail about the trip. But since I moved to Germany we have hardly had the opportunity for these moments.

In 1998, Birgit gave me a turquoise bead bracelet which is supposed to give me health, strength, energy, and success. It has been my lucky charm. I have worn it on my left wrist on all my expeditions. She first gave it to me for my Cho Oyu trip, which was organized by the Alpine Club in the spring of 1998. This trip eventually became the official expedition of the Friends of Nature of Upper Austria, for which we received financial support. At the beginning of April, thirteen Upper Austrians flew to Kathmandu and continued on to Lhasa in order to scale the 8188-meter peak known as the "Turquoise Goddess"—the name stems from its turquoise glow in the afternoon light. Even though Cho Oyu is technically not so difficult (it is known as the least challenging 8000-meter peak) it is still the sixth-highest mountain in the world. For me, this meant climbing 200 meters higher than I had last time. I was very excited to go back on expedition and explore Tibet. But the price I had to pay for this expedition was painfully high: I had to quit my job at the hospital. I did so with a heavy heart. I had already worked around the clock to get the four weeks I needed for Ama Dablam; taking two months off was simply impossible.

I didn't worry too much about getting another job, but I knew it would be difficult to find one that would allow me to go on expeditions. I was sad to give up my work as a nurse because I really liked it. My interest in this profession began in my early childhood when I visited my eldest sister at the hospital during her night shifts. I also loved helping people. I liked working as part of our friendly team at the hospital, I didn't mind the responsibility, and I got so much back from the patients. On our ward, I looked mainly after chronically ill patients—cancer patients, diabetics, and stroke patients. Apart from my professional skills, my greatest strength was my patience in talking with the patients and spending time with them. I remember some difficult moments with them, but also beautiful ones.

I often think about an elderly patient from Admont. I noticed her immediately when she arrived at the hospital; she had a bright sparkle in her eyes, which you don't often see in people her age. Her tanned skin made me think that she must have spent a lot of time outside. I soon found out that she had been a mountaineer. She told me all about the routes she had climbed when she was young. She had amazing stories! She even took part in an expedition to the Hindu Kush in Pakistan, which was almost unimaginable for a woman when she was young. I devoured every moment with her and she soon became very close to my heart. She was fairly fit for her age. She never took the elevator, using the stairs instead. But during the nights she was often mentally confused, reliving her past. When she was unable to sleep she would leave her room, and then it was always difficult to get her back into bed. Once she imagined that she was on expedition. She thought that the storm had blown away her tent and she was now freezing to death. I tried to calm her down, but she suddenly pulled the mattress from her bed, put it on the floor, and said, "There is the tent. You can go back into your sleeping bag." And then she slept the whole night. In the morning she didn't remember anything, and my morning-shift colleagues were a little surprised to find her on the floor.

At the end of 1997, the time had come for me to say goodbye to the hospital, and I had a party at the Bosruck Hut. On that evening, a big snowstorm raged, but it was warm inside. I spent a lovely evening with my colleagues and friends, who surprised me with wonderful presents. I was overwhelmed by happiness and sadness at the same time, and couldn't help but shed a few tears—and I was certainly not the only one: I was saying goodbye not only to the hospital but to Austria, too. The Cho Oyu expedition was not the only reason for my departure. There was another reason: a man. Before I had left for Ama Dablam in fall 1997, I had bumped into Francesco, whom I had met during our K2 trek in 1996. He had been a member of the Italian Broad Peak expedition. When he found out from Siegfried that we had split up, he got in touch with my mother to find me. After she had given him my contact details we met up, and it didn't take very long for us to fall in love. The problem was that Francesco lived in Italy, in Padua. After we had spent a lot of money on telephone calls and put many miles on our cars to see each other on our days off, I decided to stop this long-distance relationship and move to Italy.

The first stumbling block I faced was the language. Apart from Francesco, the rest of his family spoke only Italian. I took a language course in Padua and was extremely motivated to learn. I had always liked the southern lifestyle, and so it was not difficult for me to adapt to my new life. I enjoyed my Italian year to the fullest, hardly missing anything from home—except for the good Austrian whole-grain bread, of course. I never got used to the Italian white bread or the *pane integrale*, so the bread maker that one of my former colleagues had given me came in very handy.

I was not sure whether I would enjoy life in the city, but I found that I did, probably because Padua was a great place for training. We lived only a few miles away from the Colli Euganei National Park, home to several spa towns, including Abano Terme. In its beautiful volcanic hills I could run or bike across flowery meadows to my heart's content. I could also go mountain biking all through the winter, as it never snows in Padua. On the weekends we would go ice climbing in the Aosta Valley or in Chamonix in France, or quickly nip over to the Dolomites which were essentially on our doorstep. Still without work, I had plenty of time to train for Cho Oyu but knew that I needed to earn money after the expedition. Working as a

TOP: In spring 1998, I reached the summit of my first 8000-meter peak as a member of the
Friends of Nature Cho Oyu expedition; I am the fifth in the back row from the left.
BOTTOM: Summit push from 7100 meters *(Photo by Herbert Wolf)*

nurse in Italy proved pretty difficult because of the country's complicated point system. During my time in Rottenmann I had taken a crash course in massage, so I applied for a job as a masseuse at the Abano Spa which was very popular with the Germans. I was hoping to get some work there in the summer.

But first I was going to Cho Oyu. On the flight from Kathmandu to Lhasa I saw the peak as well as Everest and Lhotse for the first time. At an altitude of 3650 meters, Lhasa was cold, and we could definitely feel the thin air. We stayed there for four days, using the time to acclimatize. We visited the most important sites of Tibetan Buddhism, or rather those sights the Chinese didn't destroy during the Cultural Revolution. Drepung and Sera were once the biggest monasteries in Tibet, and having survived near-annihilation in the past they now have a growing number of monks practicing there again. We also visited the Jokhang Temple as well as the Potala Palace, which was the Dalai Lama's home until 1959. This massive building, comprising thirteen floors and almost a thousand rooms, has been turned into a museum. In the afternoons, I would go for a stroll to the market or sit on a wall to look around and absorb the scenery. As in earlier travels abroad, I was deeply impressed by this new culture, but also found it challenging at times. Once, for example, we were served soup laden with chicken heads and feet, which I could barely eat, only spooning up the broth.

We drove about 530 miles across the Tibetan Plateau to get to the base of the normal route up Cho Oyu, the northwest face that was first climbed in 1954 by Herbert Tichy, Pasang Dawa Lama, and Sepp Jöchler. During the long, tiring jeep drive we stopped to spend one night in Shigatse and two nights in Tingri, which, at 4400 meters, is a good place to acclimatize to the increasing altitude. Back then, the lodge where we stayed was still quite simple: One room was full of hectic chickens, there were mice everywhere, and the ceilings were damp and mildewy. But the open-air toilet made up for all these inconveniences, offering the most amazing views of Cho Oyu in its full glory. On our rest day we went for a nice splash in the hot springs near Tingri, but I soon got itchy feet and wanted to leave the dusty road behind me and just get to the mountain.

After four days, we continued with our fifty yaks and all our equipment to Advanced Base Camp (ABC) at 5650 meters, while our liaison officer stayed at Chinese Base Camp at 4900 meters, which we had reached by jeep. We spent one night at an interim camp at 5300 meters for acclimatization. After a few days at ABC we climbed up the killer slope, a scree slope where you go one step up and two steps down, carrying our gear to Camp 1 at 6400 meters. The ascent was strenuous with our heavy loads. Feeling hot and sweaty, I rolled up my sleeves for the descent to ABC. There was a fresh breeze, and when I reached the big boulders I was a bit chilly, but couldn't bring myself to stop and put on another layer—a decision I would soon regret. Two days later I woke up with a sore throat, a cough, and a temperature. I felt miserable and could hardly walk to the toilet. I knew that my chances of recovery were pretty slim at this altitude. At 5650 meters, Cho Oyu base camp is very high. Most of my teammates no longer counted on me; I heard them saying things like, "She will never get better. She can forget it." But I never stopped believing that I would make it. Thomas Prinz, our expedition doctor and now a good friend of mine, treated me with antibiotics and acupuncture, and I did steam inhalations to release the pressure in my sinuses. My tent mate Herbert Wolf, whom I had known from the Alpine Club for quite some time, brought me food and tea and even waited for me when the others had already left to climb higher on the mountain.

It took four days for me to get back on my feet, and my legs were still shaky when Herbert and I left ABC for Camp 1. We had initially planned to split the team into two groups to save tents at the higher camps, but Herbert and I had now created a third group with a completely different rhythm. I consciously walked slowly, had a good night at Camp 1, joined Herbert in carrying our gear to Camp 2 at 6800 meters, and descended back to ABC. We negotiated the 200-foot-high ice wall between Camp 1 and Camp 2 without any problems, felt great at Camp 2, and even basked in the sun in the open air for about an hour. As we really wanted to capture the moment, we asked a Russian climber who had been at Camp 2 for a few days to take a photo of us. He did as he was asked, but seemed rather strange and abruptly disappeared back into his tent without saying a word.

Back at ABC in the evening, we found out that he had died. I couldn't believe it. Why had someone had to die again, on this expedition? The Russian must have had altitude sickness. Later, when we looked at the photo, we saw that he had only captured our legs, which was an indication that he must have already been feeling very uncoordinated.

After a few rest days at base camp we headed off again, but this time with the summit in mind. The weather kept changing from sunshine to wind and snow. There was a lot on my mind and I was thinking about the nights ahead at the high camps, the strong winds, the cold, and the final steps to the summit. I knew that everything would be all right, and although I was still shaken by the death, I had not lost my optimism.

As Herbert and I had acclimatized well and moved fast in our team of two, we were able to catch up to the first group. We still carried our own tent since we were worried we might not find a space at the high camps. On May 3 we climbed to Camp 1 and on the following day continued to Camp 2, where I spent what seemed to be an endless night. I lay awake in my sleeping bag with countless thoughts buzzing around my head.

While we headed up toward Camp 3 on May 5, four other people came up from Camp 1. One of them was Sepp Hinding, the most experienced climber in our group, with whom I got on very well. We found a perfect place for our camp and pitched our tent at 7120 meters, which was a little bit lower than the usual site at 7400 meters. Little did we know that this would become a problem. While our expedition leader at Camp 1 wanted us to set up another camp at 7400 meters, we thought the weather would turn. Back then we had neither a satellite phone nor an up-to-date weather forecast to rely on, so we wanted to start the attempt from 7120 meters instead of risking the higher camp. Of course, we knew that ascending more than 1100 meters in one go would be a stretch, but we thought that it might be our one and only chance. Even though we couldn't come to an agreement over the radio, we decided to give it a go by following a direct line to the summit and not Herbert Tichy's route, which went left to the last camp and then veered back to the right over the Yellow Band.

This agitated discussion was happening against the backdrop of an incredibly beautiful evening sky: It was simply wonderful to be up there.

At 8:00 p.m. I was tucked into my sleeping bag, already feeling the freezing cold. When I woke up at 3:30 a.m., the thermometer had dropped to –41 degrees Fahrenheit and I had my doubts as to whether it was actually still working. It was impossible to go out in this cold. Neither of us owned a down suit, so we decided to depart a little bit later, at 6:00 a.m. Our ascent route was on the west side of the mountain, which meant that the sun wouldn't hit our tents until 10:30 or 11:00 a.m. We couldn't wait that long.

We started walking in the bitter cold. I could feel the chill penetrating my long johns through to my bones. The snow was knee-deep, and the cold made breaking trail even more exhausting. The dawn grew lighter around 8:00 a.m. Having lost all feeling in my fingers and toes by then, I stopped to get warm, concentrating on wiggling my toes inside my boots. There was still no sign of the sun.

We took turns at breaking trail, with the snow in some places coming up to our thighs. The summit got closer, the air got thinner, and my breathing came harder and quicker. At around 8000 meters, we climbed out of a rocky and technically difficult gully and continued across a long flat plateau, slowly ascending toward the summit. Fortunately it was wind-swept, which saved us breaking trail. It took ages to finish the ascent. I kept checking the time: half an hour, one hour, one and a half hours. Step by step. I knew that we would be on the summit only when we could see Mount Everest.

When Rudi Hofer, Sepp Hinding, Herbert Wolf, Thomas Prinz, and I reached the summit in the afternoon of May 6, I was over the moon. I had never been so high in my life: I had just reached the first main summit of an 8000-meter peak. Everest felt almost within touching distance.

"Gerlinde, doesn't it look terrific?"

"Herbert, I am so happy!"

Admittedly, our dialogue was not exactly profound, but I guess this is the case with most conversations at high altitude. Despite the exhausting ascent, I felt much more aware of my surroundings than when had I stood on the false summit of Broad Peak. I was thinking about my family and Birgit, wishing that they could share this moment with me. We didn't spend a long time on the summit. We had set off late in the morning and lost a lot of time getting through the deep snow; now we had to hurry up to get down. On the descent, the sky was dipped in a beautiful red glow. When I close my eyes I can still see dusk creeping in slowly and the sun setting behind Shisha Pangma. When I stood on the top of Cho Oyu I already knew that I wanted to climb that impressive mountain, and as so often happens in such moments, a new plan was born: I would stand there, too, one day.

We reached our high camp after dark. While Ernst Michelak met us with a big flask of tea and congratulated us on our summit success, the rest of the second group, who had ascended to Camp 3, gave us a rather cool reception. The following day, they set off toward the summit but the high winds forced them to abandon their bid at 7500 meters. Indeed, we had been lucky to make use of the last good day. Unfortunately, my summit joy was a bit marred; some of the expedition members who didn't reach the top accused us of not being team players because we had gone straight to the summit rather than setting up another Camp 3. In view of the bad weather forecast, I didn't think this accusation was justified. At the same time I couldn't bear the tension in our team and urged our team leader to talk with the group. We didn't rekindle our initial team spirit, but we had a good discussion during which we found some mutual understanding of our separate positions. This incident made me realize that adjusting spontaneously to the conditions on the mountain would always be a problem in big teams due to their rigid organization and time schedules. But this was exactly what I thought was important for a successful high-altitude expedition: grabbing the opportunity, especially when it comes to the weather. Despite this realization, I never expected that I would ever go on a major expedition without a big group, because of the money and the logistical organization required for such a climb.

On our way back to Chinese Base Camp I started getting excited about going home. During the long jeep and bus journey to Kathmandu, Sepp Hinding and I talked a lot about Shisha Pangma and I started dreaming of that mountain. Without knowing exactly when I would be able to go there—I had neither the time nor the money—I put it next on my wish list.

But first I had to go back to Italy. I would meet Francesco in Austria and then return to Padua with him.

Our friends met us at the airport and drove Francesco and me to my sister Brigitte's house, where I always used to stay when I was back in Austria. Brigitte and I talked in the car about my future plans. When Francesco, who hardly understood any German, heard the name, "Shisha Pangma," he perked up his ears. I immediately noticed that he didn't like the idea. He had imagined that we would stay with Brigitte for a day or two and then go to Padua, get married, and start a family. While I was enthusiastically thinking about the next mountain, he wanted to have children.

Francesco had to get back to his printing business in Padua, but I stayed at my sister's for a few more days before I returned to Italy. The more Francesco talked about his family plans, the more I felt suffocated. Then I found out that I hadn't gotten the job in Abano. I soon returned to Austria. Brigitte had arranged for me to do a vacation replacement at the hospital in Kirchdorf for six weeks, which was great; I urgently needed money. The geographic distance contributed to Francesco and me my growing farther apart.

In the end, I moved back to Austria for good. Francesco and I had different goals. High-altitude mountaineering had become a central part of my life. I constantly longed for the freedom I felt at high altitude, and no matter how hard I could have tried, I knew that the thought of an idyllic family life would never replace that feeling.

Climbing up to Camp 1 on Makalu *(Photo by Herbert Wolf)*

CHAPTER 3
SHOCK

My temporary job in Kirchdorf was finished; my head was full of mountains, but my bank account was empty, at least in Himalayan terms. Finding a job was not the problem; what was difficult was finding a job that agreed with my expedition life. I was offered a very tempting job as a head nurse in a nursing home in Bad Goisern. After a one-day work trial I was completely torn between having a professional life and going climbing. On one hand, it would have been an interesting new challenge and a good career move; on the other, it would have been impossible to leave a management position for two months at a time. This job would have put an end to my expedition life, and so at the last minute I decided against it. I guess Brigitte's comment that Bad Goisern had the highest suicide rate in Austria, due to some kind of claustrophobia caused by the proximity of the mountains, didn't really help, either.

I eventually found a job as a nurse in the geriatric unit of Buchberg Hospital, primarily caring for older patients in Traunkirchen in Austria. There was a friendly atmosphere in this slightly dilapidated hospital with its many nooks and crannies, and I really enjoyed working there—not least because my supervisor allowed me to take long vacations in return for my working extremely tightly scheduled shifts. After nine months at Buchberg Hospital, Nik Rafanovic, with whom I had been in regular contact since our Broad Peak expedition, asked me whether I would be interested in working for his outdoor company as a sales representative. I didn't have to think twice. The prospect of flexible working hours plus being able to get enough time off for my expeditions was tempting enough to make up for the salary cut I was prepared to take. After an initial training period I became the sales representative for K2, the ski producer, and Tatonka, a backpack company, covering Western Austria from Salzburg to Voralberg. This job was certainly not easy for me. I knew a lot about the products, but I was not a natural saleswoman. I didn't like having to talk anybody into buying anything, but I was under pressure as my commission depended on my sales. I was good at selling backpacks because they were part of my world, and I enjoyed a good sales chat, but all the glamor and fuss surrounding the products and trade fairs were just not for me. Ah, the things one accepts in life just to get to the mountains one yearns for. . . .

Apart from a career change, I was also going through a personal transition. After our Cho Oyu expedition, Herbert Wolf and I had met up a couple of times. We had known each other for a while from the Alpine Club, but now I began to look at him differently. Apparently he had already been interested in me on Cho Oyu. We saw each other more often and went climbing together. When we realized that the relationship was becoming more serious I moved to Ebensee, which was very close to the village of Gmunden where I worked whenever I was not on the road visiting sports shops all over Austria. Towering above Ebensee, Feuerkogel was our local mountain. The altitude gain of 1200 meters was perfect for my training, and I climbed either on my own or with Herbert. In winter when it was already dark we would skin up on our skis after work, enjoy a quick apple strudel on top, and ski down with our headlamps on.

In the summer of 1999, Herbert and I went on our first major trip together to South America. We were going to climb Alpamayo, a 5947-meter mountain in the Cordillera Blanca, as well as a few 5000-meter peaks for our acclimatization. Naturally, I also wanted to see Machu Picchu. We booked a flight to Lima, packed our backpacks, and headed off without organizing any other logistics in advance. It was surprisingly easy to arrange for a hotel, a bus to Huaraz—the starting point of our climb—a pick-up for our luggage, and finally the donkeys for our approach trek. Our acclimatization climbs on Nevado Urus and Nevado Ishinca went very smoothly, and we soon returned to Huaraz. We had fallen in love with the Andes and its gigantic ice walls, even though they were a lot smaller than the ones in the Himalaya. The advantage in the Andes was that the approach routes were shorter, which enabled us to get back to civilization sooner between expeditions.

Many climbers deem Alpamayo one of the most beautiful mountains in the world. Its steep fluted summit pyramid is shaped by a combination of sun and humidity rising from the rain forest. There are several routes leading up the flutes on the southwest face. We had opted for the Ferrari Route, a 60-degree ice wall named after Casimiro Ferrari, who first climbed this route in 1975. It was up to us to arrange our gear transport and hire a base camp cook for Alpamayo. When we returned to Huaraz after our acclimatization climbs, we met four mountaineers from Bad Goisern in Austria who were also bound for Alpamayo. One evening over dinner we decided to join forces. The next day we visited a trekking agency to organize the transport. When we asked for a cook, the trekking agent simply walked out onto the street and stopped the first person who came along.

"Do you know how to cook?" he asked him.

"Yes," the man answered.

"I need a cook for the next few days—do you want the job?"

There you go—we had a cook! He was actually not bad, though his dishes were a bit dull, with pasta and tuna dominating the menu most days. We set up an intermediate camp to properly acclimatize and then continued to our high camp, where we were greeted by a fantastically gorgeous evening. We could see the entire southwest face with the setting sun slowly illuminating one gully after another, clearly displaying the different ascent routes: the Canadian Route, the Ferrari Route, and to the right, the French Route.

As we got ready for our summit attempt in the morning I felt very happy and excited. It was still dark when Herbert and I set off. After we had entered the gully, I was surprised to find the ice brittle and the route relatively untouched even though the Ferrari Route was one of the most popular ones. All of a sudden, it dawned on me that we must be in the wrong gully. How annoying! By the time we had climbed down and found the right gully, the others were well ahead of us, throwing down huge chunks of ice with their axes. It was a good thing that we were wearing helmets, because at one point a member of the Swiss expedition lost his ice ax. It came flying down, hitting Herbert on the head. He was lucky that he didn't look up at the wrong moment. Other than that, everything went smoothly. The conditions couldn't have been better, partly hard sugar snow and partly blue ice. We alternated the lead and made good progress. After climbing a sheer 900-foot-high wall, we had to negotiate an overhanging ice bulge before we reached the corniced summit ridge. Together with our friends from Bad Goisern, we were elated when we reached the summit. The only thing dampening our exhilaration was that thick clouds denied us a view from the top.

The trip to Peru certainly proved that Herbert and I were not only good at organizing an expedition, but that we also got along very well, even though we were together 24/7 and often faced with stressful situations. For the following year we planned to climb an 8000-meter peak, and of course it had to be Shisha Pangma! It had been on my mind ever since I had seen it in the evening light from the summit of Cho Oyu. The south face already appealed to me back then, though it still seemed a bit too ambitious for me. We opted for the normal route on the north side, and decided to take our skis to skin up as high as possible and then ski down. Asian Trekking, our local agent, organized the permit, which we shared with other climbers to bring down the cost for us all. Two Spaniards, two Americans, and four other Austrians were on our permit, but we didn't know their names. When we arrived in Kathmandu in April 2000 we were pleasantly surprised to find out that the four Austrians were Herbert's former colleagues from the Alpine Gendarmerie Service. One of them was Markus Kronthaler from Kufstein, who, sadly, died on Broad Peak in 2006.

From Kathmandu we drove to Nyalam, where we spent three acclimatization nights at 3700 meters. Nowadays I acclimatize much more quickly and no longer need to spend so many days at the high camps, but back then my body took longer to get used to the higher altitude. The next leg to Shisha Pangma Chinese Base Camp saw an altitude jump of 1300 meters, which we definitely noticed. After a few hours at camp, I could already feel how hard my body was working: Everything I did felt tiring, and whenever I bent down to put something into my tent I felt dizzy. Some people even suffer from pulmonary edema at this altitude.

After three nights at Chinese Base Camp, where we left our liaison officer, Herbert and I walked the 28 kilometers to Advance Base Camp (ABC) at 5650 meters in one go. We stayed there for a few days before we tied our skies to our backpacks and continued through the rubble along the edge of the glacier to 5800 meters. After we had crossed a difficult glacier with *penitentes* and glacial lakes, we put on our skis and skinned up to our Camp 1 at 6300 meters. We deposited our tent, food, and some gear, and skied back down to 5800 meters on pretty good sugar snow in less then ten minutes. We left our skis at the end of the glacier and walked back to ABC.

For our second acclimatization rotation we spent one night at Camp 1, set up Camp 2 at 6900 meters, and skied down. I was happy to see that my "plastic bag method" paid off. On skis, we couldn't wear our expedition boots but had to wear ski boots instead. Even though the liners were fairly warm they were slow to dry, which was a problem—they got sweaty during our arduous ascents. They would never have dried in my sleeping bag in a single night at high camp. On 8000-meter peaks, where you have cold feet anyway, it is absolutely essential to have dry boots and socks; you are more likely to get frostbite when your feet are wet. I had already come up with this solution back home: I put a plastic garbage bag and a thick sock over a thin sock and then put on my inner boots. In this way only the thin sock—which I could easily change—got wet, and the thick sock and the inner boot stayed dry.

Finally, we were well acclimatized and ready to go for the summit. When the weather looked pretty stable—we didn't have a weather forecast back then—we packed our backpacks and climbed to Camp 1. We were certainly not the only people taking advantage of the good weather. As it turned out, we all guessed wrong: The weather deteriorated during the night. A strong wind came up and by the next morning Camp 1 was covered in thick clouds. One group after another packed up their gear and descended to ABC, but something inside me felt reluctant to go down. Considering how quickly the weather had turned, I thought it would soon change again. Could it improve by tomorrow? Wouldn't it be better to ascend and be at the right place at the right time when the weather window arrived? On our first acclimatization rotation, Herbert and I had marked the route to Camp 2 and also some precarious crevasses with small flags to help us find the camp even in poor visibility. And if the weather didn't improve, we would benefit from another acclimatization night at 6900 meters. It was not easy to convince Herbert of my plan, and I invested a lot of time and effort to make him continue up to Camp 2 with me.

At times I doubted my grand plan, especially when the visibility was so poor that we could barely see our markers at the start of the big flat plateau called "the corridor" between 6800 meters and 7200 meters. Using a compass, one of us would go ahead to find the next marker, and then the other would follow. This way we made sure that at least one of us was always on the route. When we finally arrived at Camp 2, we met Stefan Jungmann and Roland Mattle from the second Austrian team. The pair had reached the summit the previous day and didn't want to descend any farther in the storm.

Herbert and I agreed that we would go back to ABC if the weather didn't improve the following day. At around midnight, I was no longer able to ignore my full bladder so I peeled myself out of my warm sleeping bag, put on my shoes, and crawled out of the tent. I was greeted by a starry night. There was not a cloud in the sky, and I could see millions of stars. I turned around to Herbert and called, "Herbert, wake up! The weather is gorgeous! We must go for the summit!"

It took Herbert only a moment to realize what was happening before he leapt out of his sleeping bag. I fired up the stove to melt snow for us to drink and put into our thermoses. We wanted to skip the traditional Camp 3 and go straight for the summit from Camp 2, which meant that we had to climb around 1100 vertical meters of altitude in a single day—a very tough undertaking at this altitude. We started at 2:00 a.m. The previous day's storm had blown a lot of snow onto the slopes, which made breaking trail even more cumbersome. We left our skis somewhere between 7250 and 7300 meters, where the slope became steep and rocky, and continued with our crampons. When the sun's first rays touched us at 7:30 a.m., we knew it would be a gorgeous day. What made me even happier was that we were completely on our own while ABC was teeming with people!

Once on the north ridge, we followed it all the way to the summit. The terrain changed from rocky climbing sections to snowy slopes where we had to wade through thigh-deep snow. One slope was particularly long and we ended up calling it the "Coke Slope," because of Herbert's cry: "I would die for a Coke. I need something sparkling and refreshing!" The last 400 meters on the ridge were extremely exhausting and time-consuming with all the trail breaking we had to do. It was getting later and later.

At the Gendarme, the landmark at about 7800 meters, the route split: One way led to the main summit, the other to the central summit. The way to the 8027-meter-high main summit veered off toward the left for about 150 meters; the steepening ridge led directly to the central summit only a few feet lower. As the traverse is very exposed to the wind and prone to avalanches, most climbers go for the central summit. When we reached the Gendarme, we noticed that the slope was heavily loaded with snow and would have been suicidal to cross. The Austrians had told us that two of them had tried the traverse and triggered a slab avalanche. They had then turned back and gone for the central summit. In addition, the relatively flat ridge between the central and the main summit was completely corniced and we would not have stood a chance to cross it, especially without a rope. Every option to reach the main summit seemed impossible, which meant that we had only one choice: to climb the central summit.

We stayed on the narrow and exposed ridge, which was completely windswept after the Gendarme, saving us the effort of breaking trail. The ridge dropped off steeply to the left and right. The highest point at 8008 meters was barely big enough for the two of us to stand on, which made our hug very delicate and undramatic even though I could have embraced the whole world. I was euphoric to have reached this point, especially after having nearly abandoned our summit attempt. The view from this summit was different: Instead of looking across countless snow-covered peaks toward the north, we could see straight down to the Tibetan Plateau. I will never forget the endless landscape, its absolute infinity with a tiny turquoise dot marking a lake at the very end of the brown plain.

After we spent a night at Camp 2 we skied down, carrying our heavy packs on our backs. Well, you couldn't really call it skiing; we had to stop after every third or fourth turn, bending over our ski poles to rest while our heavy backpacks almost dragged us to the ground. It took about five minutes for us to catch our breath and get our heart rates down before we could continue to the next four or five turns. The wind-packed snow didn't make for good skiing either. The load on my shoulders was so heavy that I could barely get up when I fell. No matter whether tent, ice axes, thermos, or the backpack itself—back then our equipment was a lot heavier than it is today. Another aggravating factor was that I had taken a lot of spare gear and emergency equipment, stuff that I would omit today to save weight.

It was already afternoon when we reached our ski deposit. The traverse through the penitentes would certainly not be a picnic in this heat, exacerbated by having to carry our skis. The small lakes on the glacier had melted. Everything felt very soft and we had to be careful not to sink in. At one point it became clear that we needed to get rid of some gear to make it through the labyrinth. We set down our skis and tents, planning to collect them the following day.

"Gerlinde, go ahead, you are lighter," Herbert instructed me. Slowly I inched forward through the ice towers and water holes. When I went one step too far at a particularly narrow point on the shore of a glacial lake, the ice cracked, and I fell up to my thigh into the ice-cold water. There was no ground beneath my feet. The weight of my backpack started to drag me down, and I thought I was drowning. I screamed for help. One of Herbert's amazing qualities is that he stays calm even in the most critical moments, but on that occasion, when I literally had water up to my neck, I resented him for it. All he could do was take out his camera and take a picture.

"Herbert, no! Pull me out, I'm drowning!"

Finally, he grasped the seriousness of the situation, dropped his camera, and pulled me out of the water hole. I was soaked to the bone. Luckily, I had a spare pair of long johns in my backpack, which I wore along with my soaked boots for the descent. It took us a few hours to find the passageway through the ice field, and we only reached ABC in the evening.

Over the next few days we had a lot of fun with our four compatriots. Markus Kronthaler, who was blessed with a lovely Tyrolean accent, told a particularly funny story, and once we knew that it had a happy ending we split our sides with laughter. He said that when he and Manfred Nagl stopped at about 7800 meters, Manfred noticed that Markus was trying to grab something with his hands in the air. He asked him what he was trying to do, and Markus replied, "Can't you see the dwarf giving us tea?"

Markus described the dwarf and how he made tea at a fireplace. He said, "Gerlinde, he was there. I saw him and he gave me a cup of tea, which I was trying to grab."

Manfred immediately knew that Markus was having hallucinations due to a lack of oxygen and that the only way to save him was to descend.

Herbert and I were very pleased about our success on Shisha Pangma. We had reached the summit on May 17, after only four weeks on the mountain. And we had done it in our team of two without the false sense of security of having a big group to support us. Everything had gone according to plan apart from the conditions on the mountain which hadn't allowed us to reach the main summit. Once again, our team of two had proved to be successful.

Back in Austria, we had just enough time to unpack our gear before we started preparing for our next expedition. In 1999, the Alpine Club had already contemplated organizing another Friends of Nature expedition for 2001. During a meeting in 2000 we decided on Makalu, and Herbert and I were absolutely thrilled about the prospect of climbing this imposing peak. In the pictures it looked gigantic, powerful, and almost impossible to climb. Scaling this freestanding mountain would be a real challenge for us. With its 8485 meters it is one of the higher 8000-meter peaks, 250 meters higher than Cho Oyu. What a lonesome giant!

This time around, I was successful in finding some sponsors. In early 2001 I had changed companies and was now working for Master Sport, looking after the Anzi Besson ski clothing line. My new boss, Karl Attwenger, was the best thing that could have happened to me. He could relate to my passion, even though he was not a mountaineer. Not only was he extremely generous when it came to vacations, he also equipped the whole Makalu crew with Gore-Tex jackets and hats. In return, I dove into my work whenever I was in Austria and invested all my energy—apart from the energy I needed for my training—into my job.

In April 2001, we flew from Kathmandu to Tumlingtar, the gateway to Makalu. The ten-day trek to base camp was long and arduous for the porters but very beautiful, passing through thick forests at a relatively low altitude of 600 meters. After we had crossed two passes we arrived at Hillary Base Camp, which was 4300 meters higher than our trek. From there we continued to Advanced Base Camp (ABC) at 5700 meters. We set up our high camps in traditional alpine style and acclimatized on the mountain by sleeping at the higher camps. During our acclimatization rotations we fixed the difficult sections with rope. We had divided our group of ten into two groups, and alternated our positions on the mountain.

At the beginning of May, four of us started our first summit attempt. During our ascent we skipped Camp 1, which we had set up for acclimatization purposes, spent a night at Camp 2, and continued to Camp 3 at the Makalu La at 7400 meters. The next morning, our two teammates decided to go back to ABC, but Herbert and I had had a good night's sleep so we continued up. We pitched another tent at Camp 4 at 7800 meters, where we wanted to rest, melt snow for a few hours, and then head up toward the summit at about 11:00 p.m. But bad weather thwarted our plans. Late in the evening we were caught in a blizzard like I had never seen before. The wind was howling and pounding against our tent the whole night, and we were scared of being blown away. I was literally shouting at Herbert; the snow hitting our tent was so loud that we were unable to understand each other. The gale-force wind pressed the tent poles down, leaving us no space to light the stove without setting the whole tent on fire. Unable to melt snow, we drank far too little. There was no way we could have left the tent for any reason. We laid in our sleeping bags, hoping the storm would abate so we could descend the next day. The summit was no longer an issue.

In the morning the wind died down, and feeling very relieved, we descended through the fresh snow. The frightening night in the storm had cost us a lot of energy. Notorious for its capricious weather, Makalu had certainly lived up to its reputation. Was it really worth getting ourselves into such a dangerous situation? For Herbert it was clear: He would not attempt the summit again. Completely worn out and dehydrated, he was more worried about his exhaustion than the weather. His decision made me sad. I would have loved to summit with him, but he had made up his mind, encouraging me to give it another go with the other group.

Apart from the Austrian expedition from Kärnten consisting of members from Lesachtal and Innsbruck, another Austrian climber had arrived at ABC: Erich Resch from Klagenfurt. He had trekked to base camp with a few porters but was otherwise completely independent. He pitched his tent next to ours. When we found out that he didn't have a cook—cooking at base camp is hard work, especially because of the water supply—we invited him to dinner a couple of times. He seemed to be an accomplished high-altitude mountaineer, having led expeditions to Cho Oyu and Shisha Pangma. Erich also wanted to try for the summit in the next few days.

For our second attempt instead of staying at Camp 4 we wanted to summit directly from Makalu La, which seemed more reasonable, saving our bodies the strenuous additional night at high altitude. Rudi Denk, our expedition doctor Karl Watschinger, and I, as well as Erich and some members of the other Austrian group, started out from Camp 3 at midnight. I knew the way to Camp 4. Steadily I set one foot in front of the other, hearing no sound but my own breathing and the crunch of the snow underfoot. The cone of light from my headlamp shrank the world to a few meters around me. It was bitterly cold and at one point I lost all feeling in my toes. I was used to having cold toes on expedition, but this time it was different, and I knew I had to do something about it. When we reached our tent at 7800 meters, I crawled inside to warm them up. Karl joined me and started massaging my toes, placing my feet in his armpits to get the circulation going. Slowly but surely the feeling came back, but I still I wanted to wait for the sun. Erich, who had also joined me in the tent to get his feet warm, waited with me while Karl and Rudi continued up.

When the sun came up between 5:00 and 5:30 a.m., Erich and I set off again, now far behind the others. I declined Erich's suggestion to share a backpack and stay together. I didn't want to be dependent on anyone on the mountain and needed to be able to get to my water bottle and equipment whenever I had to. I was also not able to judge Erich's strength. As it turned out, it was a good decision as he soon lagged behind and I lost sight of him.

At an altitude of 8000 meters I reached the French Couloir, a gully of about 200 meters of mixed terrain leading to a small plateau. The couloir was not very difficult but I was on my own and unroped, which meant that I had to concentrate hard; I couldn't afford a single mistake. Just before I reached the relatively flat plateau I bumped into the two Austrians, Karin Katstaller and Sebastian Ruckensteiner, who were on their way down from the summit. I congratulated Karin on becoming the first Austrian woman to reach the top of Makalu. They asked after Erich and I told them I assumed that he must have turned back, as he had been struggling that day. A little later I met Rudi and Karl, who were also on their way down from the summit. I congratulated them as well, and we exchanged a few words before I continued up. It was already quite late.

Getting to Makalu's false summit requires negotiating a difficult passage. A short traverse, which I frontpointed on my crampons, led into a gully of about 65 to 70 degrees. While it was only about another 30 meters up to the false summit, downward the gully ended in a bottomless abyss. A fall would mean certain death. Looking down made me cringe a bit, but I felt safe. I knew that I was a good enough climber to negotiate such terrain. I placed my ice axes safely and moved up slowly. At one point I saw an old rope, which was completely frazzled and tattered. I told myself not to touch it. Further up I found the snow stake it was attached to. It was stuck in very loose snow and would probably have held about two pounds at best.

I continued along an airy ridge toward the false summit for a quarter of an hour, and then I finally reached the main summit of Makalu—my highest point at that time. I could certainly feel the difference between Cho Oyu's 8188 meters and Makalu's 8485 meters. I took a summit picture with the self-timer of my camera, but when I looked at it later I was shocked to see how puffed up my face was. It must have been the altitude. I looked across to Mount Everest reaching even farther into the sky and wondered whether I would ever be able to climb that high. I tried to imagine what it would be like to climb another 400 vertical meters without supplemental oxygen. Even though the last few hours had been incredibly exhausting, I felt that I had not completely depleted my strength, and could still go on. But could I do another 400 meters?

Standing alone on the rocky summit of Makalu, surrounded by countless snow-capped peaks, and looking at the unreachable valleys below was an incredible sensation. I felt humble and extremely grateful. I felt like the only person on the planet, but I wasn't scared or lonely. I was in good hands in this wild, inaccessible landscape.

I couldn't spend long on the summit—it was already late afternoon. I wanted to go all the way to Camp 3, where I had left my sleeping bag and mat; at Camp 4, I would find only an empty tent. I followed the ridge back to the false summit and concentrated on the steep passage, slowly climbing down on the frontpoints of my crampons. I tried not to look down. After I managed the short traverse, I breathed a sigh of relief. The route was now pretty flat toward the French Couloir, and I relaxed a little.

But when I looked up I couldn't believe my eyes: Erich was coming up toward me. This was absolutely impossible—it was already 3:30 p.m.! Watching him from a distance, I noticed that he had trouble walking; after a few steps he collapsed onto his knees, and it took him quite some time to catch his breath and pick himself up again.

I walked to him and said, "Erich, what on Earth are you doing here?"

He didn't reply, but it seemed as if he really wanted to make it to the summit. It was not that far, but in his state and at this hour it wasn't a good idea to continue. He was completely exhausted, and I wondered how he had actually managed to come so far.

"Erich, it's late, and we have to get down as soon as possible. You have to go back with me," I said.

He kneeled in the snow, and I saw that he wasn't carrying a backpack but a kind of shoulder bag, which was weird. I could see two marker poles peeking out of the bag; one with a Nepalese flag and the other one with a flag from the Austrian state of Carinthia.

"Erich, please turn back with me—you are completely wasted."

"No," he said, his voice sounding weak. "It'll be fine. I'll be fine."

I asked him, "Do you have enough to drink?"

"No, I have run out."

There was still some sweetened black coffee in my thermos, so I gave him two cups, which he gulped down in seconds.

Once more I told him to descend with me, but he wouldn't listen. "Erich, please, go back. You are too exhausted."

"My flags! I want at least to reach the false summit so I can hoist my flags. I want to get there really badly, and I'm sure I can make it."

"Erich, forget it—you no longer have it in you."

I told him about the passage below the false summit, explaining how exposed and dangerous it was, and that he was not allowed to make a single mistake there.

"Turn around. Let's try and go down together."

He didn't budge. I couldn't get him to turn back with me. He sounded fairly clear when he said, "No, I really want to get there. I'll only climb to the false summit and turn around. Why don't you wait for me in our tent at 7800 meters? I will meet you there."

"Erich, forget it—you won't make it. Go down!"

"No, I'll make it. Wait for me. I'll be there in a few hours."

I tried everything, but I couldn't get him to come down with me, and at the time he was certainly more experienced than I was. He didn't want to descend, and I had no choice but to leave him. I couldn't take him by the hand and drag him down with me. I was also running out of energy and it was actually hard enough to get myself safely down to our camp.

I then told Erich about the old fixed rope and the snow stake and warned him not to use it. I also asked him whether he had a headlamp. "Yes, of course I have one," he said.

I gave him the last cup of my coffee. Then I had no choice but to continue downward and leave him up there. I don't think I actually knew what it would have meant had Erich gone down with me. At his slow pace the descent would have been extremely hard without a rope to short-rope him, especially through the French Couloir. I guess at some point I would have had to decide whether to leave him, or fail to get myself down. But all of this only dawned on me later. At the time, I tried very hard to make Erich descend with me because I knew deep down inside that he had no chance if he continued. When I turned around again, Erich had walked a few steps farther. Then I tried to concentrate on myself and on climbing down safely.

Just below the couloir I saw something in the snow. A thermos! Why had Erich left his thermos in the snow? It was still half full. Had he wanted to shed some weight or was he suffering from cerebral edema and unable to think clearly? A little bit farther down, I found a headlamp in the snow. It could only be Erich's, even though he had assured me that he had one. I then found his Gore-Tex jacket, which he had pegged down in the snow. This meant that he had no additional layer to protect himself against the cold. I left his stuff where it was, just in case he would need it on the descent, but I was very worried about how he would get back down the mountain without his lamp.

I reached our tent at 7800 meters at nightfall and crawled in. It was 7:00 p.m. There was nothing—no mat, no sleeping bag, and no stove to melt drinking water. I was completely dehydrated. The way to Camp 3 was relatively flat and marked, and I guess I would have found it with my headlamp, but I felt obliged to wait for Erich. I didn't even think about the possibility of him not coming back. I pushed away the obvious reality: Erich had already been in trouble below the French Couloir.

I hung up my headlamp inside the tent and left it on to help Erich find the camp. The wind was howling outside, and I was very cold. I didn't have a down suit. On my legs I wore long johns, fleecy trousers, and Gore-Tex trousers; on top I also wore several layers and a down jacket. The only thing I had with me was my backpack, which I dragged into the tent. Then I sat on it and waited. I was dying for a hot drink. The wind got stronger, reaching gale force, and I kept on hearing noises from outside. But whenever I looked out of the tent to see whether anyone was calling, I heard and saw nothing but the howling wind.

I waited and waited until time seemed to have come to a standstill. I was freezing cold and very tired, but I didn't want to fall asleep. The next time I looked at my watch it was already midnight. The wind was raging outside and suddenly it struck me: Erich was not coming back. Even though it seemed impossible and I didn't want to believe it, I knew: I would never, ever see Erich again. Suddenly I felt calm. Just like in the stormy night in the tent with Herbert a few days earlier, I accepted the situation. I knew I couldn't change it, I had to surrender. I was not the type to get hysterical in difficult situations; instead, I started to imagine what it would be like once I was back in safety, in the warmth with other people.

I was very happy the next morning when the storm abated and I could head down. I desperately needed to drink. When I got out of the tent, I noticed that I had not been alone at camp. There was an Iranian team of eight who had been so quiet during the night that I hadn't noticed them. One last time, I looked up toward the summit. I couldn't see any sign of Erich. I then turned around and slowly began my descent.

At Camp 3 I met Karl. He had been very worried about us when we didn't return to camp. When he embraced me, all the tension of the last few hours fell off me and I broke into tears. "Erich didn't come back."

Talking about it made the situation more real. I told Karl what had happened the previous day, he gave me a drink, and we packed our backpacks and started descending. I was completely exhausted and felt numb and empty. At ABC, when my team and all the other expeditions congratulated me on my summit success, I could only think about Erich not having made it. Of course, I was happy to have reached the top of Makalu, but my joy was dimmed by Erich's tragic death. Some people hoped that he would still show up—it had happened before—but I didn't share this hope. I guess he must have fallen at the steep section leading up to the false summit, the section that required such absolute concentration. Maybe he had clipped into the loose rope? Or maybe he had just sat down somewhere and fallen into a deep, infinite sleep.

The question of what I could have done to prevent Erich's death haunted me for a long time. It would have been easy for me to remove the old rope so nobody else would use it, but I didn't think of it at the time. I was busy trying not to touch the rope. Long talks with Herbert really helped. He tried to make me understand that I should not blame myself for Erich's death, that it had not been up to me to save him. Erich had been, like of all of us, responsible for himself.

Another consolation was the fact that dying was part of life—something I had definitely learned during my time as a nurse. I had often spent the last hours with a dying patient. I had already learned about terminal care at nursing school, and I later participated in a seminar on it. Even though death was often a relief after a long illness, it was always hard to say a last goodbye. On day shifts, with more staff on hand to lend support and share the vigil, dealing with death seemed easier. At night, it was more difficult. Whenever I saw the word, "dying," in the handover notes at the start of my night shift, I would be tense all night; I always wanted to stay close to the dying patients to make sure someone was with them during their final minutes. I also learned that even as a nurse I was allowed to mourn. Sometimes I cried when I informed the relatives about a patient's death. In this regard, my time at the Rottenmann Hospital was very enriching and important for my future climbing career.

It is my strong faith in God that helps me cope with the personal loss of a friend or family member. When I was fifteen my sister Brigitte's first husband died. I have no idea how I would have coped with it had I not believed that there was life after death. My other sister Manuela, who is two years older than me, was devastated. She cried for days on end. In order to help her, I told her that all was not over after death and that we would meet each other again somehow. This faith is still with me and supports me through difficult times.

One of the mountain guides from the Carinthian team reached the summit a week later and told us that he didn't find anything belonging to Erich—not even his two flags. So he must have fallen in the gully. At base camp his empty tent remained next to ours for a while, making me feel incredibly sad whenever I looked at it. In the end the Korean who had shared the climbing permit with Erich took it down.

I had never been so happy to get home after an expedition. I needed distance. Birgit was my rock; I told her a lot about what happened on the mountain. I didn't want to bother my sister Brigitte too much; she had just lost the second love of her life. It took a while for me to get over Erich's death. Losing someone on a mountain is always tragic, and having known Erich a bit better made it harder for me. I just couldn't understand why he went so far beyond his limits. At base camp he was always saying that he would never risk so much as his pinky for an 8000-meter peak—it was simply not worth it.

Continuous snowfall marked the Manaslu expedition. All teams (here just below Camp 2) attempted to reach the summit during the next weather window.

CHAPTER 4

CLOSENESS

N ever again"—that would probably have been the appropriate reaction after my experience on Makalu. But I never thought seriously about giving up high-altitude mountaineering. It was just too fascinating. Standing on the summit of Makalu for those few minutes had confirmed my sense that the Himalaya was the right place for me. Rather than thinking about giving up, I analyzed what had happened up there—not only Erich's death, but also other accidents I had seen in the mountains—so I could learn from them. It was absolutely clear to me that I wanted to go on another expedition the following year.

My resolution after Makalu was certainly not to give up. Instead I resolved: "Next time, I will go on my own." It didn't have anything to do with Erich's death. I had been on seven expeditions which were mostly big groups, with Herbert and me going twice on our own. I had realized that in a team of two we could react more quickly to the weather and other conditions on the mountain. I had learned a lot on my various expeditions and now felt confident enough to climb independently. Making my own decisions and using the tactics I deemed appropriate had become very important to me. I no longer wanted to be subject to decisions made by an expedition leader; I wanted to be actively involved in the discussions and to be treated as an equal when considering different options. Given a good match in personalities and performance, small teams can definitely avoid many problems that occur in big teams, such as conflicts of interest between members, competition, envy, and disputes about communal tasks. Who carries what? Who doesn't help set up camp? Who doesn't want to break trail? When Herbert and I were on our own it was much easier to establish contact with the locals, too, something that was and is extremely important to me. With twelve people in a group, one is less likely to connect with locals. I was very grateful for the opportunities I had had with the alpinists of the Friends of Nature, but I reached a conscious decision to climb in small and private expeditions from then on.

For 2002, I couldn't count on Herbert. After Makalu he had decided not to go back to an 8000-meter peak in the near future. We had gotten used to going our own ways, and our physical closeness had turned into good friendship. We had learned to give each other space, but we were also happy to do things together whenever we had the opportunity. I didn't spend a lot of time finding a new expedition partner, deciding instead to head out on my own. My next destination was clear. Sepp Hinding, who lived nearby and whom I had often seen since our Cho Oyu expedition, raved about Manaslu, which he had already climbed. I definitely wanted to go there. Getting a climbing permit on my own would have been far too expensive, so I had to share it with other climbers. After I found out that the trekking agent Herbert and I had used for Shisha Pangma didn't have any Manaslu expeditions, I ended up with Thamersku Trekking, which had already organized an expedition for two Australians.

The fourth person on our permit was Renzo Corona, with whom I had stayed in touch since my Makalu expedition. His Italian expedition had been kind enough to let me sleep in one of their tents at high camp, as there was a shortage of tents in my own expedition. The following summer we went rock climbing in the Dolomites, and in the winter he and his friends visited Herbert and me in Austria for ice climbing and ski mountaineering. Renzo had actually planned to climb Dhaulagiri I with his brother in 2002. But conflict between the Maoist rebels and the Nepalese government had come to a head after the shooting of the Nepalese royal family in June 2001, and due to continuing clashes between the rebels and the Nepalese Army his Dhaulagiri expedition was cancelled. Many of his expedition members chose to climb Manaslu instead, and Renzo, who knew that I would be there, also opted for the eighth-highest mountain in the world.

I too was affected directly by the Maoist conflict. After an eight-hour bus journey we arrived in Gorkha, from which my relatively small expedition consisting of a cook, Lhakpa Sherpa, and myself started the trek to base camp. Lhakpa was not a climbing Sherpa in the classic sense—I hired him to support me in setting up the high camps in case of high winds, and we agreed that we would both carry our own gear. Hiring Lhakpa was merely a safety measure; I knew I would climb on my own. Once we arrived at base camp I realized that hiring Lhakpa had not been necessary; there were so many people there. On our first three trekking days we were escorted by the military to protect us. During the nights, I was not allowed to use my headlamp, as it could have attracted the Maoists' attention. Whenever I forgot, one of the soldiers would bang his rifle against my tent in protest. I guess I felt less threatened by the Maoists than by the omnipresent soldiers, who were armed to the teeth.

When I presented my trekking and expedition permits at the checkpoint in Arughat Bazar, we got into trouble. Our liaison officer had already gone through with my two Australian teammates, and the soldiers at the checkpoint didn't want to let me go without one. They didn't listen to my pleading, and when I wanted to phone the trekking agent from one of the military posts, I noticed that the Maoists had cut the phone line. I had no choice but to wait for a day and send one of my porters back to Gorkha to get an official letter confirming that the liaison officer was already at base camp. Renzo, who had set off a day behind me, caught up with me there and we walked the last two days together.

After about a week we reached the last village below base camp: Samagoan, at an altitude of 3500 meters. We had to change our porters here, a common procedure to give the people of Samagoan the chance to earn some money. We stayed at a lodge run by the village teacher. One evening we were sitting in the common room with the family when the door flew open and a few Maoists barged in. For the first time on this trip we were faced with the "enemies." To my surprise, the situation was anything but threatening. The new guests were immediately offered food and drink, and an animated discussion was soon underway. The two climbing Sherpas of the Norwegian team told us later that the locals were in a tricky situation. If they fed the Maoists and the military found out, they would be punished; if they didn't feed the Maoists, the rebels would kill them. The two climbing Sherpas were happy to be on the mountain, far away from the village.

On my way to base camp at 4750 meters I was surprised to hear German voices. I had no idea that there was going to be an AMICAL alpin expedition on Manaslu. AMICAL alpin was the trekking and expedition company owned by Ralf Dujmovits, who, together with his Swiss mountain guide, Sepp von Rotz, led a team of fourteen climbers. In order to avoid running into Maoists, they had taken a helicopter to Samagoan. When we arrived at base camp, Renzo and I were surprised to find a lot of snow, but we were happy to finally meet the two Australians on our climbing permit, Andrew Lock and Trajce Aleksov, or Alex. I had actually come across Andrew on Broad Peak in 1994, but Alex and I were meeting for the first time. He was originally from Macedonia, but he lived in Australia. Andrew and Alex had already been on the mountain for two weeks and were well acclimatized. About two weeks after we arrived at base camp, Andrew and the two Norwegians reached the summit, which was rather reassuring given that no team had been successful on Manaslu in the previous two years.

Even though we shared the permit, base camp, and the cook and were otherwise independent, Renzo and I climbed together most of the time. The AMICAL team also climbed parallel to us, and I was not nearly as lonely as I'd thought I would be. When Lhakpa, Renzo, and I passed the German camp on our way to Camp 1, I decided on the spur of the moment to pop in and introduce myself to Ralf. Of course I had heard about him. AMICAL was a well-known operator among high-altitude mountaineers, and I had watched the live broadcast of his ascent of the Eiger North Face, where he was one of four protagonists. Some of the members of the AMICAL expedition had told me that Ralf was not so keen on visiting other camps, so I took the initiative and walked into his mess tent.

"Hello, do you know by any chance where I can find Ralf?"

I was told, "He is probably in the kitchen tent."

When I opened the kitchen tent, I saw five suntanned faces. Five pairs of eyes stared back at me. I assumed that these must be the climbing Sherpas and kitchen staff and asked in my broken English, "Sorry, I am looking for Ralf Dujmovits. Do you know where he is?"

TOP: I made a quick descent on skis from Camp 1 to base camp (Larkya Peak in the background). BOTTOM: Manaslu glowing in the morning sun, as seen from base camp.

A friendly burst of laughter was the answer to my question. One of the five introduced himself as Ralf. I had expected him to be much older. We exchanged a few words, but I politely declined his invitation to a cup of tea; I was fully dressed and ready to go up to Camp 1. I didn't think much about that meeting, but I knew that I liked him.

We pitched our Camp 1 at a safe place and spent our first acclimatization night at 5600 meters. Like some of the AMICAL members we had brought our snowblades, which can be used with expedition boots to ski over beautiful sugar snow back to base camp. It was a shame that we would only be able to use the skis on this first section. The terrain higher up was too steep and had too many seracs. On our descent we met Ralf and his group, who were on their way up. Apparently he took a video of our ski descent—something I found out only later.

One evening, the AMICAL crew invited Renzo and me for dinner. I was stunned by the comfort of their camp. They had a shower tent, a satellite phone, and a laptop with Internet access. Ralf regularly spoke to Charly Gabl of the Institute for Meteorology and Geodynamics in Innsbruck, who gave him up-to-date and reliable weather reports—which Ralf generously shared with us. I loved their good food—compared to our cook's dishes, the AMICAL meals were gourmet. Apparently, our cook had been at base camp for too long and was burned out. In any case, his cooking was pretty miserable. Once the tea even tasted of kerosene and gave me diarrhea. We spent a lovely and very sociable evening at the AMICAL camp. I talked to Sepp von Rotz, the assistant guide, and to Gianni Goltz from Ticino, the Italian-speaking part of Switzerland. Renzo was thrilled to speak Italian with Gianni. The highlight of the evening was a movie in thin air: On Ralf's laptop we watched *Erin Brockovich* with Julia Roberts. What luxury!

But soon it was time to return to the real expedition world. We went back up to Camp 1 to spend another night there and managed a gear carry to Camp 2. There were only four of us at Camp 1: Renzo in his tent, Lhakpa and I in ours, and a Korean climber in another tent. In the evening I noticed a strange hissing sound coming from outside. I had put my ski poles and ice axes in front of the tent, and the noise was certainly coming from there. I heard a crackling sound, my hair stood on end, and there was an incredible electric tension in the air. Immediately I remembered the thunderstorm with Father Tischler on Schafdach Mountain. I had never experienced a thunderstorm on an 8000-meter peak before, and the prospect of being caught in one really worried me. Manaslu was famous for its bad weather. I seemed to remember that a tent had the same protective effects as a Faraday cage in a thunderstorm, but I still snuck out quickly to move ski poles and ice axes and other metal items farther away from the tent, laying them flat in the snow.

Once I was back in the tent, the thunder and lightning continued as a blizzard came up, depositing huge amounts of snow onto our tents. I was lying in my sleeping bag, wincing with every clap of thunder, and thinking, "Please let this pass." What else could I do? We were, as they say, at the mercy of nature—there was thunder and lightning, and I was incredibly scared. In order to distract myself I wanted to talk to Lhakpa, but he was tucked into his sleeping bag and not moving an inch. The whole time I kept thinking about the South Tyrolean mountaineer, Friedl Mutschlechner, who was fatally struck by lightning on Manaslu. But he was killed on his descent, without a tent to protect him.

I was so happy when the terrifying night was over and we could pack our bags and ski down to base camp. Everyone had been very worried about us. We received a hearty welcome, and I was pleasantly surprised to see Nirkuma, who had cooked for me on the trek to base camp. He must have come to replace the other cook, with whom I had not been so happy. I later found out that this change was thanks to Ralf, who had worked with Thamersku Trekking for a long time. After our chat over dinner, Ralf had contacted the agency and done everything humanly possible to make sure that I would get a better cook. That evening, Nirkuma spoilt us with fresh vegetables and yak meat, which he had brought up to base camp and buried in the snow next to the kitchen tent to keep it fresh.

On our next ascent, we could finally continue to Camp 2. We had to negotiate a long icefall, but luckily Andrew and the Norwegians had marked it with flags, which made finding the route a lot easier. After a night at 6600 meters, Renzo, Lhakpa, and I returned to base camp. As forecast, it clouded over during our descent, and a bad weather front with gale force winds and humidity moved toward us. But we didn't expect that the bad weather would last five days, with constant snowfall. Base camp was literally drowning in snow. If we had not gotten up in the middle of the nights to shake the snow off our tents and partially dig them out, we would have had a hard time getting out at all in the mornings. And if the tents had been completely covered, we would probably have been deprived of oxygen. We had to shake the snow off our mess tent, too, to keep it from getting crushed. The world around us was entirely white: Contours had disappeared, the snow was swallowing every sound. We had entered a muted world, isolated from the other teams. Everyone was busy keeping their camps free of snow, and it would have been too hard to plod through the deep snow to the neighboring camps for a visit. My life was reduced to shoveling snow, chatting to Renzo, eating, sleeping, reading, and listening to music. Though I often long for such empty days back home, at base camp they seemed to drag on.

On the third day I began to worry. We were experiencing exactly what Manaslu was notorious for: huge masses of fresh snow in a very short period of time. There had been seasons when people had gotten stuck at base camp due to too much snow and avalanche danger, had lost all their high camps, and were unable to collect their equipment from the mountain.

On the fourth day it was still snowing. Every time I looked out of the tent I faced a huge disappointment. The snow cover kept on growing inch by inch, but I didn't give up hope. I thought that the weather had to improve eventually.

But on the fifth day it continued to snow! This was ridiculous. I had read all my books and needed to move. I paced up and down the mess tent like a tiger in a cave. When would it stop?

On the sixth day I looked out of the tent and couldn't believe my eyes: I was greeted by deep blue sky and brilliant sunshine. Getting out of the "snow cave" of the tent and feeling the warmth of the sun on my body was fabulous. The camp was waking up, and soon everyone was shoveling snow. I got the sense that all the other camp dwellers were busy shoveling, but the snow walls were so high that I could barely see them. As soon as the sun hit the mountain, we could hear the avalanches rumble higher up.

Manaslu was roaring all day, an overpowering spectacle of nature but also very dangerous. I was happy to be safe down at base camp. Renzo and I agreed that we would wait at least two days for the snow to settle. We kept ourselves busy with chores like digging for Nirkuma's meat deposit, which we located only after several hours with the help of another shoveler.

On the third good day, May 1, literally the entire base camp headed toward Camp 1. We were all eager to see what the heavy snowfall had done to the mountain higher up. After many hours of breaking trail and wading through deep snow we reached Camp 1. I was confused: Camp 1 seemed to have disappeared. I didn't know whether all the tents were buried in snow or had been blown away by the storm. As it turned out, they were still there but completely covered and crushed by more than three feet of snow. Lhakpa and I shoveled for hours to find and then dig out our tent. The weight of the snow had broken the poles and torn the tent walls, making the tent completely unusable. We were lucky to be able to stay the night in another expedition's tent. Ralf's tents also had some broken poles, but the team was able to fix them.

It was obvious that we would have to do a lot of trail breaking the following day and that we could only cover the 1000 meters to Camp 2 if we all worked together. We set off at the crack of dawn. At first the snow came up to our knees, but higher up it was hip-deep. None of us could break trail for much longer than ten minutes. Ralf, Sepp, Gianni, their Pakistani high-altitude porter Qudrat Ali, and I all took turns leading. Pulling one foot out of the snow, getting it high enough to put it back on the ground, and putting some weight on it with a heavy load on my back was incredibly exhausting. Whenever I had finished my trail-breaking shift it took me a while to catch my breath before I could follow the others.

It took us eight hours to get to Camp 2, which we also had to dig out. While most of the climbers descended to base camp the next day, our tried and tested trail breakers checked out the route to Camp 3. The higher we got, the less snow we encountered; the wind had blown it off. After a short distance we walked on sugar snow and ice. Even though we were now on easier terrain, we were forced to stop at 7150 meters by the rising wind. We spent another night at Camp 2 before going back to base camp.

Charly Gabl had predicted good weather until Friday. As he usually did, he analyzed the international satellite images and sent us regular updates. Being a high-altitude mountaineer himself, he knows how to interpret the conditions on the mountain and is even able to consider other elements such as a wind-protected spot or the jet effect in the valleys. It is a real privilege for us to know that in case of emergency we can ring Charly at any time of day or night. Charly's weather forecasts have proved over the years to be among the most reliable, and he now provides the weather for mountaineers from all over the world. His precise forecasts are invaluable to us, as it is vital to be at the right place at the right time, especially on an 8000-meter peak. Situations like in 2001, when we were unexpectedly caught in bad weather and had to spend a very scary night at 7800 meters on Makalu, no longer need to happen. He may not be able to predict every detail, but he can give us an idea about the general weather and its expected development.

So we set out again on Tuesday, May 7, after only two rest days. We were well acclimatized by then and ready to try for the summit. We spent a night each at Camp 1 and Camp 2, then we set up Camp 3 in a little wind-protected icy ditch at 7450 meters. Renzo and I helped Ralf and Qudrat put up their tents, as it took a while for all their members to negotiate the steep 70-degree ice wall. The Norwegians had fixed some rope which they said we could use. In return, we promised to donate some money to rebuild the school in Samagoan. The weather was so calm in the evening that we were actually able to have dinner outside and enjoy the breathtaking views of Annapurna IV rising above the clouds and glowing in the sunset.

Camp 3 was situated at the lower end of a big, relatively flat, but heavily crevassed plateau extending from about 7300 meters virtually all the way to the summit. I couldn't help it, something was bugging me the evening before our summit attempt. I knew that finding the route in bad weather could be tricky on the plateau, where mountaineers had gotten lost, failing to find their tents and dying of hypothermia or falling into a crevasse. In the late afternoon Sepp and I climbed a bit higher to check out the route, but the ice was so hard that we couldn't place any markers. At least I had a GPS with me. Mine, which I had brought especially for navigating on the plateau, had broken right at the beginning of the expedition, but Andrew had been kind enough to lend me his.

In the end, I didn't need it. The weather was totally clear but cold when we all set out at midnight on May 10. We made good progress on the windswept plateau. I didn't even notice that Ralf had turned back with a client who was not feeling well. The last section between the false and the main summits was pretty exposed, and we had to negotiate the mixed ground using two ice tools. Finally, at 7:30 a.m. Sepp and I stood on the summit. Ecstatic, we gave each other a big hug—rather difficult in our big down suits—and shared a moment of deep satisfaction. I was incredibly happy to have made it, and only a little disappointed by the clouds that denied us a view. After our moment of joy, Sepp and I climbed back to the false summit where we sat down to wait for the others. While we were waiting, the clouds briefly parted. Part of my deep satisfaction came from the sense of community I had experienced on this expedition. It was nice to see our group from different nations join forces and achieve our goal together.

On our descent we met Renzo and Gianni, who had also made it to the summit that day. We continued downwards and then saw Alois, a member of the AMICAL expedition, in front of us. We were at about 7800 meters when Alois suddenly slipped. We later found out that an ice plate had broken off underneath his feet. I was petrified when I saw him tumble down about 150 meters over the 40-degree slope. He finally came to a halt where the slope flattened out. He was lying on his back and was not moving. Together with Sepp and two Germans from Ralf's group I rushed over to him. His face was bleeding. He was responsive but didn't quite realize what had just happened. I tried to find out whether he was injured. His shoulder and foot were in pain, but he got off reasonably lightly. The gash on his forehead was bleeding heavily, though, and his whole body was bruised. I bandaged his head and gave him something to drink. We arranged with the Germans that they would take down his gear, while Sepp and I would slowly descend with Alois.

Easier said than done. Alois was in shock and in a lot of pain. We could only support him, since carrying him proved impossible. We also had to ignore his complaints and cries—there was no help for it, we had to get him down as quickly as possible. After what seemed like an eternity we finally reached Camp 3, where Ralf was waiting for his members to return from the summit. I gladly handed over the injured climber, wanting to wait for Renzo. But when it became clear that Alois still needed medical care, we agreed that Sepp and I would continue further down with Alois while Ralf would wait for his people as well as for Renzo.

Once again Sepp and I took Alois between us. His strength was significantly fading. As he was no longer able to clip onto the fixed rope, we had to lower him. He was in a lot of pain, and when I met him on the bottom of one of the lowering sections, he whispered, "Please just leave me here. I can't go on." I was still convinced that we could get him down alive, but his words shook me down to the core. I simply couldn't believe how instantly a beautiful day could turn into a nightmare.

It was getting dark when we arrived at the bottom of the fixed lines. To make matters worse we found ourselves in thick fog and lost our bearings. Suddenly I saw a light. "It must be the AMICAL team trying to direct us!" We followed the light, but when we finally reached it we discovered that it was one of Ralf's team members, who had also gotten lost and was waiting for us. I looked at him with my headlamp and noticed that he didn't have any gloves and his hands were black and bloody. This was just what we needed!

Alois crouched in the snow. He couldn't go on any longer. For a moment I felt desperation, but only for a split second. Then I helped our new patient put gloves over his frozen fingers, lightened his backpack, and made him continue down with us. When I saw a snow stake in the light of my headlamp I knew we were on the right track and that had only to cross the snowy slope to reach Camp 2. When we reached the camp at around midnight, AMICAL's expedition doctor was waiting for us. He immediately took over the two patients. After all those exhausting hours I was incredibly relieved to hand over the responsibility to someone else.

But I relaxed too early. It was not over yet. Ralf told me via the radio that Renzo was suffering from pulmonary edema at Camp 3 and was in such a bad way that Ralf had injected him with the cortisone drug dexamethasone. In his younger years, Ralf had gone to medical school for six months and knew how to give injections. He had also given him emergency oxygen. I couldn't believe it—this couldn't be true! After a sleepless night, Sepp and I waited for Ralf and Renzo while the expedition doctor descended with Alois. The summiteers gradually ambled into camp, but it seemed an eternity until Ralf and Renzo finally appeared. We could see them coming down the last slope step by step, with Ralf continuously encouraging Renzo to carry on. We melted a lot of snow for them to make sure they could get rehydrated as quickly as possible, and then we walked toward them. Renzo needed to descend as fast as possible, so we were anxious to get him to Camp 1, but it took a lot of coaxing to make him descend further. Sepp, Renzo, and I stayed the night at Camp 1 while Ralf joined his team at base camp. At 5600 meters Renzo still didn't improve. He kept waking up, gasping for air. Hoping it would help and that we would get him down to base camp the following day, I gave him Adalat containing nifedipine, a drug that dilates the blood vessels.

On May 12, Sepp and I reached base camp along with a completely worn out Renzo. Everything had turned out well. I sat down and thought about all the events of the past few days. It had been complete madness! The excitement and physical exhaustion of the past few days had taken a lot out of me. At the same time, I had also discovered that even though I was completely depleted after the summit, I still had enough energy to help others. Sepp and I were able to do everything humanly possible to get Alois down. It was a very moving experience when he came up to us just before the helicopter picked him up from base camp, and said, "Thanks, you saved my life."

Renzo's pulmonary edema was a bonding experience for both of us—maybe in part because I had felt responsible for him. In return for having looked after Renzo so well, we invited Ralf to dinner in our mess tent. For this special occasion Nirkuma prepared a delicious feast, which I was very proud of even though I had not cooked it.

Ralf reciprocated by inviting me to Kilroy's, a restaurant in Kathmandu. Within minutes we were completely absorbed in our conversation. We even forgot to order dinner. We talked about our climbs and expeditions

TOP: Even though our attempt to climb the north face of Kangchenjunga in spring 2003 was not successful, it was still a very intense and beautiful experience. *(Photo by Ralf Dujmovits)* BOTTOM: Kangchenjunga in the evening light as seen from Camp 1

and our respective attitudes toward the mountains, and I soon realized that we were fascinated by many of the same things. In the course of the evening, we also talked about future projects.

"Would you like to join my expedition to the north face of Kangchenjunga next year?" he asked me.

Suddenly, here was this unexpected question. Ralf was planning a private expedition with friends. The normal route of Kangchenjunga is the southwest face. The north face is hardly ever climbed; very few expeditions attempt this steep and beautiful but very challenging face. It had been a long time since it had been successfully climbed.

"We are five climbers, and we need a sixth partner. I saw how you climb on Manaslu. You would fit in perfectly, not only because of your physical strength."

I was flattered by this recognition from such an accomplished high-altitude mountaineer. Climbing the north face of Kangchenjunga would be amazing. I didn't even think about how I would get time off or find the necessary funds for this expedition.

"I would love to come with you, Ralf."

At that moment it didn't even occur to me that Ralf might have had another reason to invite me on the expedition. We still laugh about it today. He wanted to stay in touch with me because he had fallen in love with me. I really liked him, but I didn't see much beyond the prospect of going to Kangchenjunga with him. I only found out later that the minute I had walked into the kitchen tent on Manaslu, he had known I was the woman he wanted to spend the rest of his life with.

I soon got used to the idea that I would go to Kangchenjunga in the spring of 2003. Once Ralf's friends had accepted me as their sixth team member, I began to train hard. I wanted to keep up with them and prove that I could break trail as well as they could. The team was a really nice bunch. Two of them were Germans, Michi Wärthl and David Göttler, whom I met at the ISPO sports trade fair in Munich before the expedition. I met the other two in Kathmandu: the Japanese climber Hirotaka Takeuchi, known as Hiro, and the Finn Veikka Gustafsson. At the beginning of April 2003, we took a small fixed-wing plane to Taplejung. We trekked through Kangchenjunga National Park, which is very scenic and rich in flora and fauna. I had rarely seen such beautiful and varied landscape on a trek to base camp. Apart from our team, there was not a soul to be seen.

After we had passed the Sherpa settlement of Ghunsa the valley started to open up, giving way to a view of the impressive Jannu, a 7000-meter peak majestically towering above us. Base camp at Pangpema at 5150 meters was an idyllic flat green space from which we could see the entire north face, though its base was still a six- to seven-hour walk farther across the glacier. We were the only base-camp dwellers, which was rather amazing given that it was the fiftieth anniversary year of the first ascent of Mount Everest, and the Everest Base Camp was bursting at its seams. We, on the contrary, had plenty of space to spread out.

At base camp we each had our own tent, but at the high camps we would share a tent with another person. As I had come on this expedition with Ralf it almost went without saying that we would share a tent; Michi and David were very good friends, and Hiro and Veikka had known each other for a long time and communicated in English, anyway. Ralf and I were virtually living in each other's pockets, which seemed perfectly natural to me. We had gotten along very well during the trek to base camp. I felt close to Ralf, and this feeling grew by the day. Every morning when I woke up I looked forward to spending time with him. On expedition, you cannot avoid getting to know a person to his or her core. It is impossible to build a wall around oneself or pretend to be someone else, as you would do back home to impress the other person. In extreme situations, you cannot fool each other. Ralf and I both saw that we were on the same wavelength in many ways, and I started to reciprocate the feelings he had had for me for quite some time. We fell in love, which added some lightness to all the exhaustion and setbacks we experienced during our difficult weeks on Kangchenjunga.

The six of us made a harmonious team. Everyone was motivated and fit enough to take turns at breaking trail, which meant we made good progress on the mountain. I enjoyed being among professional mountaineers, and I really appreciated being treated as an equal from the very beginning. We had a lot of fun together; Veikka was a fun guy, and David and Michi definitely made us laugh a lot. We were optimistic, confident that we would be able to climb the north face if the weather allowed us to.

We spent one night at Camp 1 at 5700 meters. We fixed some rope on a steep section a little farther up and established a deposit camp at 6200 meters before we descended back to base camp. At the foot of a slightly overhanging serac we fixed an ice screw and attached to it our crampons, ice tools, bolts, some more ice screws, and 150 meters of fixing rope. With this deposit, we avoided having to take down the gear we didn't need lower down on the mountain. Well, that was the grand plan. When we went back up after a few days of bad weather, we were greeted by a nasty surprise. The serac had collapsed and our gear was buried underneath it. We dug with a vengeance to find our deposit, but gave up after two hours. Our gear was gone!

Could this be the end of our expedition? The mood was muted when we climbed back to base camp. How could we possibly continue without crampons and ice tools? Of course, everyone had a bit of spare gear, but it would certainly not be enough to climb the mountain. We probably would have no other choice than to pack up and go home. I was devastated.

In the meantime, two Dutch trekkers had arrived at base camp. Apart from a biologist the Dutch had been the only visitors there. They very kindly lent us figure-of-eights as well as crampons. On the spur of the moment, Michi decided to run down to the nearby Jannu base camp, from which the Swiss climbers Erhard Loretan, Stephan Siegrist, and Ueli Steck were attempting the unclimbed north face of Jannu—a feat they didn't accomplish in the end. They had enough spare gear to help us out so we could continue our expedition.

After this unfortunate incident we set up Camp 2 at 6000 meters, but were forced back by bad weather and couldn't stay the night. We were stuck at base camp for a few days while a violent storm raged farther up the mountain. Charly Gabl told us that the jet stream would drop down to 6500 meters and that we certainly had no business being up there. Farther down the weather was not too bad so, using our sleeping mats as crash pads, we went bouldering on the big rocks near base camp, all the while hearing the wind howl across the ridge higher up.

On May 5, the wind finally abated and we went back up the mountain. This time we reached the north ridge at 7300 meters, where we pitched our three small tents in an exposed spot. The far side of the ridge offered a spectacular view into Sikkim and across to the east ridge. The Friends of Nature of Austria had attempted this beautiful ridge in 2000, but abandoned the climb at 6200 meters. After another acclimatization night we descended about 2000 meters all the way back to base camp in an approaching storm. We were ready to go for the summit; all we needed now was a decent weather window.

Once again a storm raged higher up, keeping us at base camp for a few more days. Slowly but surely we were running out of time; we had already been at base camp for five weeks. We spent our days climbing 6000-meter peaks in the vicinity, enjoying some bouldering, and devouring the delicious food prepared by our cook Maila. Whenever we were at camp, which was rather often during the bad weather periods, for both lunch and dinner he would serve a soup starter, a main course, and dessert. The food was very tasty; we were satisfied and didn't worry about the supplies, until one fine evening when Maila came into our mess tent wearing his apron.

He said to Ralf, "Sir, I am very sorry, today no soup."

Ralf asked, "Why no soup?"

"Soup finished," he responded.

We didn't mind having no soup. "No problem," Ralf said, and told him to bring the main course.

"No sir, all finished."

Our jaws dropped. How could it be? We had eaten a huge lunch and all of a sudden we had run out of supplies? Ralf suggested that Maila bring us some canned fruit instead.

"No, all finished, sir. Gas also finished."

This was impossible. We had run out of kerosene, toilet paper, sugar, and flour—we had literally depleted our entire stock. Fortunately, we were still in the possession of more than enough freeze-dried high-altitude meals, but they were a poor substitute for Maila's delicacies. The following day, our Sirdar embarked on the three-day trek down to Ghunsa to get some basic supplies such as eggs, sugar, and flour, while Maila and his assistants collected dried yak dung to make a fire for some tea. But the tea tasted of yak dung, which made it rather difficult to get down.

On May 18, we finally headed off, but we had to wait at Camp 1 for an extra day due to heavy snowfall and high avalanche danger. We managed to get to Camp 2 the following day, but after another night of heavy snowfall Charly told us to expect another eighteen inches of fresh snow. "Get down as quickly as possible," he said. The expedition was over.

It was a shame that we never got a proper weather window as everything else went so smoothly on that expedition. But even though we didn't reach the summit, it didn't seem like a failure to me. I didn't worry about the two months I had lost or the money I had spent; I looked at the positive experience I had had. And in any case I had no time to dwell on frustrations. When I arrived back home I quickly washed my laundry, unpacked and repacked my bags, and was ready to go to Nanga Parbat three days later. But before I left, I needed to talk to Herbert and tell him that I had fallen in love and that I would move out after Nanga Parbat. We had agreed that we would not stand in each other's way if either of us met somebody else, and now the time had come.

Still, breaking up was hard for both of us. Herbert has remained a good friend and we still have long, profound conversations. But in Ralf I had found a soul mate, a partner with whom I could share my passion for the mountains. Ralf shared my attraction to 8000-meter peaks. We each understood what high-altitude mountaineering meant to the other. I had found my male counterpart.

In summer 2003, I reached the summit of Nanga Parbat via the Diamir Route.

CHAPTER 5
WILLPOWER

B efore Ralf invited me to Kangchenjunga, I had already planned to go to Nanga Parbat with some Italian friends in the summer of 2003. Robert Gasser, Kurt Brugger, and I came up with the initial idea; Renzo Corona, his brother, and another friend later decided to join us. We shared a permit but I wanted to climb independently, especially since I was already acclimatized from Kangchenjunga.

The Karakorum are on the northernmost tip of the Himalaya range, far enough in the northwest not to be affected by the monsoon. For this reason, the climbing season in this part of the world stretches from mid-May to mid-August. So it made sense to make the most of my acclimatization from the spring season in the Himalaya by going on to Pakistan. I knew from the outset that I could only climb another 8000-meter peak if I was not too exhausted from the first expedition, had not lost too much weight, and still felt motivated, and this was definitely the case after Kangchenjunga. This was the first time I ever tried combining a spring and summer expedition, and I was curious to find out how long my acclimatization would last.

We had opted for the Diamir Route. Even though it is the most frequented route on Nanga Parbat, it is still absolutely beautiful and technically challenging. We traveled to Chilas via Islamabad and trekked to base camp in three days. On our second trekking day a few men stopped us in a village and asked for a doctor. They told us about a woman who had been very sick for a while. They had some medical equipment, but nobody knew how to use it. I offered to have a look at the woman and followed the men past some goats and chickens into a basic mud house, where I found her, obviously weak and dehydrated. She was lying next to ampoules of electrolyte and an IV drip. I couldn't really examine her but thought that putting her on a drip would be the right thing to do. I got out my first-aid kit, an essential part of my expedition gear, and unpacked the syringes, needles, and venous catheters. The patient was very nervous, and I needed someone to hold her hand while I inserted the drip. Foreign men are usually not allowed to enter a room with Pakistani women, but as I had already introduced Paolo as my assistant he was allowed to come in and help me. I stayed with the woman until the drip was empty, took it out, and bandaged the puncture wound.

The villagers went out of their way to thank us. When I asked them where the drip had come from they explained that every time someone went to Chilas to buy supplies, they always brought back medicines. Sometimes the climbers and trekkers would give them leftover drugs, indicating clearly how to use them. Once again I saw the lack of medical care and the need for health posts in these remote areas. As we walked on, I felt very happy that at least I had given the woman some relief. The same evening a boy came to our camp, bringing us six boiled eggs and a flask with milk tea—a gesture of gratitude for our help. I was very touched, especially considering that most people in Pakistan don't have much for themselves.

Fairy Meadows on the Rakhiot side of Nanga Parbat is famous for its beauty, but base camp for the Diamir Route is situated on another lovely meadow, which was in full flower when we arrived. We had come to a scenic place: It was sunny, a small creek gurgled nearby, and the gigantic Diamir Flank rising over 4000 meters towered above us, a breathtakingly beautiful, glittering white. Once again I had entered a different world where I knew I would want to stay for a long time. Nanga Parbat looked friendly and inviting, and the moment I laid my eyes on it I felt a strong bond. I was really looking forward to climbing this mountain.

As we were walking past the mess tent of an international expedition, we received a warm welcome. Simone Moro from Italy, Ed Viesturs from the United States, Jean-Christophe Lafaille, Ignacio Ochoa de Olza— whom everyone just called Iñaki—from the Basque country, and his Spanish teammate all shared a permit but were climbing independently.

Simone and Jean-Christophe, for example, intended to do a new route up to Camp 3. In addition to their group, there was another expedition at base camp from Kazakhstan.

I was excited to meet some of the most famous high-altitude mountaineers. Still unknown back then, I often caused consternation when I arrived at a base camp. Female 8000-meter climbers were certainly no longer out of the ordinary, but men still outnumbered women by far on the high mountains, especially women who climbed independently.

Because of this, I became more and more part of the small circle of high-altitude mountaineers. Little did I know that spending my springs in Nepal and my summers in Pakistan would become my annual routine. The international mountaineering community usually gathers in Kathmandu at the end of March or the beginning of April. It's always great to see each other, go out for dinner, and exchange stories. Of course, there are also animosities, for example against the so-called freeloaders who tag along on an expedition and take advantage of its others' trail-breaking work. But on the whole I developed good friendships with most of them. I really enjoy spending time with these other climbers whom I have gotten to know so well over the years.

Simone's girlfriend (now wife), Barbara Zwerger, accompanied him to Nanga Parbat that year. She is a competitive rock climber, but the cold and the "grind," as she calls high-altitude mountaineering, is not her cup of tea. She stayed at base camp and did such a good job of entertaining Simone and everyone else that we called her "Radio Bolzano." We chatted a good deal over the course of the expedition, and I really enjoyed our time together. Her good mood was contagious, and it was nice to have another woman in that male-dominated world.

On our first morning at base camp, a climber we called Sepp, though he was actually named Giacoma, didn't show up for breakfast. This was rather strange; he was usually an early bird, always first out of his tent. He had been very strong over the past few days, leading the pack most of the time. After breakfast I went over to his tent to have a look. I certainly did not expect to be faced with a life-and-death situation, but when I looked in I saw that Sepp's face was blue, his lungs were gurgling, and he was vomiting blood. Shouting for the others, I immediately gave him some drugs. Sepp was suffering from severe pulmonary edema. The only way to save his life was to get him down to a lower elevation as quickly as possible. But he couldn't even stand up straight. Simone, Iñaki, and three other members of the international expedition offered to carry him down. Like me, they were already well acclimatized. They took turns piggybacking him while one of the kitchen boys ran ahead to procure a horse. I quickly packed Sepp's passport and money, his sleeping bag, two sleeping mats, drugs, and a water bottle and followed them. As Sepp was gasping for air, I injected him with cortisone along the way. When the horse arrived we put him on it and I went on with the patient while the others returned to base camp.

The next village was at an altitude of 3000 meters. I hoped that he would recover at this lower elevation. The villagers were incredibly helpful; they even moved some cows out of their stable, cleaned it, and let us sleep there. I put down the two sleeping mats, Sepp's sleeping bag—I had left mine behind in the rush—and a warm jacket, while Sepp sat outside, leaning against my backpack, which was more comfortable for him than lying down. When we walked back into the stable, I couldn't believe my eyes. One of the cows must have felt homesick and snuck back in. She was leisurely chewing on Sepp's sleeping bag and had left a huge puddle on my mat. I had to go down to the river to wash the stuff before Sepp could finally lie down in our new abode. Fakir, the horseman, kindly gave us some milk tea and even provided me with a bowl of rice.

Through the night I listened to Sepp's breathing. I don't think I had ever seen such advanced pulmonary edema. I really hoped the drugs would work. At base camp it was not difficult to decide whether to give him dexamethasone or nifedipine—I had simply had to act. Had I not done anything, Sepp would have died. I didn't even question whether or not I had done the right thing; I had to try everything humanly possible to save his life. That night in the village Sepp slept deeply, but I lay awake. First, I had to keep moving because I was freezing; second, I was constantly checking Sepp's condition, using my headlamp to see him; and third, the mice probably would not have let me sleep anyway. It was a long night. At four o'clock in the morning a beautiful voice suddenly filled the whole valley: the prayer of the muezzin. The song gave me goose bumps and sent shivers up my spine.

In the morning Sepp felt a bit better, but he still needed medical care, and not only because he was at risk of catching pneumonia. Fakir said he would take him to Chilas, where he could catch a jeep ride to Islamabad and then fly straight home. On my way back to base camp I reflected on what had just happened, and it was only then that I noticed how tense I had been. I felt as if a huge weight had been lifted off my shoulders, and I was very relieved that it had all worked out in the end.

My relief didn't last very long. The following night Robert woke me up, saying that his lungs were rattling. Fortunately, his condition was not as bad as Sepp's, but Kurt Brugger took him down to one of the villages, where they stayed for a few days. It was incredible. Base camp was only 4200 meters high, and yet two members had already suffered from pulmonary edema.

After all of this I was eager to find out where I was at with my own acclimatization. Kurt and I went to the bottom of the face, where we pitched a first camp between the rocks. The next day we were already faced with the crux of the route. We had started fairly early to avoid rockfall, climbing without a rope. At first we climbed the Low Ice Couloir, a steep 45- to 50-degree gully consisting of sugar snow and ice. We then traversed left toward the Kinshofer Face. In the lower part the mixed ground was relatively easy, but farther up we moved two or three pitches in grade V, which was pretty tough at this high altitude. We found several tattered old fixed ropes, which were actually more of a nuisance than help, as well as an old battered aluminum ladder. We had arranged with some other mountaineers that we could use their fixed ropes, giving them some of our rope in return. When climbing on fixed lines, I usually use a Tibloc, a small, light ascending device, which I prefer to the Jumar, another type of ascender. Because you have to pull it up with your arm, a Jumar demands a lot more strength. With a Tibloc, I can climb normally; it just runs loosely on the rope and only locks when loaded.

Just below Camp 2 we came across a metal pillar on the left. The first successful expedition must have used it to haul up loads—I had wondered how on Earth they had managed to get all the material up here in 1962. We established our camp at about 6200 meters. Kurt had a mild headache and decided to go down. Apart from me that left five Kazakhs and Iñaki, with whom I had gotten on well right from the start. He told me that one of his colleagues had contracted cerebral edema at Camp 2 and had descended.

One of the Kazakhs, Denis Urubko, spoke English pretty well. Late one evening I heard him talking to Iñaki. It had started to snow, and they were discussing who would be breaking trail and who would be fixing the ropes. At about 7000 meters there was a dangerous traverse that had to be fixed. I was a bit perturbed when I heard them talking about six climbers—but we were seven! They simply didn't count me as part of the team! After Denis had left I asked Iñaki what that was about. He just laughed and told me to calm down.

"Gerlinde, don't take it so seriously. The Kazakhs are used to their women being at home in the kitchen looking after the family, not going climbing."

I was furious. That same evening I grabbed the two ropes, used them as my pillow, and put them into my backpack the next morning. I wanted to actively contribute to the rope fixing. The men had planned to start at 8:00 a.m., so I made sure that I was ready to leave well before then. After a good night's sleep, without a headache, I started off plodding behind them. Nobody was talking. The snow was knee-deep. Whenever we changed lead, the first person would step out of the track, the next one would move up front, and the person who had just broken trail would go to the back.

When the guy in front of me stepped out of the track, the Kazakh behind me quickly overtook me and broke trail. I was flabbergasted. Once again, nobody talked to me, just as if I wasn't there. I was not prepared to accept this! I stepped out of the track, overtook the Kazakh in the front, and started breaking trail. Fortunately I was well enough acclimatized to do this. Overtaking someone in deep snow costs a lot of strength and effort, and all the Kazakhs were very strong climbers. There was nothing they could do to stop me from breaking trail all the way to Camp 3 at 6650 meters.

When we reached camp, one of the Kazakhs asked me for my name. Well, at least somebody was taking notice of me. They later told me that they had thought I was a trekker when I first arrived at base camp. In the end, I corrected this assumption.

The next day Denis, another Kazakh, Iñaki, and I climbed farther up to fix the traverse. Iñaki and I, at the front, secured a rope to a big rock. The rope was too long and had to be cut, but we didn't have a knife. In the meantime, Denis had caught up with us.

"Denis, do you have a knife?" I asked.

Denis hesitated. He was probably already freaked out that a woman was helping out with the rope fixing, and now I was asking him for a knife. But he had one, and he threw it to me. Stupidly enough, I didn't notice that his knife had a spring release. When I tried to open it, I used too much force and broke it.

"Typical! Never give a woman a knife!" Denis shouted in Russian. This definitely proved his point that women had no business up there.

After we had fixed the traverse, Iñaki and I went back to base camp. The Kazakhs, who were going for the summit, stayed at the camp. I was content: I had climbed all the way to 7000 meters and felt great. I was definitely still acclimatized from Kangchenjunga. But a voice inside me told me to go down one more time. First of all, I had not brought my down suit, and secondly, I was not mentally ready to go for the summit. Over my climbing years I had adopted a method of familiarizing myself with the mountain and connecting with it before I tried for the summit. Just outside base camp I found a huge flat boulder where I could sit and gaze at the Diamir Route from the Low Ice Couloir all the way to the summit. This was the right place to focus on my goal.

Denis came back to base camp a day later. He had been to the summit with some of his teammates. I gave him my Swiss Army knife, which he really appreciated. He had found out that I was a trained nurse and asked whether I could help him—he had lost a filling. Robert's wife, a dentist, had given me some dental equipment, and my own dentist had provided me with some instant filling paste. Barbara and I agreed to do this "operation" together, but we were not sure how to stop the saliva flow during it.

Then Barbara had a stroke of genius: "Wait! I have an idea—I'll be back in a minute."

She came back with a few tampons. We cut off the obvious blue cord and inserted one into Denis' mouth, which made it a lot easier for us to put in the replacement filling. Had Denis known what we had put into his mouth, he would probably have run for the hills.

Nanga Parbat was the first expedition where I used a satellite phone; Ralf had lent me his. We used it to get the weather forecast, and I also talked to Ralf, whom I missed very much. On Tuesday, June 17, Charly Gabl predicted two days of mixed weather. According to his weather forecast Friday was the only possible summit day, with bad weather moving in right after. So Friday seemed to be my summit day. Unfortunately, that only gave me one rest day instead of the planned two or three. I had to pack all of my summit gear on Tuesday. On Wednesday I would climb to Camp 2, go straight to Camp 4 on Thursday, and try for the summit on Friday. When Iñaki came to our camp for a cup of coffee I told him about my plan. He decided to join me, which was great news.

During the night it snowed a lot at Camp 2, and we had to work hard to break trail the following day. It was especially deep in the Bazhin Hollow. The snow kept falling and visibility was extremely poor. It took us ten hours to cover the 1200 meters to Camp 4, where we found the two tents of the Kazakhs between two boulders. We had arranged with Denis that we could use one of them and deposit our own tent nearby. In the other tent was another Kazakh who had repeatedly tried to get to the summit. He had been at 7400 meters for three nights. Even though his toes were already blue and frozen, his expedition leader, who was at base camp, told him to try again for the summit.

Iñaki suggested a rest day because we were both tired after the strenuous ascent to Camp 4, but in view of the weather forecast, I talked him out of it. I knew I would not recover at this altitude, I would only lose strength. I wanted to go up, with or without him. At about 3:00 a.m. we started out together, and so did the Kazakh. After about an hour and a half, I could tell by the Kazakh's headlamp light that he was going back to the tents. I briefly stopped. It was cold, −29 degrees Fahrenheit, and I could see lightning toward K2. The route led steeply through the rocks, and Iñaki and I were literally digging through deep snow. We took turns at breaking

TOP: Breaking trail just above Camp 2 was hard work   BOTTOM: Descending with Sepp, who was suffering from altitude sickness

trail, and I was glad that he had joined me. I would not have been able to do this on my own. It was actually only another 800 vertical meters to the 8125-meter summit, but breaking trail was so time-consuming that we made very slow progress.

For the final stretch we first had to climb through a gully and then negotiate rocky ground which was fairly windswept. At around lunchtime, I stood on the highest point of Nanga Parbat on my own. Iñaki had fallen behind. I discovered a little metal tube on a chain fixed to a rock. It contained a tattered note from Reinhold Messner saying that he had summited on his own on August 9, 1978. Other Nanga Parbat summiteers, such as Willi Bauer and Rudi Wurzer, whom I knew very well, had also signed the note. They had stood here twenty-five years before me, and fifty years before me Hermann Buhl had become the first person to reach the summit of Nanga Parbat, also on his own—an amazing achievement, given the equipment they had back then. At that moment on the summit, I was very much aware of the rich history of Nanga Parbat and felt incredibly grateful to join this elite and be up there.

Looking down to the green valleys below, I couldn't believe that I had actually made it. I don't think there is another mountain where you can see the altitude difference of 7000 meters as dramatically as on Nanga Parbat. Surrounded by beautiful mountain ranges, I could see our base camp in the distance. Toward the northeast across the Karakorum I could see thick clouds gathering already, and the weather was obviously deteriorating. The summit of Nanga Parbat is rocky, which made it possible for me to put my camera on a boulder and take a photo using the self-timer. Before I started my descent I took two little rocks. One was for myself and the other was for my brother-in-law Walter, Brigitte's husband, who had encouraged me to come here.

On my descent I met Iñaki, and after we had exchanged a few words I was back in the summit gully. With the copious new snow, which would certainly act as a brake, I thought I could slide down part the gully on my backside. The gully was steep at the beginning but flattened out farther down.

"Come on, let's just give it a go," I thought to myself.

I sat down and slid down for a bit. The going was pretty fast, but I was able to brake with my crampons.

"Wow, that's great," I mused.

Then I climbed down for a bit but soon wanted to slide some more. I had my ice ax prepared to break a possible fall. My crampons filled up with snow very fast, which made stopping a bit harder. Suddenly I sped up quite significantly. I rammed my ice ax into the snow to break the slide. I came to a halt but found myself in a thick cloud of down feathers. I had ripped my down suit—the first down suit I'd owned—with my ice ax. This was the price I had to pay for a quick descent. I had covered 300 meters of altitude in just a few minutes and had reached Camp 4 in no time. Only later did I realize that Sigi Loew had fallen to his death in this gully. Had I not been able to brake in time I would probably have slid toward a precipice at high speed.

Thinking about it today makes me feel sick. It was an irresponsible and dangerous thing to do, and I would never ever do it again.

Maybe it was my eagerness to get a drink that drove me to speed toward camp. I had filled my water bottle and my flask for the ascent but in the morning's rush I had left them in the tent. I had not drunk anything the whole day and was feeling very dehydrated.

When I got to my tent, both my bottles were empty! It must have been the Kazakh quenching his thirst. He obviously felt so bad that he had no energy to boil some water himself. I fired up the stove and started to melt some snow. When Iñaki got back, we drank as much as we could. We had no energy to eat.

The next morning we headed out in poor visibility. We wanted to get back to base camp and recover as soon as possible. We had to persuade the Kazakh, who was very apathetic, to come down with us. He was very slow and kept on falling behind. Just above Camp 3 we met Ed Viesturs and Jean-Christophe Lafaille. Jean-Christophe and Simone had just opened a new route. We congratulated Jean-Christophe, had a quick chat, and continued on our way down. We kept on turning around to look for the Kazakh, who was still moving at a snail's pace.

When he finally reached the Bazhin Hollow, he disappeared for a while. Iñaki and I decided to wait for him to reappear to make sure he was following us. We waited for one hour . . . two hours . . . but he didn't show up. I was slowly getting nervous. We couldn't leave him up there! At one point I got fed up with waiting, left my backpack, and climbed back up to look for him. Iñaki joined me. As soon as I started going up, I noticed how tired I was. I was completely and utterly exhausted. The only thing on my mind was to get down as quickly as possible.

When I reached Ed and Jean-Christophe, I could finally see the Kazakh coming down. The other two moved toward him, while I took a short rest before he reached me, and we continued down together. Iñaki rushed ahead to Camp 3 to melt snow. As the Kazakh was completely exhausted, I offered to carry his pack.

"I would rather die," he said, "than give my backpack to a woman."

I thought my ears were deceiving me. He had been above 7000 meters far too long, he was completely exhausted, but he was still too proud to give me his pack.

"OK," I said, "but then at least take my walking poles!"

He didn't object to taking my poles, but it still took us ages to get to Camp 3, and it was obvious that we would not get any farther that day. He had a bad cough, and when I noticed a slight gurgling in his lungs I gave him some drugs to prevent pulmonary edema. He felt a bit better then and talked to his expedition leader on the radio. "The boss says I have to go farther down." I could feel my anger rising. Someone with no clue what was happening up here should not be making the decisions.

"Let me talk to him," I said.

"No, this is not possible—you cannot talk to him."

He would not give me the radio, and the expedition leader continued coercing him to go down. But then suddenly Denis was on the radio. I was at least allowed to talk to him. I explained the situation and told him that his colleague was too exhausted to continue down. Denis explained to me that they were organized differently, and that they had to follow the expedition leader's orders. It was driving me mad. "Denis, this is impossible. He has hit rock bottom! Let me talk to your boss."

I am not sure how it happened, but then the Kazakh expedition leader was on the radio. I tried hard to be friendly as I explained the situation. I dramatized it a bit, telling him that it was a matter of life and death. Denis translated for me.

"Trust me, we will get him down safely tomorrow. We have drugs here, and if you send some people up to meet us tomorrow, we can make it!"

"Okay, we will come toward you tomorrow." I was stunned. He had just allowed a woman to convince him!

All through the night we checked on the Kazakh, urging him to drink as much as possible, which paid off—he was able to walk down himself the next morning. He kept on losing his balance, so I grabbed him from behind by his backpack to keep him stable. Getting him down was a very cumbersome undertaking. He collapsed every few steps. I talked to him as if he were a sick cow, trying to motivate him to get up and keep going. Iñaki and I were absolutely exhausted. Step by step we inched our way down. On the Kinshofer Face we had to keep checking to see whether the Kazakh was clipped in and had screwed up his carabiner properly. Iñaki rappeled down the fixed ropes first and made sure the Kazakh changed over correctly at the anchor points. Finally, at the traverse in the Low Ice Couloir, three of his mates came toward us and took him under their wing. They were extremely grateful for our help. Someone had fixed the ice gully in the meantime, which meant that he could descend relatively safely.

Slowly but surely, the tension of the last few days fell away. When we arrived at the edge of the glacier, Iñaki and I received a hearty welcome. Our base camp team was waiting for us with flower garlands to put around our necks and drinks to celebrate our summit success. I felt a roller coaster of emotions. So many things had happened in the days since I had arrived at base camp. It had all been very intense: the worry about my teammates, the extreme exhaustion, the intense moments on the summit. I was exhilarated that everything had worked out in the end, and it felt good to be recognized by the other climbers. I was also pleased to find that my previous acclimatization had paid off. I later learned that it lasts for two weeks, starts fading during the third week, and is completely gone after twenty-one days. But the second acclimatization is usually quicker than the first.

The Kazakh expedition leader came to our camp to thank Iñaki and me for bringing his climber down the mountain. While we were gone the whole meadow had started blooming, and he gave me a colorful bunch of handpicked flowers as well as a bottle of vodka. In return, I visited the Kazakh camp to see how the patient was doing. He was obviously better and thanked me with very simple words—yet another emotional moment for me. Then Denis came up to me. He told me that they were going to K2 afterward, and on behalf of all the expedition members he invited me to join them. There would be enough time to organize the permit for me. I was speechless. K2! I couldn't believe that they were inviting me, considering they hadn't taken any notice of me at first. I was very happy that they had finally recognized me as a person as well as a mountaineer.

Going to K2 was extremely tempting; I was acclimatized and still felt strong. I called Birgit to discuss it with her, but I already knew what I wanted to do: I wanted to go to K2. I only had to talk to my boss to see whether I could stay a bit longer, and then I had to tell my sister Brigitte. Almost ten years older than me, Brigitte has always been one of the most important people in my life. She is my link to the rest of my family, keeping them informed of what I'm up to. I asked Brigitte how she was. She said she was well, but I could tell by the sound of her voice that something was wrong. Was it because of the great distance? I told her about my success on Nanga Parbat and said that I would like to stay and climb K2. When she heard that, she started to cry and begged me to come home. Her husband, Walter, who had been suffering from diabetes, had died after being in a diabetic coma for five days. Only a minute ago, I had been so happy about my success on Nanga Parbat. Now I fell into a deep hole. I wanted to go home immediately. I packed my bags and left, very worried about my sister.

When I arrived with Birgit at her house in Spital am Pyhrn I was almost too scared to go in. Brigitte told me later that she had been waiting for me. Losing the person you love is incredibly difficult, and Brigitte was experiencing this painful loss for the third time. I wanted to be there for her and give her all the support I usually get from her. My family is my rock.

Whenever I'm on expedition, I need to know that my parents and siblings are well. I think about them when I get into difficult situations on the mountain; knowing that they are with me in their thoughts gives me a lot of strength. Being with my family at home in Austria is a welcome change to my public life as a professional mountaineer. When I am with them, I don't have to deal with extreme situations—I just enjoy everyday life. My siblings, nephews, and nieces accept me the way I am; I am not constantly questioned or enviously criticized. For them, I am simply Gerlinde. It does not matter whether or not I reach a summit; the most important thing is that I return home safe and sound. I feel protected by my family so I can be myself.

With six children, there was certainly never a dull moment in our family. Like my father, my mother worked full time, so from a very early age we children were left to our own devices during the day. Brigitte, the eldest, was responsible for us younger brothers and sisters. I loved playing in the outdoors with Manfred, who was three years older than me, and Manuela, who was two years my senior. We dressed up as Indians or Robinson Crusoe and Friday, hid in the haystacks, and played with the other children in the neighborhood. Manfred loved building huts and tree houses. Since we often stole the wooden planks from somewhere and took my father's tools and nails, which he was not too happy about, we didn't want our parents to know what we were up to. For this reason we sometimes left behind the youngest member of the Kaltenbrunner Gang, namely my brother Günter, three years my junior, as he could be a bit of a tattletale and occasionally told our parents about our shenanigans.

We also liked munching the strawberries from our neighbor's flowerbed and picking young corn on the cob from the Kukuruz field, which gave my mother more than enough reason to tell us off. Solidarity was very important among us siblings. Even though we argued quite a lot, we would never tell on each other. For example, we loved playing in the Wur, a hilly forest where barracks from the Second World War were rotting away. The ruins, covered in thorny bushes, were the ideal place for bold adventures, but unfortunately it was a no-go area. Our parents would have punished us had they known that we went there. Of course, we ignored their warnings and played there anyway. During one of our reconnaissance tours—it was summer and I was wearing sandals—I accidentally stepped onto a wooden plank with a long rusty nail sticking out. The nail went right through my shoe into my foot and came out the other end. I screamed my head off. Günter plucked up all his courage, grabbed the plank, and pulled the nail out of my foot.

What now? Our parents were not allowed to find out where we had been. I bit my tongue, limped home with my siblings, and washed and bandaged my foot before my parents came home. During dinner, I didn't say a word, pulling myself together so as not to show the agonizing pain. That night I couldn't sleep a wink; the foot was throbbing with excruciating pain. In the morning, a red line had appeared on my skin moving up from my foot, and the pain had become unbearable. I discussed the next steps with my siblings. Whether I liked it or not, I had to drop my "no pain, no gain" approach and come clean with my parents. My mother was more shocked than angry and immediately took me to the hospital, where they treated me for the onset of blood poisoning.

As it turned out, this experience was not enough to teach us a lesson. One of the rules in the Kaltenbrunner residence was never to walk barefoot in the wood storeroom down in the basement. When four of us were sent to the basement to get some wood, Manfred, who loved playing Tarzan, ignored that rule. After all, Tarzan didn't wear shoes in the jungle. Manfred hung off the wooden beams, swinging back and forth, screaming like Tarzan, and then to give his performance a suitable finish he jumped off. Unfortunately, his calculations went wrong and he landed on top of the rake. Two spikes went straight through his foot. Once again we didn't tell our parents about the accident, and once again a member of the Kaltenbrunner clan ended up in the hospital with blood poisoning.

I loved sports from a very early age. Even before I was enrolled in school I had joined the skiing club. Later I became a member of the swimming and athletics clubs too, and I guess I would have probably joined other sports clubs as well had there been any others in my home village at the time. Like my sister Manuela, I went to a different training every night, all voluntarily. Exercise was everything to me.

I won a couple of medals in country races through the ski club. Being an enthusiastic skier, I was very keen on going to skiing high school after primary school. There was a financial hurdle, though: Boarding school, equipment, and so on were all expensive. At first it seemed unlikely that it would work out, but at Christmas when I had just turned eleven I was allowed to change over to the Skiing High School in Windischgarsten. One of the coaches, Hubert Fachberger, managed to get me into the school as a day student. He gave me a ride to Windischgarsten every day and drove me back to Spital after dinner. He also gave me skis. I was happy to be able to exercise so much. Our daily routine looked like this: rise at 6:00 a.m., run for an hour at 6.30, have breakfast at 8:00 and then start school lessons; in the afternoons we did more training, and in the evening we had another lesson. In fall and winter we went on countless training camps. The last two years of school I was able to board, which made me feel much more part of the team, as I was finally able to spend time with my schoolmates in the evenings.

The ski competitions put a lot of pressure on me. During the races my friends became my competitors, inevitably creating tension. I had to learn how to put my foot down and build my self-confidence. I also had to meet my mother's expectations. Since my parents were paying for such an expensive school she wanted to see results, which I didn't always deliver. Sometimes I took too big a risk, fell, and got disqualified. I was one of the few students who were not supported by their parents during the races. My parents didn't ski, and with six children at home, they didn't have the time to come to every race. It was usually my schoolmates' parents who took my ski jacket and pants from the start to the finishing line.

While most other pupils owned a racing suit, I still skied in jet pants and a woolly sweater. I tried to fix this situation by writing to the professional ski racer Sylvia Eder, whom I had seen on television many times. I asked her whether she had an old racing suit for me. A few days later, she phoned me to find out which suit I would like. I didn't care—the most important thing was that it was a racing suit. She sent me a white suit with red stripes. Of course, it still bore the emblem of the International Skiing Association (FIS), which was almost embarrassing. The suit was a tad big for me, especially around the thighs. Sylvia, who was five years older than me, certainly had an advantage when it came to leg muscles. I was very excited to have the suit, though I attracted some attention in it, as my skiing performance didn't quite match the professional look.

Not long after I graduated I gave up racing. I was simply not good enough and felt too nervous before the races; in addition, I considered it a loss that racing was all about competition, not camaraderie. For my development, though, skiing high school was very important. I later benefited greatly from exercising my motor skills along with comprehensive weight and conditioning training, and it certainly helped me to gain more self-confidence.

During my time at skiing high school, two significant events defined my future life and choice of profession. My brother Dietmar, who was nine years older than me, suffered serious brain injuries from a motorbike accident. He ended up in a coma for two weeks and spent nine months in all in the hospital. I remember paying sad and confusing visits to his hospital bed during his coma. When we had almost given up hope, he woke up. With the admirably energetic support of my grandmother, who visited him every single day, he learned anew how to swallow, speak, walk, and write, and is now able to lead a totally independent life.

But our joy over his recovery was soon followed by more bad news: When I was fifteen, my parents decided to split up. At primary school, I had always been shocked when other kids told me, "My parents are getting a divorce." I had hoped that this would never, ever happen in my family; I felt sure that I couldn't cope with it. But then I found myself in exactly that situation. The worst thing was that my mother didn't allow me to see my father, which I simply couldn't accept. I felt closer to him than to her, and so I saw no choice but to pack my bags and move in with Brigitte.

Brigitte was twenty-five, living on her own and working as a nurse. My relationship with her was very special. From the early age of ten, she had looked after all of us younger siblings when our parents went out in the evenings. When she had felt scared in the middle of the night, she had taken me out of my crib and put me into her bed to help her feel less lonely. Maybe it is because of this close physical contact that we share such a strong bond. I always turned to Brigitte when I was upset or needed her to help mediate between me and my mother. She was my rock as well as my professional idol. After I moved in with her I sometimes accompanied her to the hospital for her night shifts. I followed her like a little puppy, observing the procedures and carrying out small tasks until I collapsed on a bed in the nurse's room. I knew early on that I wanted to follow her footsteps and become a nurse.

At fifteen I was too young for nursing school, so I went to social services school in Rottenmann for two years. These two years in Rottenmann counted for one year at nursing school, which meant that I could go straight into the second year of my official nursing training. I was too young to do the training in Upper Austria, where the minimum age was seventeen, so I had to move to Vienna.

At the age of sixteen I arrived in the Austrian capital with two suitcases and moved into a room at the boarding school of the Rudolfstiftung Hospital. I was one of the first students to arrive, and I remember feeling completely and utterly lost in the massive building. I found refuge on a bench in front of the building and sat down. Loneliness and homesickness brought tears to my eyes. An elderly lady asked me why I was crying, and I explained my "destiny" to her. She consoled and encouraged me, telling me that I would soon get used to my new life. It did me a lot of good knowing that there was at least one person who was willing to talk to me in the big city.

During my first few weeks in Vienna, I felt like a country bumpkin. I greeted everyone I met in the streets and was surprised that nobody greeted me back. I jaywalked and was surprised when drivers honked their horns angrily at me. I missed nature, the mountains, the forests, and the meadows of home. The weeks from September to Christmas were very hard for me; I only lived for the next trip home. I started hatching an escape plan. One thing was clear: I didn't want to stay in Vienna.

On one of my weekends at home, I told my sister that I had probably taken the wrong career path and would like to become a waitress. In this way, I could kill two birds with one stone: I would not have to go back to Vienna, and I would be financially independent, autonomous at last and no longer accountable to anyone. Brigitte was shocked. She told me to get my act together and finish my training. So I went back to Vienna and continued to think about how best to get away from there. Next time I would have to play my cards better.

The dentist in Spital am Pyhrn was looking for a dental assistant. I secretly applied for the position and ended up getting the job. By then, I had taken my first exams in terminology and health law in Vienna. Before Christmas, I would have to take two big exams in anatomy and pathology. The rule was that if we got the equivalent of two Ds, we had to take an extra exam, and with a third D we would be thrown out of school. Yes, this was the solution! If I failed the exam, Brigitte would have to accept that I was just not meant to be a nurse. I studied for both tests, though, as the subjects really did interest me. During the exam I drew a question card, which I then had to answer in front of the examination board. Even though I knew the answers, I blankly handed the cards back to the board, saying, "I am sorry, I don't know the answer." Now, I only had to wait for the letter saying "failed" to land in my sister's mailbox.

And it landed. But it didn't say "failed" it said, "not attended." Brigitte immediately knew what had happened, so I put my last card on the table and told her that I had found a job as a dental assistant in Spital.

"Gerlinde, this is impossible," she said. "Pull yourself together and finish your training. You are not a dental assistant—it doesn't suit you."

This was Brigitte's only comment to me. Then she called the dentist to explain the situation, and so put an end to my dental career. The dentist actually encouraged me to finish my nursing training. After this episode I started to think differently. I wanted to be strong and reach my goal. My ambition grew, and when I started my work on the wards caring for patients I enjoyed the training. In the summer I took my exams in anatomy and pathology and did pretty well. But I still took the elevator to the hospital's fifteenth floor, where I could see the peaks outside the windows on a clear day. I so longed for the mountains, and dreaming of them filled me with energy. I also continued saving my pocket money for the train tickets home.

In my third year, the work was more practical and the subjects of internal medicine and surgery dominated the curriculum. I threw myself into studying. After I had started my fourth year, I could finally see the light at end of the tunnel and was happy to know I would soon be leaving Vienna. I knew that the big city was not for me, and I was looking forward to working in a rural hospital surrounded by mountains. I was now aware of how much I loved my job. I finally earned my diploma with merit, and my sister and father came to my graduation in Vienna. It was a lovely feeling knowing that my family was proud of me.

Whenever I stand on top of an 8000-meter peak, I often think about my relatives. I always want to share my amazing experiences up there with them. They have a hard time understanding what I feel up there and why on Earth I spend so much money to exhaust myself. Now that I take videos rather than just photos they understand better how slowly we move at high altitude and how relentlessly the storms can rage. Nevertheless, high-altitude mountaineering remains an unknown world for them.

When I visited my father a few weeks after my Nanga Parbat expedition he asked me whether I had heard my new nickname. After Nanga Parbat, the Kazakhs went on to K2, and Simone, Jean-Christophe, and Iñaki attempted Broad Peak. Rumor had it throughout the Karakorum that the Kazakhs now called me "Cinderella Caterpillar" because of the way I had broken trail on Nanga Parbat. From Broad Peak base camp, Barbara sent me an email telling me about my new title. But how did my dad find out about it? As it happened, he was at the Bosruck Hut and over-heard Gerfried Göschl's father talk about Cinderella Caterpillar. Gerfried had been part of an Austrian expedition that was in the Karakorum at the same time. It was particularly funny for my dad, as he used to work in a plaster mine driving a digger. He would never ever have dreamed that his youngest daughter would in a way follow his footsteps one day.

Climbing steep ice of about 70 degrees on the south face of Shisha Pangma *(Photo by Robert Bösch)*

CHAPTER 6
COURAGE

luffy white clouds drifted across the deep blue sky below us. The shadow of our airplane moving across the clouds was the only reminder that we would eventually get to our destination. The turbines' monotonous drone insulated me from the people around me. I closed my eyes.

Usually I cannot wait for a flight to be over, but my journey back from Pakistan to Austria made a welcome break. I had nothing to do and plenty of time to get lost in my thoughts. Apart from my concerns about Brigitte, I was worried about something else. This was the first time I had been away for three and a half months in one go. So many things had happened in the meantime, and I was struggling to catch up. The shock of losing our gear deposit on Kangchenjunga and the worry about other mountaineers' lives were pushed away by moments of exuberant happiness: I was in love and looking forward to seeing Ralf again. But first and foremost I knew that I had to change jobs. The thought of getting into my car and presenting the latest outdoor collection to one sports shop after another almost made me cringe. I had not really been happy to work as a representative for outdoor gear, and I no longer wanted to do it. Mountaineering made me happy and had become the center of my life. If only I could make a living from climbing!

First I had to move house. Luckily my sister had invited me to live with her in Spital am Pyhrn. There was enough space in her house, and I also hoped that I could help her get over the loss of Walter. Jobwise, I had to find a new direction. Professional mountaineers such as Ines Papert or Stefan Glowacz didn't work as mountain guides but got support from sponsors.

Ralf, who made his money organizing trekking tours and expeditions, had contracts with sponsors allowing him to pursue his own personal goals. Up until then I had never thought about the significance of fame or the marketing value of a mountaineer, but when I sold my first photo to the Austrian magazine *Land der Berge* I was very excited that I could actually make money from climbing—even though it was only thirty euros. Would I be able to convince outdoor gear companies to give me sponsorship contracts? Gear sponsorships alone would not be enough, though; I had to be able to live from mountaineering, as financial independence was my first priority.

After my return from Nanga Parbat I got some media attention that certainly helped me. For the fiftieth anniversary of Hermann Buhl's first ascent, the Austrian media reported extensively on Nanga Parbat. My being the first Austrian woman to reach the summit raised some media interest. The German magazine *Klettern* published the first article about me; *Alpin*, another German climbing magazine, introduced me to its readers; and some of the national newspapers mentioned my summit success. I was also asked to do slide presentations. This new development gave me hope. Ralf and my employer Karl Attwenger encouraged and supported me to become self-employed. At the end of the day, it wasn't a huge risk. I would not have to make big investments, and if it didn't work out I could always go back to my job as a nurse. In the fall of 2003, I set up my own company.

Around the same time, Ralf organized a modeling job for me with an outdoor clothing company. The Swiss photographer Robert Bösch was doing a photo shoot for an outdoor company in the Monte Rosa region. It was fantastic—I could do what I loved doing all day long and get paid for it. I completely forgot that it was actually work. By spring 2004, I had signed my first two sponsorship contracts guaranteeing me a fixed annual income over the next few years. It was a wonderful feeling to know that both companies had faith in me from the very beginning, and I am happy that I am still with them today. With them I can count on good cooperation based on mutual respect.

My first appearance on a talk show on Austrian television triggered further interview inquiries. Back then, I had no idea how much media interest I would attract over the years; I was just happy that my company had gotten such a great start with two solid supporting pillars, the sponsorships and my presentations.

As a professional mountaineer I no longer had to feel guilty when I neglected chores and went biking for hours on end or did my other training sessions. I was now able to spend more time exercising, organizing my day more generously for longer sessions. Training, especially endurance and weight training, had become part of my job. It was definitely easier than sitting in front of the computer for more than three hours, which I had always found difficult. I didn't have to force myself to train. I love exercising and have always been keen on sports. The only thing I sometimes struggle with is going to the indoor climbing wall, which just does not compare with climbing outdoors.

I need to exercise; if I don't, I can be a real pain for the people around me. My psychological well-being depends on staying physically active. On the other hand, I also feel that I need a break after four or five days of intense training. I completely rely on my gut feeling and not on a training schedule. I never use a heart rate monitor when I run; I can feel my pulse perfectly without it. Resting is also a big part of my training, which I normally do in the sauna or by listening to relaxing music.

After the eventful year of 2003, Ralf asked me to go on a climbing trip to Thailand with him. He had been there before and had been enthusing about it for a while: After the cold in the Himalaya, he said, it felt great to enjoy heat and quiet, which made Thailand a good place to recharge your batteries. It took me a while to get used to the hot weather in Tonsai, but once I was "acclimatized" I really enjoyed life there. In the mornings and evenings we would go climbing, and during the day we would lie on the beach. The food was delicious, even though Ralf had a few bad experiences with the Thai cuisine. After one of our morning climbing sessions in Railay we went to a small beach restaurant. Ralf ordered a seafood cocktail, and I chose rice and vegetables; I am usually a bit careful when it comes to fish. After lunch we went for a swim and lay down on the beach. Ralf didn't feel well; needing to vomit, he ran off to find the restrooms.

"Do you want me to come with you, Ralf?" I asked.

"No, no—I'll be right back."

I waited on the beach for half an hour, three-quarters of an hour, an hour. Ralf still hadn't come back, and I started to worry. I looked around for him, but there was no sign of him anywhere. Suddenly I saw a Thai man who seemed to be looking for something. When I noticed the piece of paper he had in his hand, I knew that he was looking for me. I ran toward him. "You are Gerlinda?" he asked me. I nodded.

"Your husband almost die," he said.

I was shocked. I asked him to take me to Ralf. We walked into the jungle, where Ralf was lying in the shade of a coconut tree surrounded by a lot of people. Had the man not taken me there, I would never have found him. Even though Ralf was not unconscious, he was in a pretty bad way, as white as a sheet and only able to groan. He didn't seem to notice me. I panicked and called for a doctor, but the next health post was a forty-minute boat ride away in Krabi. I felt helpless. Desperately trying to make him vomit, I stuck my finger down Ralf's throat, but he didn't react. What was I supposed to do?

A Thai climbed up one of the palm trees and cut off a coconut. He opened it, poured the milk in a glass and slowly dribbled it into Ralf's mouth. I was very grateful that at least someone was doing something, as I was at my wit's end. The coconut milk made Ralf vomit, which made him feel better. He was responsive and able to sit up. A huge weight was lifted off my shoulders. In the afternoon, we took the longtail boat back to Tonsai. Ralf, still shaky, ate only rice and couldn't really do anything for three days. Happy that everything had turned out well, I vowed to myself that next time I would bring a small medical kit for such incidents.

After Ralf had recovered completely, we went climbing again for two or three days. One evening, I couldn't believe what I heard when Ralf ordered fish again.

"But Gerlinde," he said, "look how delicious it looks."

"Ralf, I don't think this is funny. You have just recovered from fish poisoning, and now you want to eat fish again. Why don't you have a rice dish?"

"Gerlinde—I have had enough rice the past few days. I want fish."

Ralf is an enthusiastic fish eater, and there was no way I could talk him out of it. But he promptly fell sick again during the night, with vomiting and diarrhea, and I was extremely angry. He was flat out for two more days. Instead of going climbing I spent my time reading. When he had recovered again, we took a trip to Ko Phi Phi. For a change, I got seasick on the small ferry. The center of the island was far too touristy for my liking, but the climbs were great. We took a little boat to the bottom of the routes, some of which were multipitch, and climbed back up. The only thing I felt uneasy about were the monkeys. Once a whole pack of monkeys tried to steal our rope bag as well as Ralf's T-shirt. Another time, I was just about to get annoyed with Ralf for keeping the rope too tight when I saw two monkeys pull on the rope above me.

One afternoon we rented a kayak and went for a paddle. We had a tailwind and paddled to a lovely bay where we went for a swim. There was a big bolted rock in the water, and we wanted to have a closer look on our way back. Though the wind had picked up, Ralf insisted on kayaking around the boulder, behind which the open sea began. When we approached the rock I noticed that the wind was stronger and the waves were getting higher. My gut feeling told me to go back as quickly as possible, but Ralf was unperturbed, leisurely looking at the climbing routes. I felt extremely scared and stressed. When we finally started paddling back, the waves came much higher than our kayak, sweeping over us. It felt as if we were paddling for our lives, and the more we paddled, the more we seemed to drift toward the open sea. Synchronized paddling proved very difficult; after all, it was my first time in such a boat and both Ralf and I were pretty stressed. It was a very strenuous effort, we barely moved, and I pictured us drowning in the sea. For the last few hundred yards we swam, pulling the kayak behind us. When we finally got back we were completely exhausted: Our one-hour trip had turned into five hours of torture. The guy from the boat rental was also very worried about us. Once again, I felt extremely relieved; I had been truly worried that we would not make it back. I love the mountains; I am not a great fan of the sea.

Just before our departure we went to a restaurant in Tonsai, where Ralf had his eye on a huge ray displayed on ice. Ralf was immediately enthralled by it.

"Look Gerlinde, how nice. I have to try a piece of this."

I didn't believe my ears. "Ralf, you are definitely not eating fish tonight."

"But Gerlinde, it is completely fresh. I have to try a piece of it! Ray is something very special—you don't find it every day."

I gave in to my fate and decided to have some ray as well. At least we would be sick together, which meant that I would not have to look after Ralf. I have to admit that the ray was absolutely delicious, and fortunately we didn't get sick from it.

Shortly after our return we decided to make our lives a bit easier. The distance between Ralf's hometown in the Black Forest and Spital am Pyhrn was 700 kilometers, which we managed either by driving or taking long complicated train trips. I was fed up with weekend relationships. The only way to get to know the other person properly is to live together. As Ralf was tied to his hometown—partly by his son Joshi, who lived with him half the time, and partly by his company—I moved to the Black Forest at the beginning of 2004.

I didn't hesitate, as I was convinced that our partnership would last. We have an intense relationship with many ups and downs; I guess we both need to be challenged by our partner. We often disagree, but we like discussing our differences. And mountaineering has always provided a strong bond between us.

My move to Germany didn't only distance me geographically from my family, it also changed my training. In winter, it was impossible to quickly nip up a mountain on my skis; the real mountains were much farther away. The good thing about the move was that Valais in Switzerland or Chamonix in France were now only three or four hours away by car, instead of the eight to ten hours I was used to. Ralf and I like going to the Swiss Alps for backcountry skiing or ice climbing whenever we have time. We also love cross-country skiing, especially skating. In the summer I go mountain biking, which allows me to cover long distances and enjoy beautiful surroundings. As the Black Forest is pretty hilly I clock up a lot of altitude meters, which makes my training more effective while offering me a significant view of the beautiful Rhine valley. Ralf now shares my enthusiasm for mountain biking and in return I go running with him. We like alternating our training sessions, which can also include swimming, climbing the Battert crag, or training on the ergometer if the weather is bad. I first had to get used to the rock at Battert, which is porphyry. Ralf grew up climbing there and knows Battert like the back of his hand.

I love training with Ralf. We have a lot of fun pushing each other. Even if we plan to take it slowly we never do, as we speed each other up. Sometimes, however, I like to train on my own. I love getting lost in thought while my body is working hard. When I am out biking on my own, I usually have my best ideas and reach decisions.

Ralf used to train more systematically than I did. Now we discuss whether we want to go, for example, on a long run or do interval training instead, and usually we follow our gut feeling. I listen to my body and base my decisions on how I feel. Maybe I could get more out of my body if I trained more strictly or according to a training schedule, but that is not important to me. I just want to enjoy what I do.

Now that Ralf and I were living together, we spent a lot of time exchanging ideas for future projects and making plans. I told Ralf that I had dreamed of climbing the south face of Shisha Pangma since I had first laid my eyes on it in 2000, and as it turned out this climb had also been on his wish list for a long time. So what was more obvious than that we should make this dream come true? When Ralf's Japanese friend Hiro found out about our plan for 2004 he eagerly committed to joining us, and Ralf's good friend Röbi Bösch soon became the fourth climber in our team. We decided to climb the face alpine style, meaning that we would climb from base camp to the summit in one go, without using fixed ropes or high-altitude Sherpas and—this goes without saying—without supplemental oxygen. This style of climbing does not require fixed high camps; instead, we would use small, light bivouac tents which we could carry in our backpacks along with our food and other equipment. Climbing in this particular style required acclimatizing on a different mountain, since our climb would not be considered alpine style if we had already climbed the route before our summit attempt. We are still big fans of this style, in which we travel light and fast; in fact we prefer to climb alpine style as long as conditions allow.

For our acclimatization we chose the 7221-meter Xifeng Peak, which lies in the shadow of Shisha Pangma. We found out that only one expedition from Japan had climbed this beautiful freestanding 7000-meter peak. Xifeng Peak and Shisha Pangma's northern route share a base camp as well as a Camp 1 before the route to Xifeng Peak veers off to the right. After having scaled Xifeng Peak, we wanted to change over to the south side of Shisha Pangma. If time allowed after our ascent of the south face of Shisha Pangma, we also planned to climb Annapurna I in Nepal before Ralf would go off to lead an AMICAL expedition to Gasherbrum I in the Karakorum in the summer. Without a doubt, this was an ambitious program.

Even though the weather was highly changeable on Xifeng Peak and we had to deal with a lot of wind, snowfall, and fog, our acclimatization rotation worked out very well. The only incident happened on the walk from Chinese Base Camp to Advanced Base Camp (ABC), when something must have gotten into the yaks; they started jumping up and down like crazy. Unfortunately, one of the leaping yaks was carrying the entire egg supply for our and another AMICAL expedition to Shisha Pangma. Hundreds of eggs broke. The cook, who only saved a few, was so upset that he cried. Ralf immediately got on the phone to call our agency and order more eggs, as omelets are a very popular breakfast on expedition. It didn't take very long before another "egg yak" was on its way. But as fate would have it, the second egg yak got stuck on a rock at a narrow section of the path, and most of the eggs were lost again.

On Xifeng Peak, the route to Camp 2 started off flat before it turned right across a very rocky section that eventually led to the knife-edge southwest ridge. There were big drop-offs to the left and right, and we had to concentrate hard not to trip with our crampons. Röbi was happy to get so many photo opportunities, but whenever he took a picture he had to sit down and straddle the ridge as if he were sitting on a horse—that was the only possible position. The ridge seemed endless, but after few more yards of climbing in grade III we finally reached the summit. Despite having no view, the four of us were overjoyed and fell into each other's arms.

On our descent we acclimatized another night at Camp 2 at 6600 meters before we returned to base camp at the end of April. On our drive to the south side of Shisha Pangma, we stayed three nights at Nyalam at 3750 meters; Ralf had to recover from a bad throat infection, and I had bronchitis. The only hotel there, the Snowland Lodge, was pretty basic—it didn't even have a shower. But the public bath in Nyalam was rather rustic and interesting. You had to sign up in the morning to use one of the three showers in the afternoon. The public bath also seemed to be some sort of common house. We enjoyed the hot water with only a paper-thin wall separating us from some Tibetans watching a Bollywood movie,

On the third day we started the two-day journey directly from Nyalam to the southern base camp of Shisha Pangma. The trek across green, flowery meadows where yaks grazed was stunning, and base camp proved to be the absolute highlight of the trip. Lying at an altitude of 5100 meters, it was situated in the middle of a meadow in a remote spot by a small lake, which provided us with drinking water. The only other people there were Rolf Bae, another Norwegian, and their cook. They had also planned to climb the south face, but first they encountered bad weather, and then they both fell so violently ill that they had to abandon their expedition, leaving us and our cook alone at base camp. We were well acclimatized, the conditions on the face seemed perfect, and Charly Gabl had forecast a few days of good weather: It couldn't have been better. Excited, we packed our bags. We sorted out how many ice screws and pitons and how much food we would need. We even weighed our backpacks to distribute the loads evenly, as Röbi always carried a bit more with his camera equipment. In the end, everyone's backpack weighed around 40.7 pounds, which as we found out later was far too heavy for this face.

The 2000-meter high south face looked extremely steep. We had studied the various routes prior to our expedition and decided to go for the most direct one, which was first climbed by Doug Scott, Alex McIntyre, and Roger Baxter-Jones in 1982. This route resembles a beautiful line all the way to the top. We had planned to descend via the Polish route, which is

TOP: Climbing in Thailand with Ralf was totally different than the snowy giants of the Himalaya. I loved the rock and the routes, but 98 degrees Fahrenheit was simply too hot for me. *(Photo by Ralf Dujmovits)* BOTTOM: Climbing the exposed ridge to the summit of Xifeng Peak *(Photo by Robert Bösch)*

also on the south face but not as steep. We set up our first bivouac on the bottom of the wall. From there we were able to have a closer look and identify sites for further bivouacs on the face. Röbi, who is a very good climber, had found a great boulder close to our camp, and bouldered wearing his down suit and heavy high-altitude boots. But it didn't take him long to discover that exercising was challenging at high altitude. Our team had a relaxed atmosphere from the beginning to the very end.

The following day, we set off early. The climb started off fairly easily as we ascended through frozen sugar snow in gorgeous sunshine. It couldn't have been better; fresh snow or hard ice would have cost us a lot more energy. We intended to climb from 6000 to 7000 meters and set up a bivouac there. We also wanted to climb most sections without a rope to make better progress. But at an altitude of about 7200 meters, we had to negotiate a few difficult rocky sections with brittle rock; we had to climb roped up over a few pitches. Afterward we moved on to mixed ground with a gradient of about 50 to 55 degrees.

The broken rocks higher up were one of the reasons why we headed off first thing in the morning. An early start bought us time before the loose rocks, which freeze to the wall at night, would come tumbling down. This is also why we wore helmets. At one point there was a big rockfall lower down, but it was far away and didn't worry us. The compact sugar snow gave way to blue ice farther up the face. There were sections of 60 to 65 degrees and some short passages of 70 degrees, in between which it got a bit flatter. We were making good progress and were nearly at our next bivouac.

At about 6850 meters as we were traversing a 45-degree slope toward the left, Ralf suddenly cried out and crouched. His scream pierced my bones. I had no idea what had happened. I only knew that we were not roped up and if Ralf lost his balance, he would probably fall to his death. I couldn't help thinking that he would tumble down any minute and quickly prayed to God that he would be able to hold on. I then saw that Ralf was hanging off both his ice tools with his crampons anchored to the ice. Röbi and I were a little ways above and below Ralf, respectively, and could support him. Hiro had gone a bit ahead. At first, we couldn't understand what was wrong with Ralf, who was still in excruciating pain, until he said that he had been hit by a rock. A single fist-sized rock had come out of nowhere and hit him on the inner part of his left calf, just above the shoe shaft. It happened when he was just about to start the traverse. Ralf managed to edge along a few more meters, where we found a better place to stop. No matter how bad the situation might be, I was extremely relieved that he was still alive.

"It'll be okay," he said. "I just have to sit down for a minute. I'll be fine." Ralf uttered these words with such a pained face that I didn't quite believe him. We descended to a flatter spot where Ralf could sit down on his backpack and I could have a look at his leg. The rock had hit his calf, which was badly swollen, through four layers: gaiters, down suit, fleece pants, and long johns. I bandaged up his leg and gave him something to drink. Even though he was in so much pain that he could hardly stand up straight, he refused to accept that this was the end of the expedition for him. He didn't want us to turn back because of him and actually managed to continue for a while. But the more often we had to frontpoint on our crampons, the more unbearable his pain became, and just below 7000 meters he had to accept that carrying on was not possible. It would have been too dangerous for him, and I was not willing to give him any more painkillers at this altitude.

I too could not believe that this was the end of our expedition. Everything had been perfect: the weather, the conditions . . . and then it had all changed in a split second. From one second to the next, I had to deal with a new situation and change plans. It was very sad, but it was what it was; it was clear that I would descend with Ralf. We both tried to convince Röbi and Hiro to go on, but they refused. On our descent we noticed how slow we had been, which was another indication that we should not have continued. Descending on frontpoints over about 1000 vertical meters was torture for Ralf. He inched his way down, needing to stop for a few breaks. In the very steep sections we put him on belay. We were all relieved when we finally reached the bottom of the face and arrived at our bivouac site just before nightfall.

It had been such a short outing. What a shame. But my disappointment soon turned to relief that nothing worse had happened. What if Ralf had lost his anchor, or if he had looked up and the rock had hit him in the face? I didn't even want to think about it. This could have been the end of him! I finally looked at the bright side of things, but it was more difficult for Ralf. This was the first time that a high-altitude expedition was abandoned because of him, especially in perfect conditions. However, the rock could have hit any one of us.

Once we were back at our idyllic base camp, we all agreed that we were definitely eager to go back to the south face, and we wanted to do it soon. Unfortunately, Röbi would not be able to come again as he had too much work and no time off; he was also unable to join us for Annapurna I. We discussed what we might do better next time; our backpacks would have to be lighter, and we would have to be quicker. We were over our initial disappointment. We could let Shisha Pangma go and turn to Annapurna I—hopefully with Ralf.

Due to the serac fall, climbing the north face of Annapurna I was probably one of my riskiest undertakings. *(Photo by Ralf Dujmovits)*

CHAPTER 7
FEAR

At 8091 meters, Annapurna I is only the tenth-highest mountain in the world. In 1950 it became the first 8000-meter peak to be successfully climbed. Despite its beauty, it is the least-often climbed of all fourteen peaks rising above the magical height of 8000 meters. By the end of 2008, it had had only an estimated 150 ascents compared to more than 4000 ascents on Mount Everest. The reason for this is simple: Annapurna I is considered the most dangerous 8000-meter peak in the world. K2 may be the most difficult; Everest, with more than 200 deaths, may be the deadliest; but statistically speaking, more mountaineers die on Annapurna I in relation to the number of ascents than on any other mountain. Most of the deaths are either caused by serac fall or avalanche. On the north side of the mountain, whole teams have been buried in avalanches on the French Route, which is regarded the normal route, as well as the Dutch Rib Route running to its left.

Why was I attracted to such a mountain? Well, it is one of the fourteen 8000-meter peaks, and the grandeur of the massive Annapurna mountain range towering above the Kali Gandaki Valley had fascinated me for a long time. Climbing Annapurna I is a very risky undertaking and not many mountaineers go there, which meant that Ralf and I would have a good chance to be more or less on our own. After his attempt in 1991, though, Ralf had vowed never to return to Annapurna I. That year, a huge avalanche had thundered into base camp from the southern slopes of Tilicho Peak, and it was pure luck that he and his team had survived instead of being buried like most of their equipment. He had changed his mind partly because he wanted to be with me, and partly because of his ambition to scale another 8000-meter peak.

We had come up with a strategy to minimize the objective dangers, which are especially present on the upper slopes of the north face, where huge hanging ice seracs threaten to fall directly onto the route over a stretch of about 300 meters. Our only chance was to get through this perilous area as quickly as possible. We knew that acclimatizing on the mountain was out of the question, so in order to spend minimal time in the danger zone we wanted to acclimatize prior to our expedition. This was why we planned to climb Annapurna I straight after Xifeng Peak and Shisha Pangma. We wanted to be well acclimatized and climb alpine style: light, quick, and without fixed ropes. Thinking about it now, our worries were more than justified. Even though we did well on the mountain I wouldn't go back there for all the money in the world.

When we got back to Kathmandu from Tibet, we were actually not sure whether Ralf would be able to join the expedition because of his injury on Shisha Pangma's south face. His left calf was painfully swollen and badly bruised. The doctor in Kathmandu said the calf had been seriously bruised, but it was nothing worse. In addition to the Voltaren bandages I wrapped around his calf, massages and a bit of stretching really helped. In the end the swelling went down and Ralf felt sure that the injury was no longer a problem, but he had found another reason to doubt our Annapurna expedition. Mid-May had already come and gone, the monsoon was looming, rain was pouring down in Kathmandu, and he just couldn't help feeling that it was too late in the season to climb Annapurna I. While Hiro didn't say much, I was convinced that we still had a chance. I was not prepared to give up without having even tried, and I managed to convince both of them that we should at least give it a go.

After a massive avalanche destroyed an area as big as a football field in 1991, teams heading for Annapurna I now set up their base camp a little bit lower. The camp is now underneath the relatively safe western side of the south face of Tilicho Peak, lying at an altitude of 3950 meters, comparatively low for a base camp but much better protected. But as the trek to base camp is very prone to rockfall, it is almost impossible to find porters willing to go there. Most Annapurna climbers—and during most seasons there are very few, or none at all — take a helicopter to base camp. Since we were already well acclimatized and quite late in the season, we opted for the helicopter.

On May 21, 2004, we flew to Pokhara where we caught a small helicopter to the remote base camp. The aircraft was so tiny that it could either take two passengers or just one with luggage. Ralf went first with about 220 pounds of expedition gear, followed by Hiro and me. Unfortunately, the weather had worsened in between the two flights, and the pilot barely found a gap in the clouds through which he took Hiro and me safely to base camp before the weather closed in completely. After a few minutes he had to abandon his first attempt to fly back to Kathmandu, as the conditions were too dangerous. He was forced to stay with us, which was not ideal because he was not acclimatized. We gave him a lot to drink, but even though he had some bottled oxygen in his helicopter we worried that he would get altitude sickness. When the clouds opened up for a fraction of a second in the afternoon, he didn't waste any time: He jumped into his helicopter and flew off into the sunset.

The other mountaineers with whom we shared a permit were expecting us at base camp. We knew that Simone Moro would be there, but we had no idea who else would be in his group. I was pleased to see the Kazakh Denis Urubko, whom I had met along with Simone on Nanga Parbat the previous year. He greeted me with a warm and welcoming, "Ah, Cinderella Caterpillar!" and we all burst out laughing. A Russian, Boris Korshunov—who would turn out to be something of an interesting character during the course of the expedition—was their team's third member. Boris, sixty-nine, had once been a spaceship mechanic for the Soviet cosmonaut Juri Gagarin. He had been awarded the Snow Leopard Prize seven times for his mountaineering achievements all over the world. Unfortunately, his linguistic skills were somewhat limited. Apart from Russian, he could only master four German words: *ja, nein, bitte, danke.* We were forced to revert to nonverbal communication, but with the help of Denis, who speaks English, and Simone, who is a real linguist with his seven languages including Russian and German, we were able to exchange some basic information.

The three had been acclimatizing on Baruntse, where they had opened a new route. Simone and Denis also intended to do an unclimbed route on Annapurna I. From the second to the last camp on the French Route they planned to circumvent the traverse underneath the hanging glacier and climb via a rock pillar directly to the summit. In the end this route proved too dangerous due to rock- and icefall, and they were forced to revert to the normal route, just like Boris. Simone and the others had already looked at the lower part of the north ridge and said that a huge ice serac had collapsed in the Dutch Rib and that it was impossible to climb. This left us with no choice but to do the normal route as well.

The seventh name on our permit was that of an Italian climber, Abele Blanc. He had already climbed thirteen 8000-meter peaks; Annapurna I would be his last one. He was also at base camp after having acclimatized on a trekking tour in the Khumbu. He had intensely studied the route and conditions on the mountain. On May 22, our second day at base camp, it was snowing heavily and out of the blue he said, "Nope, I am not taking any risks. This is too dangerous for me. I am going home."

We were dumbfounded. Ralf tried to change his mind: "Abele, we are all well-acclimatized. If we work together we can do this. Let's give it a go."

Abele gave it another thought, but stuck to his decision: "No, I am not coming."

He gave each of us a red Sungdi string, which had been blessed in a Buddhist monastery, said goodbye, and walked off. I was impressed by his determination given that his goal, his last 8000-meter peak, was so near! I wondered whether we were taking too big a risk, but I listened to my gut feeling, and for me the climb still felt right. The most important thing would be to recognize the potential dangers on the way, and turn back if we had to.

The weather forecast for the following day was good, so we got ready to go. We planned on taking four days for the round trip and packed our backpacks accordingly. In order to keep our packs as light as possible we split food and gas for exactly four days, didn't bring any extra weight, and didn't plan for an extra day. We didn't want to make the same mistake as we had on Shisha Pangma, where our backpacks were simply too heavy.

The higher I go, the less I eat. In the morning, it's usually porridge; in the evening mashed potatoes; and for a snack, a waffle, a couple of cookies, or a cracker. Ralf and I had packed our two-man tent; Hiro had a light single tent. Time flew as we were getting ready for the summit.

We also enjoyed the delicious food prepared by our cook Sitaram, who was with us for the first time. His meals were amazing, but unfortunately he was so shy that we hardly ever got to see him. After the meal, he would come out of the kitchen proudly wearing his apron and asking whether everything had been all right. Denis and Boris were absolutely hilarious and entertaining during our meals. We had a lot of fun with them. Boris was a phenomenon. Among other jobs, he had worked for the Russian secret service and taken part in recruitment and survival trainings. In one such test, the applicants had to jump naked into cold water (30 degrees Fahrenheit) and stay in as long as they could. Those who managed more than ten minutes received one ruble. Before exposing trainees to such tests Boris used to take them himself, earning sixty rubles. Every single day, he entertained us with his unbelievable and interesting stories.

His wiry body revealed his age as well as his incredible strength. But his equipment was pretty basic and insufficient; his harness had certainly seen better days, and I wouldn't have wanted to entrust my life to it. Simone had lent him his new, very good high-altitude mittens for Baruntse, but even though it was bitterly cold Boris preferred to climb with his old fleece gloves that were full of holes. When Simone asked him on Baruntse why he was not wearing his mittens, Boris said he wanted to save them for Annapurna I. As a result of this, he already had slightly frostbitten fingers when he arrived at Annapurna base camp, but didn't seem too worried about them.

On May 23, six of us headed out of base camp. We wanted to cover a lot of ground that day and set up our bivouac at 5800 meters, which is usually the site for Camp 2. We knew that we had to negotiate three icefalls on our way to the summit, which could be—depending on their condition—pretty tricky. We could have circumnavigated the first one, but doing so would have led us across a rocky section which we would have had to fix for our rappel. This would have been pretty time-consuming, and since we didn't want to climb expedition-style we decided to climb all three icefalls. Contrary to our expectations, we got through the first icefall relatively easy. We found a good route, which we marked with little flags so we could find it again in poor visibility or snowfall. As Hiro had an upset stomach and needed some time to recover, we had no choice but to stay at the site of Camp 1 at 5000 meters.

While Denis and Simone continued through the deep snow up toward Camp 2, Boris indicated that he also wanted to stay at Camp 1. We had not made any arrangements for him to stay with us, but with him obviously unpacking his things we guessed that this was his plan. Over the next few days, we had to guess many things from his behavior; without Denis or Simone to translate, our conversations with Boris were reduced to sign language. When he wanted to take a picture of us and his camera was not working, he looked at us with a questioning glance indicating that he needed spare batteries. We didn't think much of it, but told him that unfortunately we didn't have any.

Our camp was on rocky ground, which had the advantage of water running between the rocks, making cooking a whole lot easier. While we made tea and cooked our dinner, we saw that Boris had also assembled his cooking set, but he was obviously looking for something. Suddenly, he pointed his finger at our pot and then down to base camp, which made it blatantly obvious that he had left his pot down there. Shortly afterward, he disappeared behind a rock. Half an hour later he returned with a wide grin, holding an old rusty tin in his hands. Even though we had finished by then and had offered him our pot, he preferred to cook in the tin. After a short while, we found out that he hadn't brought a water bottle, either; every time he was thirsty—in my view, he drank far too little—he would unpack his cooking set, put snow in the tin, melt it, and drink the water from the tin before he would continue to climb.

It had now become cloudy and cold, and Ralf and I withdrew to our tent. We left the tent door slightly unzipped so we could observe Boris, who gave us another sample of his forgetfulness. He started off by arranging the rocks to make a suitable platform for his tent. His progress was excruciatingly slow; it took him a long time to put up the flysheet. Suddenly he walked over to the place where we had left our ski poles. He grabbed one of the poles, took a second one, looked into our tent, and asked us with wild gesticulations whether he could use them. We made him understood that he could, but we were rather surprised when we saw him use them as tent poles. Of course, he had left his tent poles at base camp too! There was no doubt that Boris was physically very fit, but I couldn't help thinking that his brain might have suffered from his high-altitude mountaineering—or had he just wanted to save on weight?

The next morning Hiro felt much better, so at 5:00 a.m. we started out. Thanks to the trail Simone and Denis had broken on the flatter sections, we made good progress. The second icefall was a lot steeper and technically more difficult to climb. We often had to cross crevasses on narrow snow bridges, which we had to probe to make sure they were strong enough to bear our weight. It goes without saying that we were roped up on the glacier. Well, at least that was the case for Ralf, Hiro, and me; Boris, who kept a safe distance behind us, was not on the rope. Ralf offered to rope him up with us but he refused categorically, insisting on his independence.

At Camp 2 we met Denis and Simone, who were having a rest day after having broken trail for a day. Camp 2 was in a safe spot: There were a few crevasses, but the most important thing was that it was relatively well protected from serac fall. Unfortunately, the weather clouded over again and started snowing at midday, so we had to deal with a lot of fresh snow the next morning. Given the poor conditions and the bad weather forecast for the next two days, Simone and Denis decided to go back down to base camp. We, on the other hand, were eager to continue and, avalanche danger permitting, wanted to find a way through the third icefall. Despite our light loads—we had planned to go back to Camp 2 the same night—this task turned out to be very hard physical labor. The approach route to the icefall was heavily crevassed and the snow was so deep that we could only break trail for a short time before we had to switch. We also had to rope up on some of the traverses due to slab-avalanche danger. At about 6600 meters we were standing on the bottom of an almost vertical icefall of about 50 meters. I managed to climb up and fix some rope before we retreated to Camp 2. Our initial contentment was slightly marred by the snow that started falling again in the afternoon. We hoped that our hard trail-breaking work had not been in vain!

Very early on May 26 we left Camp 2, which we had initially envisioned as our first bivouac. We had already been on the hill for four days, longer than anticipated, and we were slowly running out of supplies. The fresh snow had settled, but our trail was gone with the wind and we had to start breaking trail all over again. The snow was up to our knees, and this time we had to break trail with our heavy packs on. Boris continued to follow us at a safe distance: He adapted to our plans but made us understand that he was independent. Getting over the third icefall posed a few problems. The slopes were either completely covered in drift snow, difficult to break trail in, or they were steep and covered in blue ice. We were repeatedly faced with big crevasses, and it took a lot of time to find the routes through the seracs in this difficult terrain. I could not stop thinking that we were directly underneath the huge hanging glacier and would have to speed up significantly to get through safely.

In the afternoon, Dhaulagiri peeked out of the clouds. Under the protection of an ice wall we stopped to have a drink. Boris got out his rusty tin and fired up his stove. Ralf started to talk about his Dhaulagiri expedition in 1990. The summit unfolded beautifully in front of us, and this was the moment when I started to feel drawn toward that mountain. I said to Ralf, "One day, I would also love to climb Dhaulagiri I." It would take another three years for that day to come. We didn't stop for very long as we were all pretty tense. From this point onwards, Dhaulagiri I was always in my view; in front of me towered the summit of Annapurna, and to my right I could see Dhaulagiri.

In the afternoon, the spectacle was over. Clouds moved up from the valley and our visibility dropped to about 10 meters. At around 6800 meters we reached a huge crevasse, the bergschrund underneath the ramp leading to the looming hanging glacier. The crevasse was about 150 to 200 meters long and its upper edge overhung slightly. In thick fog, we tried to find a place to cross the crevasse at its upper left, but it was about 3 meters wide, and there was no way to cross it there. We then walked back toward the right, but there was no suitable place to cross there either. We found no obvious place where we could get across, and we had no idea what it would look like higher up. Ralf and Hiro suggested pitching the tents underneath the overhanging edge and continuing our search the following day. But I couldn't let go: I didn't want to lie in my tent wondering the whole night whether or not we could get over the bergschrund. In some years it had not been possible at all. I needed to know! I insisted that we traverse over to the right again. We found a place where spindrift snow had accumulated to form a little snow mount on the crevasse's lower edge. It looked pretty stable, and I said to Ralf, "I will see whether I can get across here."

He put me on belay and off I went. The upper edge of the crevasse was slightly overhanging and I had to move up dynamically, almost in a jump. After I had slammed both ice tools into the ice above me, my feet followed, and I was on the other side. It was only one critical moment before I entered easier terrain again. I moved up another few meters and put in a marker. Just as I was about to place an ice screw to facilitate our crossing the next day, I heard a loud roar of collapsing ice above me—a noise I will never forget. It pierces through my body whenever I hear it. One thing was certain: Something was collapsing above me and it was not just a small piece of ice, but tons of it.

I stood on the frontpoints of my crampons and looked down to Ralf. My mind raced as we looked into each other's eyes, "Is that it? Is this the end? Is this our last goodbye?"

Describing that moment is almost impossible. Everything happened so quickly—literally in nanoseconds. I knew the ice would crash down on top of me any second and then I heard Ralf scream, "Gerlinde, jump! Jump!"

I hesitated for maybe half a second before pushing my feet off the ice and jumping. I was on belay—Ralf would hold me. I landed softly on the little snow mount where I had started. The overhanging serac offered some protection from the ice blocks that were tumbling down. We were lucky that they didn't collapse directly above us but a little farther to the right. The falling ice thundered and roared for a while until it had all come down. Ralf and I looked at each other. I knew that this had been a matter of seconds, and that it could have gone terribly wrong. I was in a strange state, a mixture of shock and relief. I had to force myself not to imagine what could have happened. Had the ice avalanche hit me in full swing, I would have been dead.

While we set up the bivouac, we discussed whether it was wise to continue the following day. We would have to traverse the ramp for one and a half hours during which we would be constantly exposed to the dangers of the hanging glaciers, which could collapse again any minute. Usually Ralf and I don't have intense discussions on the mountain, but this situation was different; it was emotionally charged. We talked about it in the evening and spent a sleepless night. For Ralf it was clear that he would go down.

"Gerlinde, this is impossible. The risk is too high. I have a fourteen-year-old son. I have responsibilities."

I absolutely understood the strong responsibility he felt for Joshi. I knew that I had been extremely lucky and that the risk was too high with the hanging glacier threatening to collapse any time, day or night. It was certainly wiser to go down. Hiro, who is usually prepared to take higher risks, didn't say a word. I felt torn, and in the end I decided to wait and see what my gut feeling would say.

The night was calm. We couldn't hear any ice avalanches, but a lot of spindrift settled on our tent, and in the morning it was covered in snow. The night's calmness made me want to carry on. At 5:00 a.m., when my full bladder forced me out of the tent I could already see that a beautiful day was about to break. The fog had disappeared, it was calm, the deep blue sky was cloudless, and Dhaulagiri I looked toward me, saying "Hello."

I shouted: "Ralf, have a look, it's a gorgeous day." I looked up and saw the hanging glacier, which was at arms' length, as well as the little marker that I had put in the previous day. I knew that we could do it, I could feel it.

"I would like to continue," I said to Ralf.

"Okay," he replied, "but I'll go down. I don't want to take this risk."

Prior to the expedition, we had made an arrangement: if one of us wanted to turn back and the other one wanted to carry on, we would go our separate ways as long as we were both happy with the decision, nobody was injured or sick, and it would be responsible to leave the other person to his or her own devices. If the opposite were the case we would help each other, just as we help other team members and climbers from other teams. We were both independent mountaineers and could make our own decisions; we should certainly not miss out on our summit chance due to consideration for the other person. We were responsible for ourselves, and we wanted to give each other that freedom.

I accepted Ralf's decision as fully as he accepted mine. He was going to descend to base camp, because waiting on this wall would have been far too dangerous. Hiro followed me when I packed my tent and continued up—and so did Boris. After having done it once, I found the crevasse crossing was a lot easier and faster; once we had reached the other side, we were in the middle of the ramp, which was about 45 to 50 degrees steep. It was windswept and hard; the shiny blue ice surely didn't make for an easy ascent. Even though I had left camp feeling confident that my gut feeling was right, I had an adrenaline surge. For the next hour and a half we would have to traverse across the ramp toward the left before we could continue to climb up on the left side of the icefall. We would be right below the huge hanging ice serac the whole time. There was no safe place, no refuge: We were absolutely exposed to the icefall, which could collapse at any minute. Speed was our only chance, and this is why we were unroped—everyone was climbing independently. From that point on, I had to concentrate hard. Even the tiniest mistake could be fatal.

I don't think I have ever felt as tense as when I climbed the ramp of Annapurna I. I placed my ice tools mechanically and followed them with my crampons. I knew that Hiro and Boris were behind me, but I didn't turn around. I only wanted to get through this death trap. On the sloping traverse I moved fast, completely out of breath. I couldn't have kept up that speed for long, as we had already reached 7000 meters. The 45-degree terrain was actually not that technically difficult for us, and the climb had already been dangerous in the lower part of the route, which was also exposed to the hanging glacier. There was no way we would find a safe place to bivouac underneath the hanging glacier. But still, the frightening events of the previous day had changed something inside me. I was constantly worried that the seracs would tumble down again, and I couldn't help being scared that I would again hear the roar of the falling ice blocks.

When I turned around to look for Hiro and Boris, I saw Ralf coming up behind them. For a split second I was moved to tears, but then my happiness turned into mixed feelings. On one hand, I was overjoyed that we would attempt the summit together, but on the other hand I was very worried that something would happen to him and that I would feel responsible. I could never, ever forgive myself if something were to happen to Ralf.

"Please, let everything be okay! Please don't let anything drop down on us!" I kept chanting these words like a mantra all the way.

Nothing fell on us. Every once in a while we got dusted with snow, which was blown across the ramp, but that was it. When I got out of the danger zone I waited for the others. Ralf came toward me beaming with joy and relief. We hugged each other as if we had not seen each other for weeks. How lucky I felt to be there with him!

After this brief intermission we carried on in deep snow. Though breaking trail was exhausting, I felt a lot more relaxed than I had felt underneath the ramp. After another 150 vertical meters, we found a good spot for our fourth bivouac, just below a crevasse with an overhanging edge. As the space was too small for three tents, Boris crawled in with Hiro, which was quite amusing with the huge language barrier between them. We had now been on the mountain for five days—we were just about to spend our fifth night up there—and no matter how deep we dug into our backpacks, all we found was disappointment over having eaten most of our food. As happy as we were to have left the dangerous ramp behind, we were very worried about our supplies. When I fired up the stove to melt some snow I knew that the gas would last only another five minutes. The water—just enough to make some porridge and still have something to drink for the evening, the night, and the following day—was only tepid when the flame began to flicker and die out. Ralf and I had three spoonfuls of porridge left for breakfast.

As we felt fine, we agreed to go for the summit as long as our physical condition was still good the following morning. We showed Boris on our watch that we were leaving at 5:00 a.m.; he nodded and laughed. During the night a storm came up, covering our tents in drift snow. Our ascent route

TOP: We had to get through the last icefall above base camp quickly since collapsing ice towers posed a constant danger. *(Photo by Ralf Dujmovits)* BOTTOM: I experienced mixed feelings of joy and apprehension while with Ralf on the summit of Annapurna I. *(Photo by Hirotaka Takeuchi)*

was covered in fresh snow with several sections of blue ice on a 40-degree slope. We made good progress until we reached a rocky outcrop wedged between two gullies. Ralf, Hiro, and I immediately agreed that the right gully would lead to the main summit, but Boris insisted on taking the left one.

"Boris, Boris, this is the way." All our shouting, waving, and gesticulating was in vain: Even though Boris had seen where we were going, he pointed at the summit above him and took the left gully. Sure that we were right, we stayed on the right side. Hour by hour we took turns breaking trail through the gullies, slowing down significantly as our exhaustion from the past few days finally set in, along with hunger and thirst. A long sloping traverse took us to the start of the summit couloir, where we had to break trail again before we set foot on a windswept, rocky slope that led to the summit toward the right.

On May 28, 2004, Ralf, Hiro, and I embraced each other on the summit of Annapurna I. In the beautiful afternoon light, we enjoyed a magnificent view from the top. Below us, at about 6000 meters, a thick blanket of cloud covered the nearby valleys, with countless mountaintops peaking through. It was a glorious scene. Machapuchare and Annapurna IV, which I had already admired from Manaslu, made for a stunning view, and a little below us, separated by numerous pointy ridges, we could see Boris standing on the 8012-meter east summit. His stubbornness had taken him to the false summit.

Later at base camp, he told Simone that he would have liked to reach the main summit but that the east summit was not a bad achievement either. After all, he was now the fourth person to summit that peak solo.

Of course, I was very happy to have reached the highest point of Annapurna I, but worries about the descent were intruding on my joy. I am always aware that the summit is only halfway and that I have to get down safely, but on top of Annapurna I, I was even more worried than usual: the dangerous traverse, the icefalls. . . . I felt subdued. The risk was too imminent for us to stay on the summit for long, and when I realized that it was already 3:30 p.m. I urged that we start down as soon as possible. We took a few summit photos, radioed Simone and Denis at Camp 1, and began our descent.

After three exhausting hours we reached our two tents at 7200 meters. The weather looked good for the next day and we decided to leave as early as possible in order to avoid dangerous icefalls during the hottest time of day. I was ravenously hungry and thirsty that night, but having run out of gas, we couldn't melt water so we had to lick ice. I dreamed about *Kaiserschmarrn* (scratched pancakes, an Austrian dish) and fizzy drinks—I was dying for an endless supply of something refreshing and completely obsessed with drinking.

On our descent—it was another 3000 meters to base camp—we bumped into Simone and Denis. They had abandoned their plan of opening a new route and were on their way to climb Annapurna I via the normal route, this time using our trail. In the end, Simone didn't reach the summit due to an upset stomach. We were eager to get down as quickly and safely as possible, and we all descended individually. When all four of us had crossed the ramp I was finally able to relax a little. We stopped for a while at the relatively safe spot of our third bivouac; Denis and Simone had told us that they had left a little bag with candied sugar there, and with their permission we scarfed it down like hungry wolves.

Finally, we said, "Boris, let's go."

We wanted to continue, but Boris wasn't moving. He indicated that he would be with us shortly. When I turned around, he had already gotten up and was fiddling with his backpack, so I didn't think anything of it. The only thought on my mind was to get down as fast as I could. Between 6500 and 6000 meters we disappeared into a cloud; the fog became increasingly thick as we got lower until we could hardly see anything and had to find our way using the little markers we had left. At 5900 meters we waited for Boris to cross the second icefall with us. We waited and waited, but Boris didn't appear. It was getting late, and we still had to negotiate two icefalls and wanted to continue farther down. We called him, but we didn't hear anything. Given the state we were in—completely dehydrated, hungry, and exhausted from the summit—we couldn't go back up to see what was going on. We did walk back on the flat plateau for a while, but couldn't see anything. We then radioed Simone and Denis, who were at our last camp, and explained the situation. Night was falling and we had no choice but to pitch our tents and spend another night on the plateau. We were seriously worried, thinking that Boris must have fallen into a crevasse. We kept in constant radio contact with Simone and Denis, who planned to go down the following day to look for him. We would go up and do the same, even though our hunger had become unbearable.

At around 8:00 p.m., we heard a rustling sound outside our tent. We looked out and saw Boris sitting in front of Hiro's tent, just as exhausted as we were. I rushed toward him in joy and asked him gazillions of questions, which he didn't understand. Wanting to know what had happened, we gave him the radio so he could talk to Simone. Simone translated for us that Boris didn't understand the big fuss; he had simply taken a short break higher up and was here now. At first I couldn't believe my ears. We had been so worried about him. Later, we laughed about Boris, especially about his forgetfulness, but at that moment I was livid. The reasons for my anger were obvious: There was always something wrong with him; he always held us back; he had nearly thwarted Denis and Simone's summit plans. The situation was no longer funny, but pretty serious. Given the increasing intensity of the sun at the end of the season, every day counted in the icefall. But when we later found out more about his solo shenanigans back in Russia and Kazakhstan, we could understand his reaction a little better. He was simply not used to other people looking out for him. In his circle, everyone looked after him- or herself. In his view, we should not have felt responsible to help him.

The next day—our eighth on the mountain—we desperately wanted to reach base camp, but first we had a 2000-meter descent ahead of us. We started at 5:00 a.m. in thick fog, which made finding the way through the ice maze even more difficult. The second icefall had changed completely over the past few days, and our little markers had become completely useless. Seracs had collapsed and buried our ascent route; snow bridges had collapsed or become impassable. Because there were so many crevasses, we roped up and insisted on Boris joining us. But he refused even to put on his harness. Well, Boris was definitely not prepared for Ralf's wrath; he screamed at him in German, telling him that we would have arrived at base camp a long time ago if it had not been for him.

Ralf then grabbed Boris and tied him into our rope, mumbling, "I am tying him on now and will certainly not let him go until we get down. I don't want to lose him again."

As I was the lightest, I took over the lead; it would be easier to pull me out of a crevasse if I broke in. I did break in a few times, but fortunately never really deeply.

Just before we reached our bivouac spot at 5000 meters we reached a little bowl with water running down the rocks. We fell on the water like people who are dying of thirst in the desert. I drank like a camel, but couldn't get enough before we carried on. We still had to cross the lower icefall, and it was getting warmer. Our ascent route, which we had marked, was completely gone: Huge ice towers had collapsed on top of it. At first we did reasonably well, but then we were wincing at the horrific sound of tumbling ice blocks.

"This is like descending into hell," Ralf shouted.

He was right: If we didn't want to be crushed by collapsing ice chunks, we had to get through this labyrinth of wedged ice blocks as quickly as possible. In order to avoid these flying chunks of ice we took off the rope, but doing so demanded more concentration on not losing each other in the maze. The crossing was extremely stressful. We shouted at each other, trying to indicate where to go through. One reason for the shouting was the deafening noise of the collapsing ice; the other was that we felt tense and frightened when we saw 20-meter ice blocks collapse just in front of us.

We stopped short at the edge of a precipice. It was about 100 meters long, and the terrain below it looked a lot better, but we only had a 50-meter rope with us. The ice was slightly overhanging, which made it hard to make a belay point for the rappel. So we had to go back into the icefall, but we thought up a new strategy: We waited for an ice tower to collapse, then quickly ran across the big chunks of ice, trusting the statistical probability that another tower would not collapse in the same spot within such a short period of time.

We ended up at another break-off edge. This time we had no other choice but to rappel. Ralf placed an ice screw. Once again, the ice was slightly overhanging, but with the rope too short to reach all the way to the bottom it was impossible to double it up. We would have to leave the rope, hoping that this would be the last rappel. Ralf went down first to look for the way. He had to cross a crevasse on the rappel, but did so without problems. Hiro and I followed him as fast as we could. Then came Boris. I thought that he would use the figure-of-eight rappel device that was hanging off his harness, but what was I thinking? Boris preferred the Russian method and wiggled the rope around his mitten to arm-rap. In this overhanging terrain that would have taken superhuman powers, and I was sure that none of us had any of those left, so I called out, "Boris, no, no, no!"

My warning came too late. Boris started to arm-rap down. In the last meters above the crevasse he ran out of steam, could no longer hold himself, and crashed right into the crevasse. Great! Now we had to see how we would get him out of there. As if we didn't already have enough on our hands! Luckily, the crevasse was relatively wide on top, narrowing into a big V where Boris got stuck with his big backpack. But we had left our rope at the rappel. . . .

I slowly crawled toward the crevasse with Hiro holding my feet to stop me from falling in. Using joined forces, we heaved Boris out of the crevasse and felt enormous relief when he emerged unharmed.

After then climbing across a steepish slope, we were finally out of the danger zone. For a moment I felt relaxed, but when I noticed the broken ice on the path, I realized that the danger of serac fall was far from over. We ran for our lives—first Ralf, then I, then Hiro, followed by Boris. I didn't turn around or listen for the others; the only thing on my mind was getting down as soon as possible. I scurried over big chunks of snow and ice before I reached flat rocky terrain. Finally, I was safe!

After everyone had gotten through this dangerous section safely, we all sighed with relief and hugged each other warmly. The mountain certainly hadn't spared any effort to show us why it was considered one of the most dangerous 8000-meter peaks in the world. We knew that we had been very lucky, and being free of all the tension of the last few days was an incredible feeling. I was brimming with joy that I had summited Annapurna I, but I knew that the risks we had taken were disproportionate to our summit success. As I do so often, I had listened to my gut feeling and relied on my inner voice, but by doing so I had put Ralf and myself in danger. I knew that I must not push my luck this way again.

After a short ascent across a moraine we reached the path to base camp. On a big flat rock I discovered a can of beer and three cans of Coke. I thought I must be dreaming—my dehydration was making me hallucinate. I had been longing for ages to put a fizzy drink to my lips, and here it was. I kneeled down, examined the cans, and couldn't believe that they were actually real. As we later found out, Sitaram had put them there for us a few days earlier, thinking that we would be back after four days on the mountain. We gave Boris the beer and drank the Coke—what a treat! Boris, who was a big handsome man, came over and gave me a bear hug so powerful that I could hardly breathe. This was his way to say thanks for helping him. After gulping down his beer he lay happily in the grass, not moving an inch. Ralf, Hiro, and I also felt huge relief. When we walked past the original base camp, we were reminded once again that it was not a matter of course to get up and down that mountain safely. Base camp is now a memorial site where numerous rocky mounds and engraved stone slabs pay tribute to the climbers who have lost their lives on Annapurna I.

We could hardly wait to get to base camp and were especially looking forward to a good meal. Sitaram cooked an amazing dinner, which he served on a nicely set table: sausages, pizza, pasta, different kinds of vegetables, and yak meat. I was so hungry I didn't know where to start, but unfortunately I felt full after about three bites. My stomach had shrunk so much that I could hardly get anything down. The only thing I could do was drink and then sleep.

Late in the afternoon Simone and Denis came back, telling horror stories about the lower icefall. It was even warmer when they went through, and apparently everything had moved in there. When an ice block collapsed right beside them, they saved themselves by jumping into a crevasse. They had gone through hell and back, but luckily they came down safely in the end.

A Japanese expedition on the same route in the fall of the same year was less fortunate. Two of their members were killed by falling ice. When I found out about them, all my fear returned; I could certainly understand how something like that had happened on Annapurna I. I had a similar sensation in spring 2005, when a big Italian expedition acclimatized on the north side of the mountain. Abele Blanc was a member of this expedition. Veikka Gustafsson, Ed Viesturs, and Silvio Mondinelli reached the summit, with Ed finishing all fourteen 8000-meter peaks. The South Tyrolean climber Christian Kuntner would also have finished all fourteen, but sadly was killed by a falling ice block. While Silvio was able to get to safety, Abele was seriously injured.

This expedition gave Ralf and me another reason to discuss what to do if one of us wanted to turn back and the other one wanted to go on. Being in a relationship changes things; unlike climbing with a friend, deeper emotions are involved. I usually worry more about Ralf than myself, but I guess that's normal. It is understandable not to want to leave your partner alone, but at the same time you don't want to be responsible if he or she gets hurt. Discussing these principles made us agree that if one of us wanted to turn back he or she should do so and stick to his or her decision whether the other likes it or not.

Annapurna I also changed my way of making decisions. Up until that point, I had always followed my gut feeling. Ralf taught me how to take realistic criteria into consideration in my decision-making. I no longer wanted to rely solely on my intuition, even though it had worked for a long time. I have a sense of basic trust—this is my way of life. I guess a healthy mix of basic trust and rationality would be best, and maybe this is how Ralf and I complement each other, especially on expeditions.

Annapurna I left me deeply grateful that everything had turned out okay, that I had experienced such an intense time there, and that I had reached the summit. But our trip was not quite over, and our pain threshold was once again put to the test on our way home—a story we still laugh about today. At Munich's main train station we loaded our 175 pounds of expedition gear onto the train to Baden-Baden. While I stayed with the luggage on the train, Ralf thought it would be nice to have a newspaper for the long trip. He took my wallet—his was empty and packed up somewhere—and bought a copy of *Spiegel* and some fresh pretzels, a special treat after an expedition. I sat on the train wondering where Ralf was. Suddenly the doors closed, and when I anxiously looked out the window l saw Ralf standing on the platform, gazing at the departing train. I will never forget the expression on his face and how he waved goodbye when the train slowly pulled out of the station without him.

For a split second, I was upset that Ralf had missed the train because of a stupid magazine. But when I thought about Annapurna l, all anger and panic vanished. I didn't have any money, but I had my ticket in my breast pocket. I was only worried about changing trains in Karlsruhe, where I would have to move all our expedition gear by myself.

Ralf had the great idea to rent a car to follow me, but at the car rental he discovered that this would be quite tricky without his driver's license, which was in his wallet on the train. So in the end, he had to take the next train an hour and a half later.

To make matters worse, it had been raining so hard that a landslide had buried the train tracks between Ulm and Stuttgart. My train stopped and we had to take a bus to Stuttgart, where the train would continue. How would I possibly be able to get the 175 pounds of gear from the train onto a bus? While I was considering whom to call to help me with the luggage, I suddenly remembered that I had no money and couldn't pay anyone, so I would have to do it myself. It took me three trips from the train to the bus stop, and when I was finally done hauling the gear the bus driver told me that I couldn't possibly take it all on his vehicle. I had to use all my charm to convince him to accept our luggage. Drenched in sweat, I phoned Ralf, who told me that his train was taking a different route to Stuttgart and that he had asked his brother Martin to pick us up from the train station there.

When I arrived in Stuttgart, completely and utterly exhausted, a very relaxed Ralf waited for me with his brother Martin. I was so happy to have Martin drive us home to Bühlertal, where we arrived at 1:30 a.m. As usual when we go on expedition, we had arranged for the house key to be left for us. But there was no key in the arranged spot! We couldn't get into the house, so once again we had to call Martin, who came back from the neighboring village to pick us up. At four o'clock in the morning we finally fell into a very deep sleep on Martin's couch.

Due to the deep snow in the Japanese Couloir, we had to get out our shovels just below Camp 3 on Gasherbrum I. Step by step, we dug our way up. *(Photo by Ralf Dujmovits)*

CHAPTER 8
DISTRESS

After Annapurna, we spent about ten days in Germany before we set off to climb in the Karakorum. Ralf was leading an AMICAL expedition to Gasherbrum I and one of his mountain guides, Hajo Netzer, was going to take a group to Gasherbrum II at the same time. Hiro and I were on both of AMICAL's permits and could use their base camp, which is shared by both mountains. We intended to climb independently, while Ralf was leading his group. We felt sure that we were still acclimatized well enough to climb Gasherbrum I alpine style. And weather, time, and energy level permitting, we might also have a go at Gasherbrum II.

Ralf, Hiro, and I were quite motivated after our success on Annapurna I. None of us had gotten sick, we were still feeling strong, and everything boded well for another successful climb. We traveled and trekked to Gasherbrum base camp with fifteen others. This was the first time I had attempted an 8000-meter peak as part of a commercial expedition, and it took me some time to get used to these new dynamics. The start of the Askole trek saw us facing our first problem: We couldn't find enough porters to carry our 180 loads to base camp. Most porters in the valley were busy carrying for the many expeditions en route to Concordia for the fiftieth anniversary of the first ascent of K2. We had to leave eighty loads, mainly food, in Askole to be flown in to base camp by helicopter a few days later.

Weather-wise, the expedition to the Gasherbrums was not blessed. It snowed heavily on our trek to base camp, forcing the porters to wade through knee-deep snow on our last day. After we set up base camp, it snowed for three consecutive days. We had to get our heads around the fact that we would have a lot of trail-breaking work to do. The weather remained unstable throughout the expedition, with continuous periods of rain and snow. Even though at 8080 meters Gasherbrum I is one of the lower 8000-meter peaks, its upper slopes are quite steep and exposed. The fresh snow would make it more difficult to break trail and of course increase the avalanche danger.

For Hiro and me, the unstable weather also meant that climbing alpine style was out of the question. The long periods of snowfall forced us to leave high camp and descend to base camp, but the constant up and down was important to keep the track open despite the heavy snowfalls. After twenty-one days we had also lost our acclimatization and had to start again from scratch. This was actually not such a bad thing, as Ralf needed some support with the difficult conditions on the mountain. Hiro and I helped him break trail and set up the high camps; we carried up the ropes and helped fix the Japanese Couloir, the crux of the route. Though we didn't use the fixed ropes for our ascent and carried our own lightweight tents, Hiro and I had now become part of the commercial AMICAL group. Since I knew three of its members really well, I actually felt quite comfortable.

The 600-meter-high icefall between base camp and Camp 1 was fairly demanding. Because the constant fresh snow had increased the risk of breaking through, we roped up when we moved through this maze of ice towers and crevasses. We sank in particularly deep in the upper, flatter part of the icefall. Ralf, Hiro, and I were able to take turns in breaking trail with Hajo and a guide from another expedition, since the routes for Gasherbrum I and II are the same up to Camp 1, which is situated on a big plateau. Whenever we went through the icefall, we left base camp at around 2:00 a.m. to get through the danger zone as safely as possible. When the sun was out, it beat down relentlessly on the icefall, and the heat was almost unbearable. But no matter whether we started at midnight or at 1:00 a.m., we were always woken by the beautiful yodeling of Erich Weitlaner, a member of a Gasherbrum II expedition from Eastern Tyrol. Those lovely morning calls never failed to put me in a good mood early in the day.

On the other side of the plateau, the route led very steeply to the Gasherbrum La, the pass between Gasherbrum I and Gasherbrum II, where we set up our Camp 2 at 6500 meters. After a period of bad weather, Ralf, Hiro, and I went up to Camp 3 one day ahead of Ralf's crew to fix the rope in the Japanese Couloir on the north face. There was so much fresh snow in the gully, which was 500 meters long and 55 degrees steep, that we were forced to climb a rocky rib on the left side of the couloir. We could only get into the couloir at its narrowest point; otherwise we would have been too exposed to avalanche danger. The fresh snow cover, hip-deep in places, made it difficult to place pitons to fix the rope. At 6850 meters, we ran out of rope and returned to Camp 2. The following day we descended to base camp in yet another whiteout, and were happy that our markers guided us down. Who knows whether we would have found the way without them!

When we arrived our kitchen crew and high-altitude porters, who were almost all Hunzas, were busy preparing a celebration dinner in honor of Aga Khan. On July 11, 1957, he had been named the spiritual leader of the Ismailis. The Hunzas, who follow this relatively liberal Islamic faith, celebrate this date with a feast, singing, and dancing.

On July 12, we started another summit attempt. From base camp we went straight to Camp 2 only to find the upper part of the Japanese Couloir completely covered in snow. As we didn't want to risk getting caught in a slab avalanche, we went back down without having achieved anything. Once again we were stuck at base camp waiting for the snow to settle. While it was snowing at base camp, the wind blew hard near the summit. At this point we had been in Pakistan for seven weeks. Hiro and I had expected to summit within three weeks and were slowly running out of time. The official expedition time was also coming to an end, and only a few members could get more time off to extend their stay. At the end, the only climbers left for Gasherbrum I were Ralf, his client Peter Fessler, the Pakistani high-altitude porter Qudrat Ali, Hiro, and I. Base camp was slowly clearing out, with one expedition after the other pulling the plug and leaving; in the end we were one of the few groups left.

I was still sure that we would get another chance to summit. I tried to think positive and keep my eyes on my goal, no matter how fed up I was with waiting at base camp. The weather looked good for July 24 and 25, so on July 22 we climbed to Camp 1 in heavy snowfall. As the avalanche danger was high, we only continued to Camp 2 in the afternoon of the following day, wading through deep snow. And on July 24, the weather was indeed as clear as forecast. By the time we reached the end of the fixed rope, the snow was so high that we had to plough through it meter by meter. When it was my turn to lead, the snow reached up to my hips and I had to dig up the snow with my hands to make progress. At one point, Hiro even used his avalanche shovel to clear the snow on a steep section. Even though it was incredibly exhausting, I did this work with great enthusiasm. We knew that the snow would be very deep in the couloir, but we hoped that the route would be windswept farther up.

It took hours to get through the couloir and we finally set up camp at 7000 meters. Our hard work was rewarded with a stunning panorama of the Karakorum. Although I was exhausted, I enjoyed sitting in the tent with Ralf, melting snow, and absorbing the amazing view of the surrounding peaks and the gorgeous evening scenery. Shortly after us, a Dutch couple, Katja Staartjes and Henk Wesselius, as well as a Spanish team with Carlos Pauner, arrived at Camp 3. I had known Carlos from previous expeditions, but had only gotten to know his teammates Guillermo (William) Barbier, Raquel Pérez, and José Antonio Lopez over the past few weeks. José was the last to reach camp, and though he seemed very tired, he enjoyed the magnificent view.

July 25, our potential summit day, started with clear skies but was bitterly cold. We set off at 2:00 a.m. Despite wearing my down suit, I had been freezing in the tent during the night: It was −9 degrees Fahrenheit inside the tent, and outside it was even a few degrees colder. As we had planned to leave in the middle of the night anyway, and I wanted to save weight in view of the upcoming trail-breaking work, I had left my sleeping bag at Camp 2. Hiro had done the same. It took a long time for me to warm up; as usual, I had very cold toes. Wading through deep snow on the summit flank, which was about 50 degrees steep and 2600 feet high, felt even more exhausting than the day before due to the higher altitude. Finally, after eight exhausting hours, we stood on the highest point of Gasherbrum I in perfect weather at a few minutes before midday.

TOP: On the highest point of Gasherbrum I: Qudrat Ali is on my left; Ralf, Hiro Takeuchi, and Peter Fessler on my right. *(Photo by Katja Staartjes)* BOTTOM: This beautiful view across the Karakorum compensated for all the effort of wading through deep snow on Gasherbrum I. *(Photo by Ralf Dujmovits)*

We had been able to enjoy stunning views during the breaks on our climb, but the panorama we could see from the summit was indescribably beautiful. One mountain range linked to the next, and spectacular peaks filled our eyes and our minds to the point of utter bewilderment. A long way down, we could see the gigantic glaciers merging into one, and we could look into the remote Shaksgam valley to the north.

The prominent summits of Broad Peak and Gasherbrum II rose directly in front of us, and a little farther behind, the mighty summit of K2 towered another 500 meters above us. From our perspective, Gasherbrum II looked incredibly steep and attractive. What Hiro and I had thought increasingly impossible over the past few weeks—namely, that we would also climb Gasherbrum II—suddenly became very real. But first and foremost, we were incredibly happy to have made it to this summit with joint effort and on such a beautiful and perfect day. Katja and Henk also had reason to celebrate: They were the first Dutch people to reach the summit of Gasherbrum I. We stayed on top for about an hour and took our time taking photos. Compared to Annapurna I, where I had been very worried about the descent, I was feeling pretty relaxed.

We were still aware, though, that the descent would be steep and we wouldn't have any room for mistakes. Just as on the ascent, we would negotiate the descent of the summit flank without a rope. Down to 7000 meters the route was very exposed, with a constant danger of falling. Near our last camp, it flattened out before it got steeper again leading into the Japanese Couloir.

I always climb knowing that one single mistake could be fatal. When the five of us left the summit, I told myself that I had to fully concentrate, but I didn't really expect anything to happen.

Ralf and I descended together, keeping a safe distance between us. Hiro, Peter, and Qudrat were a little ways above us. We climbed down facing forward with our crampons gripping pretty well in the relatively deep snow. We had probably covered a third of the summit flank when I suddenly heard Ralf yell, "Gerlinde!"

At the same moment, he grabbed my arm and pulled me over to his side. I had been concentrating on my steps and now I was terrified; everything was happening very fast. The next moment, something flew past me with incredible speed: something red—a body. In fact, it was a human body thumping onto the ground, spinning through the air, and landing on the ground again. Petrified, I looked down, unable to move. It must have been someone from the other group. But who? All I had seen was a red down suit, but almost everyone at base camp, no matter whether Spanish or Dutch, was wearing a red down suit. Only Ralf and I wore yellow. Within seconds my brain scanned everyone and the color they wore. Peter wore a blue anorak; Qudrat a green one. Hiro's down suit was red—but he was still standing above us, frozen with fear.

My summit joy was gone. I was terrified to have seen someone fall right before my eyes. Someone I knew—it was horrible. The body flew so fast that I would never ever have had the chance to self-arrest had it hit me. Had Ralf not accidentally turned around to look out for Peter, he would not have seen the falling body out of the corner of his eye nor pulled me over to his side, which means I too would have fallen.

"Ralf, oh my God."

I could hardly utter a word. All the way down at the end of the gully, which widened a bit toward the end, I could see the person in the red down suit. It was very unlikely that anyone could survive a fall of more than 800 meters. Was it Katja? Or Raquel, the lovely Spanish lady? Or Carlos, whom I had known for a long time? And how could this have happened? The person must have made a mistake—there was no other explanation. Maybe he or she had tripped after a crampon got tangled up in the gaiter of the other foot—a fatal mistake on such territory.

Even though there was not much we could do, we had to go down to find out who it was. My whole body was shaking, and I had to be really careful not to make a mistake. On the descent, I found a crampon. It was a Grivel, but again, everyone was wearing this brand. Further down, I found a piece of boot, which wasn't much of a clue, either, as everyone had the same orange boots.

The lower down I got, the less inclined I was to look at the body. I could already tell from afar that the face would be unrecognizable. As a nurse I was used to dealing with death, but now I was scared. I was scared to see

the disfigured face and find out that it might be someone who was important to me. Ralf volunteered to identify the body, while Hiro and I waited
a few meters away.

"Ralf, who is it?" I didn't look. "I think it's José" he replied.

José. He had already been tired the day before; he must have lost concentration for a moment. It was terrible—a young man horribly disfigured, his
life snatched out of his fingers. This was different from facing death in the
hospital, where I had seen many bodies and was not afraid to touch them.
José had not been incurably ill; death was not a salvation for him.

Henk arrived shortly after Peter. He had come down ahead of Katja,
and when he saw the red down suit tumble down, he thought it was his
partner. In his shock, he didn't turn around but simply ran down as fast
as he could. He shouted out her name, crying. Ralf managed to calm him
down until Katja arrived. This scene made me realize what it would be like
to lose someone you love.

I just stood there a few meters away from José, staring into the void. My
whole body was numb. This was simply impossible. The day had started so
beautifully and had taken such a horrific turn.

Ralf suggested I go ahead to Camp 3. He wanted to wait for the Spanish
team and take photos of José. This may sound morbid, but it is important for the relatives and the authorities, as well as for insurance. It was
obvious that we would not be able to get José's body down the Japanese
Couloir, so Ralf wanted to bury him with the help of the Spanish team.

I was happy to leave. Lost in thought, Hiro, Peter, and I started our
descent. Ralf came back late, which gave me time to sit in our tent and
ponder what could have led to José's fatal accident. Did he not keep his feet
wide enough apart as he walked? Opposite our tent, the Karakorum was
glowing in the evening sun just as beautifully as it had the previous day;
just as if nothing had happened.

It was a difficult night. Ralf too was traumatized by the incident, but
only noticed it now that everything was done. Neither of us slept a wink.
As I had left my sleeping bag at Camp 2, I was shivering with cold until
four o'clock in the morning, when João Garcia from Portugal started his
summit attempt and gave me his sleeping bag. At least I could warm up for

one hour before we packed up our gear at 5:00 a.m. and descended. While rappeling down the Japanese Couloir, nobody said a word. We were all in our own worlds, mourning.

We wanted to bring down all the AMICAL gear that was still at Camp 2. In order to save Ralf from having to go up again to collect everything, I put as much gear into my pack as I could, but my body could hardly carry the 88 pounds; after three consecutive expeditions I only weighed about 121 pounds. It was impossible to stand up on my own with the big pack on. There were a few moments when I seriously considered throwing in the towel and going back, but I fought on.

Hiro and I deposited some of our gear at Camp 1. Since the two Gasherbrums are right next to each other, we wanted to keep the option open to maybe try for Gasherbrum II after a few rest days. We marked our deposit with little flags and continued down to base camp. But we never got the chance to try. Some of the high-altitude porters from another expedition excitedly told us three days later that they had brought our equipment down from Camp 1, but unfortunately it was the equipment we had deposited in the hope of climbing Gasherbrum II. They had meant well, but that was one of the rare moments when I nearly lost my temper. The calm and serenity I had felt after Annapurna I had completely gone. Physical exhaustion combined with the mental stress triggered by José's fall had been too much for me. Hiro and I decided to leave it and go home. In hindsight, it was definitely the right decision. We wouldn't have had a chance; the weather never improved. In the end the porters' action was a blessing in disguise, saving us from having to carry down our equipment.

Once again, a terrible accident had opened my eyes to the deadly side of high-altitude mountaineering. Of course I had known the dangers of climbing an 8000-meter peak, but it was different to see someone fall to his death in front of my very eyes. José had died, and I had barely escaped death myself. Had Ralf not pulled me aside I would have fallen too. High-altitude mountaineering is not only excitement, challenge, and pure happiness—it is also desperation and loss.

The almost vertical, rocky, and brittle rib was certainly the crux on the south face of Shisha Pangma. *(Photo by Ralf Dujmovits)*

CHAPTER 9
HOPE

The faint sound of yak bells reached us higher up. Making progress through the deep, heavy snow was hard work for the animals. Around lunchtime a storm came up, blowing freezing cold snow into our faces. Even the calls of the yak herders were not as jolly as usual; they had a hard time getting the sixteen animals to move. We knew that the winter in the Langtang Himalaya had been a harsh one with lots of snow, but we had not expected it to be this bad. The snow had started from just behind Nyalam, the starting point of our journey, and it was so deep in places that it came up to the yaks' bellies. Due to the long, harsh winter, the animals were not as well-fed as usual and could only carry about 90 pounds apiece instead of the usual 130 pounds. Our progress was far too slow.

It had looked so different a year ago! When we attempted the south face of Shisha Pangma in 2004, we were surrounded by lush meadows. Back then, we were not only mesmerized by the south face of Shisha Pangma but also by our remote lakeside base camp, to which we desperately wanted to return the following spring. And now we were wading through deep snow, and the yaks were even hauling their own fodder as there was nothing for them to eat higher up. When night fell after ten hours of walking, we set up camp though we had not reached even our intermediate campsite. The yak herders doubted that we would make much progress the following day. The night was clear, but so cold that the yaks' scruffy fur was covered in icicles by morning. We tried a new strategy of shoveling a path for the yaks, but it didn't stop them from breaking through the snow cover. Inch by inch, we slowly made our way across the moraine.

The yak herders had wanted for a long time to turn back, and finally we could no longer get them to keep going. They repeatedly tried to convince us to go back with them, claiming that it would be a bad year anyway, that there was far too much snow, and we would not stand a chance to succeed on the mountain. Our trek stopped about 450 meters below last year's base camp, which was still about a five-hour walk away. We were forced to set up our base camp in a ditch in the moraine in the snow. Unfortunately, our efforts to dig for the stream were in vain. Without running water we would probably get into trouble, as we had not planned on having to melt water at that altitude. In our frustration we took a black tarpaulin and an expedition barrel and constructed a snow melting system which actually worked very well, thanks to many days of sunshine.

We had not expected our expedition to start like this. It wasn't only that our approach trek to the south face ended up taking so long; we couldn't even see Shisha Pangma from our base camp. Studying the mountain is a very important part of an expedition for me; I have to connect with the mountain and identify myself with my goal. For a short time I lost motivation, but once we got used to the situation, we started acclimatizing. After climbing a nameless 5550-meter peak, we spent a night at the summit testing our 3.3-pound three-man tent, which Hiro had had specially made for this expedition. As usual, we were climbing alpine style and so we needed to keep our backpacks as light as possible.

A few days later, we acclimatized on Pungpa Ri, a 7000-meter peak right next to Shisha Pangma. We passed our old base camp, where we had a good view of the south face and could actually see how far we had made it last time. Fortunately, the higher we went on Pungpa Ri the less snow we encountered, and the less snow we could see on Shisha Pangma's south face. We didn't climb all the way to the summit of Pungpa Ri; we were not acclimatized well enough and preferred to spend two nights as well as a whole day at 6650 meters. With our ice axes we hacked out a platform big enough for our tent. Both nights were very stormy and cold, and when we woke up the inside of our tent as well as our sleeping bags were covered in ice.

After depositing our tent, sleeping mats, and sleeping bags at the starting point for the south face we descended, looking forward to one of Sitaram's delicious dinners. But just below the original base camp clouds swirled in, and with visibility of less than five meters we had trouble finding our way. We had no choice but to stop and wait for the weather to improve—an undertaking that was pretty uncomfortable without a bivouac. We huddled up on three boulders in the snowfall. Despite the cold, I kept dozing off. I was very tired and wanted only to sleep.

At 11:30 p.m., Ralf jumped up and said, "It's clearing, we've got to go!" Indeed, the fog had lifted enough for us to find our way by the light of our headlamps. Then a gigantic figure appeared suddenly in front of us. It turned out to be an oversized cairn that Sitaram and his Tibetan kitchen assistant had built to help us find our camp in the fog. Unfortunately we didn't see the Coke and beer they had also left there for us. When we finally arrived at base camp at 12:30 a.m., Sitaram immediately fired up the stove and prepared pizza, pasta, and rice for us.

We intended to tackle the south face after a few days of rest, but the weather turned and tested our patience over the following nine days. We shoveled snow, read and ate a lot, worked on the laptop, listened to music . . . and shoveled snow. When we were no longer able to charge our electrical equipment—our solar system was not getting enough sun—Hiro said, "We may not use fixed ropes, but we certainly use a lot of cables."

Ralf talked regularly with Charly Gabl, who repeatedly told us that the weather would remain unstable. I tried to stay focused on the south face of Shisha Pangma and not get distracted by the north face of Everest, which we intended to climb afterward. We were early, we had plenty of time, and I really didn't want to be distracted from my present goal.

We set off on May 1. Charly's forecast predicted moderate winds, high humidity, and snowfall in the afternoons. We said goodbye to Sitaram and Pintos, the kitchen boy. They knew that they might be waiting for us for quite some time, since we didn't know whether we would descend via the south face or the north face and return to base camp from the other side. In order to make sure we had something to eat on the face, Sitaram gave us two kilos of potatoes fried with onion and garlic. They smelled and tasted delicious, but we ate them before we even got onto the face; our lightweight regimen didn't allow us to carry extra food. We were only allowed one tube of sunscreen between the three of us, and Hiro and I even cut off the handles of our toothbrushes to save weight. The only thing Hiro didn't want to do without was his pocket mirror, which was great as it also allowed me to get a glimpse of myself every once in a while.

After we had spent a night at our deposit camp and packed our gear we continued to the bergschrund underneath the south face, which we reached at around noon—the perfect time of day for a delicious snack. Simone Moro had told us where he and Piotr Morawski from Poland had put their food barrel during their winter expedition to the south face in January 2005. We managed to find it and gorged on cappuccino, Polish chocolate, sausages, and dried fruit. The weather still looked good so we decided not to sleep right underneath the exposed face, but to climb up the first steep section. Unlike the previous year, it was now difficult to get over the gaping bergschrund, and it took us a few attempts to cross it. We climbed up another 150 meters and dug a platform right next to a big rock to which we secured our tent. Our first few hours on the face ended with a beautiful sunset, but the clouds gathering lower down didn't bode well.

The next day we started early and made good progress despite the ever-changing conditions, sometimes wading through deep snow, and sometimes climbing on blue ice. But the constant frontpointing was exhausting. We all climbed independently, side by side and unroped. I was completely absorbed in my climbing: First I placed my ice tools and then systematically followed with my feet. Even though we were not attached to a rope, I never worried about slipping. As Ralf was taking stills and film, he was a bit behind me, while Hiro was in front of us. At that point, I'd say the face had a gradient of about 65 degrees.

"Argh, Gerlinde!"

To this very day, I can still hear the horrifying sound of Ralf's scream. It was filled with desperation and fear, definitely the scream of someone falling. I felt a stabbing pain and my first thought was, "Ralf is falling." I turned around, feeling absolutely terrified.

Ralf was still there, hanging off his ice axes.

"Ralf, what happened?"

"I lost a crampon!" He was completely flustered, standing on the front-points of his other crampon and unable to move.

"Stay calm. I'm coming down."

Ralf was about 15 meters below me. Slowly I climbed down, breathing heavily and trying to get my emotions under control. I had to place my ice axes very carefully; there was no room for a single mistake. When I reached Ralf I fixed an ice screw for him to clip into. We had not brought any spare crampons due to our strict weight regimen. Luckily, I saw Ralf's crampon dangling about 80 meters below us. It had come to a halt at just about the only snowy bit on the blank ice.

"Ralf, I can see your crampon. It's down there! I am going to get it!"

In my excitement I forgot to fix a second ice screw for my backpack. I climbed down with my heavy pack on to get the crampon and was thrilled when I finally held it in my hands. Then I climbed right back up to Ralf and put the crampon on his boot, which was rather difficult to do while he was hanging off this steep ice cliff.

We both took a deep breath. Ralf was crestfallen; something like this was not supposed to happen. It was also inexplicable. His crampon had a safety bar, making it almost impossible for it to come off. Had he not cleared the snow off his boot meticulously enough?

"Gerlinde," he said, "I don't think the mountain wants me. Last year it was the falling rock, and now this."

"If the mountain didn't want you, you would have fallen," I said, trying to encourage him. We continued climbing. I felt relieved that nothing bad had happened, but Ralf remained silent and introspective. After we had climbed for a while longer, he suddenly asked me, "Where do you get your strength from?" He meant the mental strength one needs to do the right thing in such a stressful situation. I couldn't answer his question.

The day started off overcast with precipitation in the afternoon. Keeping your bearings on such a big face is difficult even in good weather; you don't have the overall situational awareness you get when you look at a mountain from afar. Routefinding was hard, and after about 450 meters the fog eventually forced us to find a place to bivouac and sit out the bad weather. Luckily, we found a good well-protected ledge and with great effort managed to flatten it enough for us to pitch our tent. We were huddled like sardines on the huge face and could only move wearing our crampons—even to the toilet. While the two men had a pee bottle, I had no choice but to go out into the cold to do my business. With the three of us squeezed together, the tent was far too small for me to use my Nalgene bottle or funnel. As it was a single-skin tent the inside kept freezing, and every time one of us moved it snowed in the tent and left a lot of moisture on our sleeping bags.

Since Charly had forecast snow showers for the afternoon, we started early the following day. The face was about 70 degrees steep until at about 7000 meters, where we reached an almost vertical rock face. We were now higher than we had gotten the previous year, and it was getting interesting. We climbed a few pitches, putting each other on belay. The route was not obvious until we found an old fixed rope which must have been there for a long time. Considering that the first successful expedition had climbed this route alpine style, it made us a bit sad that a later commercial expedition had left their gear on the mountain. Unfortunately, the rock was very friable—probably the most friable rock I had ever climbed! Sometimes I didn't know what to hold onto as most handholds just crumbled away in my hands. Climbing with big gloves was almost impossible, yet using my thin ones didn't work, either; they soon got so soaked that I had to take them off. And without gloves it was simply too cold. We were all relieved when we were finally back on ice and snow, reaching the start of the 800-meter ice gully leading to the summit. It went straight up and was impossible to miss.

At about 10:30 a.m. clouds were swirling in, just as they had the day before. With increasing snowfall and decreasing visibility, we were able to climb for only another few hundred feet. This time it was not a loss of direction that forced us to bivouac, but the fresh snow triggering small avalanches in the couloir. This was our third night on the face. We set up our bivouac in a safe place at the edge of the ridge.

When we woke up it had stopped snowing, but after a few hours of climbing it started again. We had to get out of the snow-laden gully, which got narrower farther up. We tried to dig out a platform three times, but every time we hit either blue ice or rock on the 50-degree face. And the thundering sound of avalanches was all around us—it was exasperating. Ralf remembered a little niche he had seen in the rocks about 100 meters farther down. We had to descend back to 7300 meters, where we found that the niche was just big enough for our tent, and so we spent a fourth restless night in the storm and heavy snowfall on the face.

Our fifth day on the face was dawning. Throughout the night we had heard the disconcerting rumble of avalanches. We had hoped that it would stop snowing so we could continue our ascent, but a glimpse out of our tent dashed our hopes. The blizzard was still raging, and there was no way we could continue up the gully. In the confined space of our tent we spent the whole day in our wet sleeping bags, which had no chance to dry in that weather. I could live with our tent not being particularly cozy, but waiting for better weather was mentally strenuous. We couldn't get a satellite signal in the gully, so we were unable to call Charly for a weather update. If the snow continued, we would be trapped. Given the high avalanche danger in the gully, we could neither go up nor down. But we couldn't stay where we were forever. Learning from our past experience on Annapurna I, we had brought spare gas but only one cylinder, and our food would not last forever, either. We all knew the deal, but nobody dared say it out loud.

Doing nothing, staying calm, and waiting for the weather to improve was not easy. I kept convincing myself that we would be able to continue our ascent—I didn't want to think about the other option. I tried not to let the difficult circumstances get me down, but to stay positive despite the tough situation. I held onto the belief that we would make it. I felt the way I do at the start of all my expeditions, when I look at the mountain for the first time and have some kind of dialogue with it. Before I attempt a summit, I sit at base camp and study the route for hours on end. I want to feel how the mountain reacts to me, whether it invites or rejects me and whether it is the right time for me to go for the summit. I study the route meticulously in my head. I listen to my inner voice, and my gut feeling tells me whether it's right or not. When we were stuck on Shisha Pangma's south face and didn't really know what was going to happen, I talked to the mountain, to nature, and to God's creation, and this dialogue certainly gave me strength.

The snow fell and the storm raged all day. When we were not busy melting snow and drinking it, we were snoozing. In the small tent, every move had to be coordinated so as not to get in each other's way. I was squashed between the two men. At one point Ralf jolted up and told me about his nightmare. He had dreamed that we had run out of gas and water and were unable to leave the bivouac, trapped there forever. Hiro also jumped up once, screaming in panic.

At 10:00 p.m. we noticed that something had changed. The sound of falling snow had stopped. The storm had become stronger, which was actually a good thing: It would blow the fresh snow out of the upper third of the gully, making it easier to break trail. We waited until the last slab avalanche had come down the gully, and then we started out at 2:00 a.m. On the first few hundred vertical feet we had to break trail, but later we followed the compressed avalanche track in the middle of the gully. We were not roped up and had to concentrate hard on not making any mistakes. The freezing wind felt even colder than usual as we had never really warmed up in our wet sleeping bags. The last few days had cost us a lot of energy.

The snow higher up in the gully was compressed, which meant that we didn't have to break trail but could climb on our frontpoints for most of the time. The closer we got to the summit, the more I felt relieved from the tension of the last few days. Ralf was filming me, and Hiro was a few meters ahead of us.

"Ralf," I said, "we are nearly there. I can see the sun coming up."

The first sunbeams on my face felt comfortably warm. I paused to take a picture. Hiro had also stopped, but not for long. He suddenly seemed to lose his balance and slipped. "Hiro! Hiro!" I screamed.

He slid past me but quickly broke his fall with his ice axes, stopping about six feet below me. I was absolutely terrified and grabbed him just to make sure he was still there. His simple comment was, "No problem. I'm okay."

When we finally reached the summit ridge, the snow was deeper again and we had to break trail to the main summit. It was a perfect day. Makalu, Cho Oyu, Everest, Lhotse, and Nuptse were in front of us against the backdrop of the Tibetan Plateau and its turquoise lakes. I was jubilant; all the uncertainty and worry of the past few days were gone. I would not let us fail to get up there, and now we had made it. A dream had come true. Climbing this gigantic face, despite all its difficulties and the bad weather, was an incomparable experience for me.

In silent agreement we had brought all our gear and summited with our heavy packs on. We were still confident that we could do a traverse; going down via the north side seemed perfectly feasible. Just as there had been the previous year, there was spindrift on the traverse to the gendarme, but a lot less. This was the reason why we didn't reach the main summit but carried on to the central summit in 2000. Now we crossed over and descended the normal route on the north side, which Ralf and I already knew. At 7000 meters we spent our last night on the mountain, using the last of our gas cylinders. Charly Gabl was the first person we called to tell him about our successful traverse. As he had not heard from us for quite some time, he had been very worried about us. He was, so to speak, the fourth member in our team, suffering along with our every step.

At Advanced Base Camp (ABC) on the north side, the cook of an AMICAL alpin expedition took us under his wing and offered us food and shelter. The following day we walked the 28 kilometers down to Chinese Base Camp, where a jeep picked us up and took us back to Nyalam. I kept turning around toward the mountain, remembering the most difficult moments up there. Climbing the south face and traversing from south to north had never been done before, and I was incredibly happy about our achievement. I felt elated and deeply satisfied all day long, and I didn't even mind having to do the long walk in my heavy high-altitude boots. I got blisters and was dog-tired, but it didn't matter. "I cannot imagine that there is a drug that can give you such an amazing feeling," I said to Ralf.

I enjoyed sharing the euphoria with Ralf and Hiro on the long walk back to base camp. This incredible feeling of happiness stays with me for a long time after a summit success, though eventually it fades. On our walk I had time to think about why I keep coming back to the mountains. It fascinates me to climb rock and ice under my own power, carrying my own heavy pack at high altitudes; and so does being outside, climbing higher and reaching the next step of my journey. I love it, despite the difficult moments when it is stormy or freezing cold. The summit is my goal and I want to reach it, even if it means taking a certain amount of risk. I don't want to exceed my limits, but I am prepared to shift them. If I am brutally honest, the unknown element in an expedition also makes it more exciting. The bumps in the road to your destination often make an experience more remarkable.

After taking down our Shisha Pangma base camp, we drove from Nyalam to Everest Base Camp. For the first time in my life I saw with my own eyes the crowds of people intending to reach the highest point on Earth via the normal route on the north side. The mountain, on the other hand, I knew like the back of my hand—at least theoretically. Up until then I had not really been interested in climbing Everest, mainly because of the hustle and bustle on both normal routes during the pre-monsoon season. My attitude changed when Ralf and I found a big *National Geographic* Everest poster displaying different routes on the mountain. I put the poster up on the wall in my workout room and studied it meticulously every time I was on the ergometer. I started to dream about climbing my favorite route, which Ralf was also eager to do: the Super Couloir on the north face, which starts at the Japanese Couloir and continues into the Hornbein Couloir farther up. The Swiss climbers Erhard Loretan and Jean Troillet were the only people to have ever climbed that route alpine style. I imagined what it might be like to climb it; to negotiate difficult 5.5 to 5.8 climbing sections between 8300 meters and 8400 meters; and to traverse over to the west ridge on the right and reach the summit from there.

And now we were here, and there was a good chance that I would realize my dream. We needed a few rest days, but as soon as we saw the overpopulated base camp we fled to our Advanced Base Camp (ABC). The starting point for the north face is on the Central Rongbuk Glacier, which lies west of the North Col; ABC for the normal route, on the other hand, is on the Eastern Rongbuk Glacier, east of the North Col. After about three hours we turned off the main route, then it took us another three hours to reach our blissfully quiet camp at 5550 meters. Apart from six Czech climbers who were also attempting the Japanese Couloir, we were alone. In pleasant temperatures and little wind, we could finally enjoy two well-deserved rest days with the stunning view of Everest's north face towering 2800 meters above us.

On our first reconnaissance to the foot of the wall at 6100 meters, which was still a five-hour walk away, we wanted to find out more about the route's current conditions. We planned to stay there for one night and use the next day to take a closer look at the face and get a feel for rockfall and avalanche danger. The Czechs, who had lost some of their motivation from being stuck in bad weather for a long time, told us about an overhanging bergschrund, black ice, and a lot of water ice. We could tell that there was very little snow on the face, which meant both more rockfall and having to frontpoint the hard ice. Rocks kept tumbling down and we knew that there would be no chance to dodge them in the Japanese Couloir. Ralf and Hiro were highly skeptical, considering the conditions on the face too dangerous, not least because we had already used a lot of our energy on the exhausting traverse of Shisha Pangma. We had intense discussions, but I was not ready to give up my goal—I was completely fixated on the north face and had actually identified myself with it. Now that I was finally here, they wanted me to give up? Before I made a decision I wanted to have a closer look, so I climbed to the bottom of the face. The bergschrund looked doable, and I suggested that we should at least give it a go.

In the end, the weather forecast made the decision for us. Charly said the high winds would continue; they would reach 110 miles per hour at 8000 meters and 125 miles per hour at 8800 meters. At 8500 meters we would have to traverse across to the west ridge, which would be impossible in such high winds. We also didn't know whether we would be able to descend via the north face. The decision was clear. We returned to our ABC, where we found that the Czech expedition had also abandoned their goal.

The only alternative was to climb the normal North Col route without supplemental oxygen. From our ABC to the North Col, we could take the route Eric Shipton and Bill Tilman took in 1938, which had only been repeated once.

The information we had about the route was pretty vague, and we had to find our way through the broken glacier. A few times, ice came whizzing down from the left, but fortunately we were all very well acclimatized and moved quickly through the danger zones. The element of the unknown made this route more exciting, and the magnificent view of the north face, Nuptse, and farther up of Cho Oyu, injected us with more motivation to follow our new plan.

When we first reached the North Col at 7000 meters, I was thrilled by the great view of the Tibetan Plateau. A Czech came up to me and asked where we had just come from; he was wondering how his compatriots were doing at the bottom of the face. I then moved a few steps forward, and couldn't believe my eyes: There were at least sixty tents! Contrary to what most people think, there were no oxygen bottles or rubbish at Camp 1 on the North Col. Over the years, the rubbish collection has been organized and now everything gets taken down. But the toilet section was a pretty dismal sight; the strong wind on the Col generally scatters the paper all over the place and immediately freezes the feces. Keeping a safe distance from the other tents, we started looking for a space a little farther up.

When I was unpacking my sleeping mat, the wind caught the stuff sack and blew it away. I was lucky, though; a little later, a Russian climber appeared with it, asking whether it was mine. I was happy to have it back, and we had a chat. Among other things, he said, "Imagine this! Down there is a Swede who wants to climb Everest without Sherpas and supplemental oxygen. He must be mad."

We smiled at each other and pretended to be outraged as well. While we were chatting, countless Everest aspirants walked past wearing oxygen masks, which some seemed to use from as low as ABC at 6400 meters. Apart from a few oddballs like us, everyone was climbing with supplemental oxygen.

On my very first 8000-meter peak, I made the conscious decision to climb by my own means and use neither supplemental oxygen nor high-altitude Sherpas. Using oxygen at 8000 meters lowers the altitude to around 6000 to 7000 meters, depending on the oxygen's flow rate. I didn't want to judge whether climbing with supplemental oxygen is good or bad; I simply knew that I didn't want to do it. I would not consider it a real ascent. I don't climb for the prestige of having reached the summit of an 8000-meter peak; I climb to achieve something personally, to have a pure and real experience. For me, this is only possible without an oxygen mask. I would also never consider training in a vacuum chamber before an expedition, like a Kazakh team had told me about on Nanga Parbat. I want to acclimatize on the mountain. If I were to find out that I couldn't climb Everest without supplemental oxygen, for whatever reason, I would happily live without the highest summit in the world.

As the storm was still raging higher up, we were forced to stay at the North Col for two nights. Charly told us to wait for the winds to abate, saying that June 1 would be the best day. The temperatures near the summit were as low as –40 degrees Fahrenheit, and the wind chill made it feel even colder. The wind at 7000 meters already felt cold, and we spent a lot of time in our cramped tent. On this occasion, we noticed what a great team we had become. We all knew our space, everything was in its right place, and every move was calculated. If Hiro and I had not been getting on so well we probably would not have been able to stand the cramped conditions. Remaining cool, calm, and collected is an important skill on expeditions.

Staying three nights at such a high altitude takes a huge toll on your body, and once again being acclimatized from Shisha Pangma was a great advantage. But when we had packed our food and gas we hadn't anticipated having to stay up there for so long, and we knew that we would soon run out of supplies. Out of curiosity and boredom, Ralf grabbed his shovel to see whether he could "organize" something. Poking around in the snow, he found several delicacies that had been left behind: two half-full gas cylinders, a few tea bags, and some small chocolate bars. Well, better than nothing.

On May 30 we finally set off. There was hardly any wind at camp and a bit of snowdrift on the ridges, and we had views as far as the eye could see. Ropes were fixed from the North Col all the way to the summit. I tried hard to ignore the other people and accept the situation for what it was. We stayed a little distance away from the fixed ropes and so were able to overtake the other climbers. Once on rocky ground we waited for one another, and as I was getting cold I used the time to put on another layer underneath my down suit. Ralf suggested that Hiro and I should go ahead to find a good spot at Camp 2 while he was taking it a bit more slowly to film the climbers on the normal route.

The weather closed in early in the afternoon. A storm came up, it got very cold, and visibility at 7600 meters was down to zero. I climbed past the tents at Camp 2, and once I had found a flat spot a little bit farther up at 7750 meters I had to find some suitable rocks to even out the ground. As we had divided the weight, I carried the tent poles and Hiro had the flysheet. When I looked down, I could see him just below the fog. I waved at him with both arms.

"Hiro! I am here. I have already found a campsite."

He looked up, but didn't wave. This was strange; I immediately knew that something was wrong. This was not the Hiro I knew. I walked toward him. "Hiro, what's up? Are you ok?"

He didn't reply and looked right through me. "We are nearly there. Do you want to give me your backpack?"

"No."

And then he collapsed. Fortunately, Ralf arrived at just that moment. We grabbed Hiro, dragged him to our tent, and lay him down. He didn't respond. I opened his down suit and saw that he was not wearing enough layers for these cold temperatures. Maybe he was just extremely hypothermic and exhausted? I wanted to take his pulse but couldn't find it. When I tried again later, his pulse was about 48, which is pretty slow for that altitude.

Right away we pitched our tent and put Hiro inside it. While Ralf was trying to warm him up by covering him with our sleeping bags and massaging him, I tried to anchor our tent in the increasing storm. Even though we were both worried and nervous, we were working hand in hand. With Hiro inside the tent, inflating and putting down the sleeping pads was a real challenge. By the time I got into the tent everything was frozen or wet from the storm.

Hiro was just lying there, staring. We could hardly hear him breathe. Ralf tried to give him some water, but he immediately threw it up; his body was obviously unable to keep anything down. Worried that he would suffocate on his vomit, we were now convinced that Hiro was not just

TOP: Central Rongbuk Glacier with Changtse and the north face of Everest *(Photo by Ralf Dujmovits)* BOTTOM: I was very worried about Hiro's condition. *(Photo by Ralf Dujmovits)*

hypothermic, but suffering from severe cerebral edema. He would have to descend immediately, but it was impossible to get him anywhere at this time and in this weather. We took off his down suit and put his thermals on; with the limited space and Hiro's inability to help us, everything took a very long time. After we had put his down suit back on and covered him with our three sleeping bags, we left one arm uncovered. When I tried to inject him with Fortecortin, it took Ralf's help to press down hard on Hiro's arm for me to find a vein.

I prayed that I would not miss.

Fortunately, I didn't. I slowly injected the drug, and then it was a matter of time to find out whether Hiro's body would respond to the cortisone, or not.

What if it didn't help? I didn't even think about it. Ralf and I looked at each other. We didn't know whether Hiro would make it or not. I contemplated giving him nifedipine to bring down his blood pressure, but I was worried that it would make his circulation collapse completely. I didn't dare. This time, I was utterly distraught. I wanted to help Hiro but couldn't do anything else for him. We were both scared that he would die.

In my desperation I grabbed the satellite phone and phoned my sister. We had arranged that I could call her with medical questions, and I needed to know whether nifedipine would help Hiro. When she didn't answer I rang Birgit, who contacted another friend of ours, an internist, and called me back. But the only thing she could tell me was that there was a certain risk with nifedipine, but that I should give it a go.

The raging storm outside made our tent cave in. While I was on the phone, Ralf set up our hanging stove and collected ice and snow from outside. The wind was so strong that I had to hold our stove while we melted the snow. We had to keep the tent flap slightly open to get enough fresh air while cooking, so a lot of snow blew into our tent. We filled our water bottles with warm water and put them on top of Hiro to warm him up as much as possible. Being so busy looking after Hiro, we completely forgot to hydrate ourselves.

The only thing we could do was wait. Time would tell whether Hiro would stay with us, or not.

"Hiro, you will make it—you are strong." Maybe he could hear me.

I imagined what it would be like if it were Ralf lying there. Would I do anything differently? Probably not, as there was nothing else I could do. In this storm, it would be impossible to get Hiro across the rocks, and he would likely soon freeze to death. We couldn't expect any help from the other climbers at Camp 2. Most of the tents were empty and were pitched a bit lower than ours. Most people on the normal route are busy reaching their own limits, and they would not have been able to help us get Hiro down. Ralf and I had done everything humanly possible. I felt helpless.

"Ralf, what are we going to do if Hiro dies?"

"I don't know, Gerlinde. I just don't know. He mustn't die."

I had lost all sense of time, but all of a sudden Hiro's eyelids started twitching—followed by a scream. He was holding his head, his face contorted with pain, but at least he had reacted to the cortisone. I imagine he screamed because the headache was unbearable. Suddenly he stopped, staring at the tent ceiling with fixed pupils.

"He is having a stroke," I said to Ralf.

Ralf called Hiro's name—but no reaction. I opened an Adalat capsule and injected the fluid into Hiro's mouth. We had no other choice than take the risk; if the nifedipine didn't help, it would be the end of him.

After a while, Hiro looked around and even tried to sit up. I sensed that he was out of the woods. Feeling a huge burden lift off my shoulders, I broke into an uncontrollable sob. We tried to give him something to drink, as hydrating was now the most important thing, but Hiro had lost a lot of liquid by breathing so hard, and he still couldn't keep anything down.

He spoke very slowly and asked us to take a picture of him—a last photograph for his wife. All my fear that Hiro would die came rushing back. Did he feel that he was nearing the end?

Finally, around midnight, he kept a sip of green tea down. We continued to give him small amounts of liquid as well as some crushed Fortecortin pills in order to keep his cortisone level up. It was sheer luck that I had put our emergency medical kit into my backpack. At the North Col we had reduced our loads one more time in order to climb as lightly as possible. Both Hiro and Ralf had urged me to leave the medical kit behind, as in their opinion nothing could happen in the next three days given how well acclimatized we were. I had decided to take it, just in case we bumped into someone else who needed it.

At dawn, Hiro was able to drink more and even started to talk a little. Ralf and I made sure we were awake to check his pupils regularly. When he was moderately stable, we started to pack our gear. It took a long time for Hiro to get dressed and put on his crampons. He kept on apologizing for the inconvenience he was causing us and thanking us for our help.

We were just about to leave when I heard someone call my name. At first I thought I was imagining it, which would not have been surprising after a sleepless and fearful night. Who could be calling me up here? Then, I heard the voice again.

"Hello! Gerlinde!"

A few meters above, I saw a crouching figure in a black down suit calling for help. I had reached the limit of my mental strength. What else was going to go wrong? As we were busy with Hiro, I told the climber to come down to us. He was more or less sliding across the scree.

"My eyes, my eyes," he complained. "I can't see anymore."

Behind the skiing goggles I recognized the Czech climber I had talked with at the North Col. He was snow blind and his eyes were very painful, probably because he had not worn sunglasses the previous day. When I got the eyedrops out of the first-aid kit I noticed that the plastic ampoules were frozen. Ralf took one and warmed it up with his breath so that we could get at least a few drops out. It was so cold that when I took off my gloves to put the fluid into his eyes, my fingers got cold immediately. I gave the Czech a few ampoules and told him to go down on his own; we were obviously busy with Hiro.

As Hiro couldn't keep his balance, Ralf short-roped Hiro across the rocky section, significantly slowing down our progress. Hiro was completely exhausted, but he pulled himself together and gave everything he had left. I also noticed that his condition improved the lower we got. At the North Col we had a long break for food and drink to help Hiro recover. Ralf and I were also able to relax a little; we felt confident that we would make it. We decided to descend to the ABC of the normal route as it was more likely that someone would help us there, if we needed it.

Russell Brice, a friend of Ralf's, said we could stay the night at his camp and invited us to dinner. Hiro hardly ate a bite; he was just sitting there, looking around without uttering a word.

The following day we embarked on the long walk to our ABC. We had to stop often, but Hiro carried his own backpack and fought like a samurai. It was June 1, our planned summit day. I kept on turning around looking up toward Everest. I knew that I would come back one day and hopefully climb the north face. I didn't regret for a moment that I wasn't standing up there. I was happy that Hiro was alive. Fighting for a friend's life had taken a lot out of me emotionally.

We never anticipated that any of us could get cerebral edema on Everest after having already climbed an 8000-meter peak. That it happened made me realize it could have been me. When on expedition I usually drink a lot, at least five liters per day, and on summit day I take two liters with me. I am convinced that this prevents edema. Cerebral edema usually comes with warning signs, like headache, dizziness, and weakness, which Hiro all described later but ignored at the time. No matter where and when, I always listen to my body and trust that I will notice the warning signs and react accordingly by going down. Could it be that women are generally better than men at listening to their bodies?

Hiro later described how he experienced the whole situation. He couldn't remember the first few hours in the tent but later could hear our voices from afar. He couldn't respond, though; his body was petrified. He had an out-of-body experience and thought he was looking down on himself. He had already resigned himself that he was going to die. I guess we really got him back at the last minute. Arriving at base camp with Hiro, even though it had seemed very unlikely at times, was the biggest success for Ralf and me. No summit could ever be greater than that feeling.

We encountered precarious conditions in huge amounts of fresh snow on Gasherbrum II. I broke trail in thigh-deep snow.

CHAPTER 10
DETERMINATION

On the jeep ride from Nyalam to Kathmandu, I reviewed the events of the past four weeks: Hiro, Ralf, and I stuck in a blizzard on Shisha Pangma's south face; the three of us standing on Shisha Pangma's main summit; my great disappointment on the bottom of the north face of Mount Everest; the horrific hours in the tent when Ralf and I feared for Hiro's life. Lost in thought, I gazed at the passing landscape from the car window. Hardly ever did a house or a person catch my eye. The last weeks had been exhausting and intense, in both a good and a bad way. But I was still full of energy and felt like climbing another mountain. I definitely felt strong physically. It was early June, and I was not quite ready to finish the 2005 season.

Of course I could have enjoyed the summer at home, but Pakistan was beckoning. On the spur of the moment, I decided to attempt Gasherbrum II, which we hadn't gotten to climb after our Gasherbrum I expedition the previous year. Fortunately, I could share the permit with an AMICAL alpin expedition which had already left for the mountain; otherwise I wouldn't have been able to organize a permit on such short notice. Booking a flight was easy, but getting a visa could turn out to be difficult. When we touched down in Frankfurt I went straight to the Pakistani Embassy to apply for the visa, requesting that they process it as soon as possible. Six days later I was on a plane to Islamabad.

For the first time, the weather in Islamabad was actually good enough to allow me to take the one-hour flight to Skardu rather than drive by jeep on the adventurous Karakorum Highway. I saved two days of traveling and had a breathtaking view of Nanga Parbat from the airplane. I could hardly believe that I had reached that summit only two years earlier.

I was sitting next to a Pakistani woman. Apart from her eyes and nose, her whole face was veiled. She didn't look at me, but I could tell from her body language that she was curious about me. I asked her whether she was from Skardu. She didn't answer—she just gave me an almost invisible nod. But when the man next to her got up and walked away, she talked to me in very good English. She hurriedly told me that she lived in Skardu with her husband and her children. Her husband was a teacher in Gilgit, where he lived during the week. The man next to her turned out to be a neighbor who was chaperoning her, as she was not allowed to travel on her own. She asked me what I was doing in Skardu. When I told her about my expedition plans, she gave me her address and invited me to her house. When her neighbor came back she immediately stopped talking to me. She was probably not allowed to talk to foreigners.

Unfortunately the address seemed to be wrong. No matter how hard I tried, I couldn't find her house in Skardu. I asked around but to no avail, which was a shame as I would have loved to talk with her in a bit more detail. While Islamabad had become more modern, with many women not wearing the veil, you rarely saw a woman in the streets of Skardu. When I first went to Pakistan in 1994 I was not only shocked by the poverty, which I experienced firsthand, but also by the subjugation of women. At least in the villages, girls had no right to education and were only meant to work in the fields or in the house. In the villages around Askole the situation had improved a little, but women were still oppressed. They were not really part of public life. I guess as a woman it was easier for me to reach out to them.

On a later expedition, Ralf and I were invited to Aga Abas's house, which was a very enriching experience. Ralf and Aga, who organizes the jeep trips from Skardu to Askole, had worked together for a long time and had become good friends over the years. While the men were sitting on chairs in the common room, I joined the women in the kitchen. Aga's wife and their four daughters, two of whom already had children of their own, were sitting on the floor and invited me to join them. Using hands and feet, we managed to have a conversation. Every once in a while their eighteen-year-old son Ali, who spoke English well, would come in to translate. The women, who were preparing dinner, were a jolly crowd and laughed a lot. I laughed with them and felt accepted by them. When dinner was served I was called back into the men's room. Ali and another young man served dinner; the women were nowhere to be seen. When we were leaving, Aga's wife gave me a bracelet and a big hug—this was our way of communicating. One of the daughters gave me a pearl-embroidered top. I was very touched by their hospitality, which was a new experience for me.

En route to Gasherbrum II in June 2005, I also experienced the other side of Pakistan. When I arrived in Skardu I had a terrible toothache. I couldn't understand where the throbbing pain in my left canine tooth came from, as I had just had a check-up before leaving on our expedition to Nepal in April. It was almost unbearable, and I knew that it would get worse at higher altitudes. I needed a dentist or I could forget my expedition.

My hotel in Skardu had had Internet access for two months, so I was able to send Ralf an email telling him about my difficulty. He replied instantly.

"Dear Gerlinde. You have to go back to Islamabad. Apparently there is a good dentist. Go there."

I didn't want to go back to Islamabad; it would have taken far too long. I could no longer bear the toothache, but I wanted to look forward and not go backward, so I told Ralf that I would look for a dentist in Skardu.

"Please Gerlinde," he wrote, "don't do this. You can do anything, but don't go to a dentist in Skardu."

I ignored Ralf's advice and called a cab. Even though the taxi driver didn't really speak English, I managed to make him understand that I needed a "tooth doctor." He indicated that he knew one, and we drove off. Then he stopped and got out of the car, and I followed him down a little side alley to a door covered by a curtain. He entered and talked to someone while I was waiting outside. I couldn't help being nosey and stuck my head through the doorway. I saw a lot of men sitting around a table. In the center of the room I could see the "doctor," who was poking around in someone's mouth. It almost made me feel dizzy. No white coat, no dentist's chair, nothing at all that reminded me of a dental practice. No way would I stay there.

"Sorry, it's men's day," my driver said apologetically. The Pakistanis even practiced gender segregation within their health system, and that day was reserved for men only. I was relieved, at least for the moment. The taxi driver knew another dentist, though, and hoped that it was ladies' day there. At least this one's door had a sign saying "Dental Doctor." As with the other dentist, there were only men in the entrance hall, where I also discovered a lot of dentures and single teeth lying on a table. Could you just pick and chose here? I was just about to relax—it was obviously men's day here, too—when I came into a room full of women. The men in the other room must have been the husbands who had brought their wives in and were waiting for them. My driver spoke to the doctor and told me to sit down, while he would go and wait with the other men.

I sat down and waited, feeling scared of being at this dentist's mercy. The other women looked around blankly. I tried to talk to them in English, but they didn't understand a word. When I pointed at my tooth, pulling my face in pain, they showed me where their pain was. I thought that if they had come here to seek relief from their pain, then the dentist couldn't be that bad. But the interior of the practice made me slightly suspicious. I could see the dentist work behind an almost transparent curtain. He had a young assistant who handed him the tools. The dentist's chair was an old tattered armchair with a wooden stool next to it. I guess this was meant for the husbands to come in and check on the dental treatment. Everything was scruffy and dirty. I was nervous, and my hands began to sweat.

When it was my turn, the taxi driver came and sat down on the wooden stool next to me. The unhygienic conditions in the practice almost made me gag; I could clearly see the traces of my predecessor in the sink. The dentist's English was pretty good, so I could describe my pain in more detail. He wanted to give me an anesthetic for the drilling, but when I saw the old syringe, which had obviously been used before, I said, "No, no. No injection."

Well, then without anesthetic. The dentist started the drill, which slowly began to move with a squeaking sound. I broke out in cold sweat. I was

TOP: Cristina Castagna climbing up to Camp 2 on Gasherbrum II. Four years later, she took a fatal fall on Broad Peak, her fifth 8000-meter peak. BOTTOM: My cook Maxud (left) and his brother Ibrahim accompanied me to base camp on Gasherbrum II.

worried about the tooth, about infection, and of course about the expedition; if the treatment was not successful I would have to go home.

"Stop! I am sorry, but I have to tell you that I am terribly scared," I blurted out. "Everything is very different from home and I am worried that I will get an infection."

"Calm down, madame," he said. "You don't have to worry. I did my training in Germany, and I am pretty cheap—only five hundred rupees."

That the treatment would only cost around six US dollars didn't really reassure me, but I had no choice but to surrender. He started drilling and I tried to be brave. As the drill didn't have a water jet it soon started to smoke and stink, which made me feel queasy again. I was very tense and anxious, probably more scared than I had been for a long time. At one point, I just closed my eyes and prayed for it to be over.

Finally, he switched off the drill. He told me that I had had an infection in my tooth and that he would now put in a white filling. I could tell that he was very professional and knew what he was doing, despite his antique-looking tools. When I paid my bill, I thanked him profusely.

"One moment, please." He was wondering whether he could take a picture of the two of us; apparently I had been his first foreign patient.

I took out my camera and asked the taxi driver to take a few photos of us. Unfortunately I later found that the pictures were all black, which was a shame as I would have loved to send him one. He really did a great job; my toothache never came back. He advised me to take some antibiotics to prevent an infection, which I did, but despite the happy ending this trip to the dentist was a traumatic experience for me. It was certainly more exciting than climbing. On the mountain, I make the decisions; at the dentist's office, I was at his mercy.

Relieved from my pain, I drove to Askole and embarked on the trek across the Baltoro Glacier, which I knew so well. Ten Hunza porters as well as my cook Maxud accompanied me. They looked after me very well and didn't even let me help put up the tents. In Paiju, Maxud slept in front of my tent to protect me from the soldiers. It was rather uncommon for a woman to travel on her own in Pakistan, but it actually made it easier for me to get to know people. Even though the porters had to work hard for me due to the masses of snow, our exchanges were always friendly. We often sat together in the kitchen tent, and with my broken Urdu I could trade a few words with the Hunzas. In the evenings we often sang together. I won them over by singing along to one of their national anthems, "Long Live Pakistan," which I had learned in 1994. I have to admit that the lyrics are pretty easy.

At base camp, I used the infrastructure of the AMICAL expedition with whom I shared the permit. With my small one-woman tent, which I carried from camp to camp, I was an independent climber. Of course I was not on my own—you are never on your own on the Gasherbrums. Fourteen different teams were attempting Gasherbrum II alone. After magnificent weather during the trek, it turned bad one and a half days after I arrived at base camp. The members of the AMICAL expedition told me that the weather had been good for twenty days. Why had the bad weather front, which sometimes lasts for a long time in the Karakorum, moved in now of all times? As we had to break trail in the deep snow, we were only able to climb short passages, going up and down quite often. Making progress, especially on the steep slopes between Camp 1 and Camp 2, was very difficult. Once we were forced to turn back halfway, as the conditions were just too dangerous. My initial plan to climb alpine style was definitely out of the question.

Finally, the weather forecast was good. On July 16 at 1:00 a.m., around thirty climbers from different countries headed off through the heavily crevassed icefall to Camp 1 at 5900 meters. In the evening it started to snow again, and by morning the fresh snow cover was about sixteen inches deep. As it continued to snow during the morning, I decided to wait at Camp 1 for a day. I called Ralf from my satellite phone and he told me that the weather was supposed to improve the following day.

At 4:00 a.m. I headed off into a clear but freezing night toward Camp 2. From the bottom of the Banana Ridge, a 200-meter-high arête, the snow was waist deep, and during my trail-breaking work I triggered the odd slab avalanche. Just before I reached camp at 6550 meters, the Italian climber Cristina Castagna and another climber helped me break trail for a short while.

After seven exhausting hours of breaking trail, I dug a tent platform, pitched my tent, melted snow, and finally relaxed. Slowly, the other summit aspirants arrived at camp. Everyone knew that the avalanche danger was precarious, and my thoughts were occupied with the upcoming day's climb.

At 4:00 a.m. I started toward Camp 3 with all my gear on my back. This time the snow came almost up to my belly. After I had crossed a crevasse I heard the muffled sound of compact snow masses settling. It was very loud, and shortly afterward a big avalanche came down, barely missing me and three other climbers. We turned back immediately and went down to Camp 2. It was just too dangerous. Back at camp, most teams packed up and descended to base camp. I didn't want to give up that easily and decided to wait one more day. The weather was good, and if the intense warmth of the sun let the snow settle I knew I could risk another attempt. I was glad that I was only responsible for myself, climbing independently. In the late afternoon Cristina's Italian team arrived at Camp 2, with the Koreans and Catalans joining us later in the evening. The Koreans actually went up for another 150 meters to break trail.

It was a starry night when I headed off. I followed the Koreans' tracks; the Italians and Catalans were right behind me. After we had negotiated an 80-degree ice slope, which demanded a lot of strength, we reached a small plateau at 6950 meters where I pitched my tent for the third time. Unlike some other expeditions that added another camp at 7400 meters, I wanted to try for the summit from there. As I had planned to start very early to allow for the slow going in the deep snow, I had left my sleeping bag at Camp 2. With melting snow and rehydrating all night, I didn't expect to sleep much. In the fading daylight I enjoyed stunning views of Gasherbrum III and IV left of "my" summit; of Chogolisa and Baltoro Kangri opposite; and of Gasherbrum I next to it.

I wanted to leave at 10:00 p.m. to have enough time to make it to the summit and back. While I drank a lot and filled up my water bottles, my head was spinning with thoughts about the upcoming climb. Would the traverse underneath the summit pyramid be climbable? Would it be possible to get to the summit via the ridge? Would we be strong enough to break trail? I was convinced that we could do it if we took regular turns at breaking trail. After all, there were sixteen of us. The moon was almost full and the night was clear, which was great for light, but it also meant that it was going to be very cold. Though it was only a matter of a few hours before I would leave, I was frozen to the bone despite wearing my down suit. My toes were so cold that I was unable to warm them up, which meant that I started my climb with already-cold toes at –4 degrees Fahrenheit.

In the afternoon we fixed a departure time. Everyone agreed with my suggestion that we could only be successful if we joined forces to break trail through the deep snow. One Korean, who was almost a head shorter than I, was fired up and kept saying, "Super Linda!" When we set off he rushed to the front to break trail. But soon the snow was waist-deep, and he almost disappeared. When I took over digging through the deep snow I noticed that only the Korean and Cristina were still with me; the others had fallen behind and were out of sight.

After five arduous hours we got to 7400 meters, where some broken poles and tattered tents peeked out of the snow: This was Camp 4. A few expeditions had lost a lot of their gear here last year when bad weather kept them from climbing up to reclaim it. We had now reached the traverse underneath the summit pyramid. After a short break I continued upward. At one point my left foot broke through, and I was barely able to shift my weight onto my other leg. When I gently poked around with my ski pole I didn't meet any resistance underneath the fresh snow. I had nearly fallen into a crevasse. This part of the route was too dangerous to do alone without a rope. I tried to find another way. I knew that if I stayed close to the bottom of the wall, where I didn't expect any crevasses, the traverse could be possible.

I started to move across. Suddenly, I heard the Korean shout from below: "No, Linda! No!" He threw his hands in the air, trying to tell me that I was going the wrong way. I wanted to explain that crossing farther down was too dangerous, and got very irritated when he continued to insist that I should turn back. I had been doing most of the trail breaking; everyone else had left me in the lurch; and now I was being bossed around and told where to go.

Not if I had anything to say about it! I turned back and descended to Camp 4, where I sat down on my backpack and waited for one and a half hours in the cold at –18 degrees Fahrenheit for the others to arrive. Once again, I pleaded with them.

"We have to work together if we want to reach the summit! I can't break trail on my own. If everyone does their bit, we have a chance."

One of the Catalans got up and started to break trail, but stopped after a few feet. When he caught his breath, he said, "I can't do it. It's just too hard and too dangerous. I'm going back."

He was right—the avalanche danger was too high, but I was still convinced that we could make it. Despite my optimism, eleven other climbers also decided to go down. The Korean said on his departure, "No chance today!"

Cristina, her teammates Claudio Pellizzari and Mario Vielmo, and I were the only ones carrying on. Claudio broke trail for about one third of the long traverse and then dropped back. Mario took over for a short time, and then it was my turn again. At around 6:30 a.m. the first sunbeams began to warm us up—a relief after climbing in the bitter cold. I could hardly feel my toes. At 7700 meters we made better progress in frozen sugar snow for the next 100 vertical meters. But our joy didn't last very long; the summit flank was covered in deep snow. At a rock I found a brand new ice ax that somebody must have lost. As it was a bit longer than mine and had an adze rather than a hammer, I took it.

At 7800 meters I gave in to my needs and rang Ralf. I told him that I was optimistic and that I would call him again from the summit. Little did I know that climbing the steep summit pyramid, where the snow was knee-deep, would take another five hours! I often had to stop to catch my breath and gather strength for the next few steps. My legs were burning, my throat was dry, but the summit was getting closer. I gave everything. During one of my stops I saw Claudio going down; it had probably become too hard for him.

We found old fixed ropes in an icy rock gully of about 50 degrees before we reached the summit ridge. It was heavily corniced toward the south, and negotiating the edge of the ridge seemed impossible. I straddled the ridge as if I were riding a horse and started to cut off the cornice, which was leaning toward the left. Fortunately the snow was soft; otherwise I would not have had the strength to work it. The ice tool I had found was perfect for this job. Holding the ax with both hands I knocked off enough snow to allow me to slide a little bit further before I did the same thing again. Bit by bit I cut down the cornice with my left foot dangling into Pakistan and my right one into China. It was an extremely exposed position. Avoiding looking down, I continued to clear the cornice with a vengeance, as we were already late. It took an hour and a half to work on the 25- to 30-meter-long ridge. Cristina and Mario waited at the bottom of the ridge, and after I had made a small path they could actually walk upright by putting one foot on the ridge and the other one slightly below.

After the ridge we had to climb some ice and rocky ground. The last few feet to the summit were very exposed and demanded full concentration. The close views of K2 and Broad Peak, which only seemed an arm's length away, made me forget for a brief moment all the hardship of the past fifteen hours. Who would have thought that one of the smallest 8000-meter peaks, with its mere 8034 meters, could be so challenging?

I hugged Cristina and Mario and was indescribably happy that I had never given up hope. As we had taken a long time for our ascent—it was already 1:30 p.m.—we didn't stay long at the summit. I wanted to descend all the way to base camp. Cristina asked me whether she could use my sat phone to call her mother. Even though she literally said only two sentences, her conversation completely depleted the batteries. Ralf would have to wait for my call.

When Cristina and I arrived at our high camp, our Italian friends gave us some tea and congratulated us on our unexpected summit success. Then I packed my tent and sleeping mat and continued downward on my own. It was already getting dark. As if on autopilot I put one foot in front of the other, using my ski poles to support my tired body. Every once in a while I had to stop, not to catch my breath but to marvel at the surrounding beauty. The sky was laden with stars and the full moon slowly rose behind Gasherbrum I. Gasherbrum I, Gasherbrum II, and K5 were all illuminated by the soft moonlight and I was immersed in a surreal, mystical atmosphere. The mountains around me, the silent glow of the snow, and the moonlight were so fascinating that I almost had to force myself to keep moving. I no longer felt tired. I was completely absorbed by the world around me, and I would have loved to take the magic of those hours home with me. It was an unforgettable descent on an unforgettable night.

At Camp 1 I took a short break. With my backpack still on my back, I laid down gazing up at the sky. Instead of melting snow to drink, I got drunk on the millions of stars.

But fatigue started to creep back, and I could feel that my toes were swollen, especially on the right foot. I couldn't really move them. I was lucky to meet an Italian team at Camp 1; they were also on their way down to base camp and I roped up with them to go through the treacherous icefall with its precarious snow bridges. When I arrived at base camp at four o'clock the next morning I had descended 3000 meters of altitude in thirty hours. I called Ralf to tell him that I had summited and that I was back at base camp. He had been extremely worried because of the high avalanche danger and had tried to get information from the AMICAL alpin expedition, but to no avail. It had driven him mad not to hear from me, but now he felt relieved.

When I got into my tent I took off only my shoes and down suit and immediately fell asleep in my socks. When I woke up I felt that something was wrong with my toes. The right sock was sticky, and when I took it off I saw that my toes were covered in huge, oozing blisters. The right toes were swollen, the left ones numb. I must have gotten frostbite on both feet. I bandaged the open wounds and then had to wear sandals for the rough trail down to Concordia. Trekking boots were out of the question.

When I was about to set off the following day, my feet were so painful that I could hardly walk. I bumped into a Pakistani on a horse, who had taken some goods to Concordia and was now on his way back. He was kind enough to let me ride his horse. At first, riding without a saddle was fun, as the horse was moving very gently. But after two hours my sore bottom forced me to continue the long slog on foot. Fortunately, my toes eventually healed even though it took a few months for the numb feeling to subside in the right foot, and to this day my right toes are still more sensitive.

I guess I got frostbite because I was dehydrated; I had had my last drink just below the summit and didn't hydrate at all during my descent. Staying hydrated is very important to keep your blood circulating. I had set off very early, my feet were stuck in high-altitude boots for thirty hours, and they never really warmed up in the deep snow. Even though I felt that my toes were cold, I didn't take the time to warm them up. After the Gasherbrum II expedition I vowed to always take a sleeping bag to high camp. My toes are certainly more important than a light backpack.

Summit joy on Kangchenjunga in May 2006: I could hardly believe I had reached the top of the third-highest mountain in the world. *(Photo by Ralf Dujmovits)*

CHAPTER 11
FORTUNE

During my expedition to Gasherbrum II, I realized for the first time that people valued my opinion as an experienced high-altitude mountaineer. I was asked what I thought about the weather or avalanche danger. When I returned home the public suddenly started recognizing me, probably because there were a lot fewer female high-altitude mountaineers than female rock climbers—and not a single woman who had successfully climbed all fourteen 8000-meter peaks. That I had already stood on the main summits of eight 8000-meter peaks made me more attractive to the press. The Spanish media especially went to town, making a race of it: Who would be the first woman to achieve this feat? They were looking for a rivalry that could be compared to the competition between Reinhold Messner and the Polish climber Jerzy Kukuczka in the 1980s.

On January 2, 2006, the weekly German magazine *Der Spiegel* published a feature article, "Queens of the Death Zone," about the Spanish high-altitude mountaineer Edurne Pasaban and myself. The story triggered a lot of media hype about me that I was certainly not looking for. Now I was famous not only in Austria but also in Germany, and journalists began vying for interviews. Even though the *Spiegel* article pointed out that I was not interested in setting a record or entering a race, many media outlets continued to talk about the competition between Edurne and me; later on, they also involved the Italian mountaineer, Nives Meroi. If you think about it, high-altitude mountaineering is not the right place to compete. As often happens, the decision to abandon a climb is a matter of life and death. I am often forced to make decisions regardless of other people's expectations. The freedom I feel in the mountains matters far too much to me to compromise it by being drawn into a race.

It was true that I wanted to climb all fourteen 8000-meter peaks, but becoming the first woman to do so was not important to me. It honestly didn't matter to me whether or not I would be the first. My ambition was about my personal pleasure and desire for challenge, which is also why I climb without supplemental oxygen or the support of high-altitude Sherpas. Even though I am a professional mountaineer, first and foremost I climb for myself and not for other people.

After the *Spiegel* article had been published I was inundated with requests for interviews and presentations. Of course I appreciated this attention, which also helped me to make a living from mountaineering. Sometimes, though, it was a bit much for me, especially when I had too many engagements and too little time to train or clear my head. Now the departure date for the next expedition was no longer just the beginning of a new adventure; it was my time to leave everything else behind and be at one with myself again.

Since we had been forced to turn back on the north face of Kangchenjunga in 2003, I had been longing to return to that mountain. Finally in spring 2006 the time had come. Ralf and I, together with Hiro and Veikka Gustafsson, intended to climb the first ascent route on the south side. This route is a bit easier than the north face, but the main reason for our decision was its directness. For this route we would not have to walk for several hours from base camp to the bottom of the face, as we had done on the north side. In April we flew to Suketar via Kathmandu and trekked in with Andrew Lock and the two Portuguese climbers, João Garcia and Toze (António José dos Santos Coelho), with whom we shared a permit. We trekked through magnificent landscapes and didn't meet any other trekkers. We met Maoists, though: In April 2006, the decade-long civil war between Nepal's Communist Party and the monarchy was threatening to escalate, and the whole country was crippled by general strikes. In order to avoid the eastern region, which was infiltrated by Maoists, we actually contemplated taking a helicopter to base camp at 4200 meters. In the end we opted for the trek, knowing it would be better for our acclimatization.

On the fourth day an unassuming elderly man—who turned out to be a Maoist—visited our camp. He was friendly but determined, demanding a toll of five thousand rupees (about fifty US dollars) per person. With this fee, the Maoists made money from tourists to finance their armed war against the government. Ralf immediately started a discussion, which was rather limited by the language barrier. He wanted to know what the money would be used for and whether it would be invested in aid projects. But he was banging his head against a brick wall with this guy, who told us only that the money would go to the party, and if we were not willing to pay he would send us home immediately. At least he gave us a receipt to prove that we had paid the toll.

Just before the start of the Yalung Glacier we were taking a break with our sixty porters when a group of porters from another expedition came back down from base camp. They told our porters that the path to base camp was very strenuous, and within minutes thirty of our staff got so scared that they simply said goodbye and left. What a mess! Suddenly we were stranded with sixty loads, wondering how the thirty remaining porters would carry our gear to base camp at 5300 meters. Under no circumstances did we want to set up camp lower down and face a long approach march to the mountain. After our Sirdar, Tonje, who also acted as a sort of liaison between the porters and us, had talked to them, they agreed to do several carries each to get all the loads to base camp. We then equipped the porters with some of the warm clothes and boots from our sponsors. Handing out the gear took the whole afternoon. Nepalis usually don't know their shoe sizes, and we had to guess what size would fit them. After a lot of to-ing and fro-ing we finally stepped onto the glacier, which was rather difficult to walk on due to snow-covered debris on the surface.

Even though we did everything to look after our porters—making sure they had enough supplies, treating their blisters, and putting cream on their feet—another ten left us after having spent the first night at intermediate camp. We knew that if all of them were to throw in the towel we would have to set up our base camp right there, even though we were still hours away from the real base camp. But we were lucky! The remaining twenty porters stuck with us and demonstrated amazing commitment, even when over the last 200 meters the terrain got so steep that Norbert Joos's Swiss expedition, which was ahead of us, fixed a few meters of rope for the porters.

Base camp was in a well-protected flat spot. In addition to our group of seven, the Swiss expedition and a Spanish team including our friend Ferrán Latorre were camped about 100 meters above us. Hiro, Veikka, Ralf, and I had initially planned to acclimatize on a neighboring mountain called Kabru and climb Kangchenjunga alpine style. But due to too much snow, with heavy snowfall in the afternoons, we had to change our plan in the end. It would also have been unfair to let the other two groups, who climbed expedition style and planned to fix rope on the steep bits, do all the work and then use their trail. There were not that many of us climbing out of base camp, so we all had to work together.

But first it was time for our Puja, the Buddhist ceremony that placates the mountain deities and makes for a safe return from the mountain. Over the years this ritual had become very important to me, not only because I respect it as a religious tradition of the local people, but also because I feel privileged to enter the world of the mountains, the home of the gods. Even before our cook Sitaram brought us our morning tea, he had prepared several delicacies to offer to the gods for the *puja*. His assistant and lama, Daba Rita Sherpa, had made religious figures of barley dough and yak butter. After selecting a place for the puja, we put up Buddhist prayer flags and built an altar there. Along with plates with plenty of offerings for the gods, we put some of our climbing gear, such as helmets, ice axes, and rope, next to the altar to be blessed. Daba Rita chanted the traditional Buddhist prayers, which sounded like music to my ears. This ceremony is almost like a meditation, and it helps me concentrate on my goal.

For our acclimatization we went up and down the mountain over the following days, spending two nights at 7200 meters. With its 8586 meters, Kangchenjunga is a high 8000-meter peak, which makes sleeping two nights up high necessary. We didn't put up fixed camps, but carried our lightweight tent from camp to camp. At 3:00 a.m. on one of the nights high on the mountain, I was woken by a loud crack coming from the glacier. It sounded as if everything was collapsing around us, and I imagined us

TOP: After the tough approach march, some of the porters needed medical attention. *(Photo by Ralf Dujmovits)* BOTTOM: Puja ceremony at Kangchenjunga Base Camp *(Photo by Ralf Dujmovits)*

tumbling down a crevasse. This horrifying noise pierced right through my skin. It was still dark outside and I couldn't see a thing, which was rather disconcerting and eerie. Slowly but surely the dwellers of the other tents woke up, switching on their headlamps. Everyone was wide awake wondering what it could have been. The sound of a moving glacier can be deafening, but despite this plausible explanation I couldn't get back to sleep for the rest of the night, listening to every crack in the ice. The next morning we couldn't see a thing on the glacier's surface.

Once we got back to base camp it started snowing heavily again. One of the Portuguese climbers, Toze, suffered from a severe stomachache. He was feeling very unwell and couldn't get up. As they had no doctor with them, Ralf and I looked after him. Suddenly I smelled odors typical of intestinal rupture. It was clear that Toze needed to be evacuated as soon as possible. Ralf called our trekking agent to organize a helicopter. Unfortunately, the helicopter couldn't fly all the way to base camp but had to land in Ramche, which meant that Toze had to be carried down 1000 vertical meters. After we gave him very strong painkillers, he descended with the help of his friend João and one of the kitchen boys. Toze was in such a bad way that they had to put up a bivouac on their way down. Fortunately the clouds parted briefly, allowing for the helicopter to fly. Toze had a ruptured appendix and was saved by an emergency operation in Kathmandu.

João came back from Kathmandu a few days later, and we were all relieved that everything turned out well. Now we were all acclimatized and ready for the summit, but the weather tested our patience. The forecast predicted a spell of bad weather with heavy snowfall. I knew that Kangchenjunga was infamous for its bad weather, and I was also aware that it had not been successfully climbed for three years, which made me doubt our chances. The weather was doing exactly what it had done three years ago. Despite the gloomy outlook we kept up our hopes, and finally we received a good weather report for May 14. Could that be our summit day? We met with the other groups to discuss our strategy. With the huge amount of fresh snow, we would have to work together breaking trail. The Spaniards didn't think we stood a chance and remained at base camp, while the Swiss were confident and joined us.

We set off on May 11, taking regular turns at breaking trail. At Camp 1 at 6150 meters we were rewarded with a beautiful scenic evening after a mediocre day weather-wise. The sun was setting just behind Jannu, Kangchenjunga was glowing in the evening light, and I was happy with the world, my faith in our summit chances restored. I didn't lose my optimism the following day, though we climbed in heavy snowfall with zero visibility and were utterly soaked by the time we pitched our little tents at 7200 meters. It didn't snow the following day, but the afternoon was very stormy. Just below Camp 3 at 7750 meters, we reached a steep section with blue ice requiring anchors. In the heavy storm and freezing cold, pitching the two small tents and digging a platform was hard work. This was the point from which we wanted to climb the remaining 850 meters to the summit in one day.

Veikka, Hiro, Ralf, and I talked to Norbert and his group and told them that we were going to leave at midnight. At 11:00 p.m. it started snowing heavily. There was no way we could have left in that weather. We waited in our tent, melted snow, and rehydrated. I was too nervous to go back to sleep. This could be the night, and tomorrow the day, for my dream to come true as I reached the summit of Kangch! The situation remained tense and uncertain. We checked the weather every hour and discussed our plans with Hiro and Veikka, who were right next to us. Because of the heavy snowfall we kept postponing our departure, first to 1:00 a.m., 2:00 a.m., and then to 3:00 a.m. When the snow still hadn't stopped at 3:00 a.m. we put our departure off until 5:00 a.m., knowing that this would be the latest possible time for us to make it to the summit and back.

Ralf and I hardly slept a wink during that night. We were too busy drinking, thinking, and hoping. But at some point we must have fallen asleep, because we suddenly heard the clinking of carabiners and crampons, which woke us in an instant. It was 5:00 a.m., and it had stopped snowing.

Our backpacks were soon packed and the only thing left to do was to put on harness, boots, and crampons. In cramped conditions and at high altitude these minor tasks take quite some time. When we were finally ready to go the others had a head start of three quarters of an hour. The younger of the two Sherpas in Norbert's team was very strong and led most of the way. Ralf and I slowly caught up with them. The snow had started again, and I was very cold. At 8000 meters the terrain got increasingly difficult: steep, rocky ground covered in snow. Negotiating grade IV climbing over mixed ground all the way to the summit sapped my energy, especially when we started supporting the Sherpas breaking trail.

As I was approaching a rocky ledge after a very steep section, I could see only sky in the background. We must be almost there! But when I reached the ledge, my disappointment was almost unbearable: There was another rocky cliff ahead of us. It was not over yet, and we still had a long way to go. We dragged our tired bodies through deep snow and across rocks for another three hours, stopping after every few steps to catch our breath. In return for our efforts, the cloud cover broke in places, the snowfall became lighter, and we could see more and more blue sky. About 100 meters below the summit we had to downclimb a 50-foot-tall chimney, frontpoint along an exposed traverse, and ascend again on rocky ground. Old, tattered fixed ropes indicated the way.

When we were nearly there, Ralf went ahead to film me climbing the last few feet to the summit. During our ascent it was almost impossible to film as the terrain was very demanding, and I was unable to repeat the individual sections for Ralf to get good footage. When I stepped onto the summit I couldn't speak, and tears filled my eyes. It was a very moving moment. I was standing on my highest summit at the time, the third-highest mountain in the world. A wonderful feeling of happiness and fulfillment spread through my body, and I felt complete. I had dreamed about this mountain for a long time. I had doubted our summit chances many times, and now, finally, we were here. I threw my arms in the air and looked up to the sky, laughing and crying at the same time. I felt like embracing the whole world.

Ralf also filmed Norbert's final steps to the summit. It was a very special moment for him; it was his fifth attempt of Kangchenjunga, and he could hardly believe that he had finally made it. The scenic atmosphere around us was remarkable. I got a brief glimpse of base camp on the north side, the meadow, which was as big as a football field, and the long glacier we had crossed to get to the start of our climb three years earlier. The hole in the clouds also let me have a look into Sikkim in the east as well as Yalung

Kang, the western summit of Kangchenjunga proudly standing about 150 meters below the main summit.

I allowed myself to succumb to this wonderful feeling for only a few minutes. With our late start it was already past 4:00 p.m., and we had to hurry now to get down safely. We didn't have a rope, having left it in the tent to save weight. It was obvious that we would end up descending in the dark, but fortunately we had our headlamps. At nightfall we were caught in a violent blizzard, seriously hampering our visibility, especially over steep ground. The only way not to lose our bearings was for one person to go ahead and call out, and the others to follow. Finally we could see lights in the tents of some of the Swiss climbers who had turned back earlier.

João had left base camp a day later and reached Camp 3 at around lunchtime. When he saw that the storm had blown away some of the tents of the Swiss, who were cramped like sardines in their remaining tents, he took ours down to protect it from the storm. It was a nice idea, but it was impossible to put back up in the storm. The tent platform was completely covered with snow, and the inside of the tent was full of snow and soaking wet. We had no choice but to crawl under the flysheet and hope for the night to pass quickly. There was no way to start the stove and have a warm drink. In the course of the night, my right arm, which I was using to support my body, got increasingly wet. My mat and sleeping bag had mutated into an unusable lump of ice. As I was lying directly on the tent floor, the wet slowly seeped through my down suit until it finally soaked my skin. I don't think I have ever been so cold in my life. My mantra was, "It will be over soon." But my efforts to get warm through meditation failed miserably.

At about 4:00 a.m. the storm abated and we were finally able to melt some snow. I was so cold that I had a hard time moving. Ralf gave me a sip of hot water, which immediately injected me with life; it was beautiful to feel the warmth spread through my body, giving me new energy. But it still took a long time for me to recover from the extreme cold.

In the morning we packed up and descended to base camp together with Veikka and Hiro. Sitaram and the kitchen boy met us halfway and gave us hot Tang, the instant orange drink that is ubiquitous in Nepal. Sitaram knew how much I loved fizzy drinks, but this time he couldn't serve us Coke; the Maoists had banned anything American and didn't allow Coke in the area. Not a single lodge along the trail to base camp had the courage to sell Coke. I never drink Coke at home due to its high sugar content, but after an expedition I need a refreshing fizzy drink. In the evening, Sitaram pampered our taste buds with a real feast followed by a delicious cake, but we were all so tired that we were barely able to eat before collapsing in our sleeping bags. We had summited Kangchenjunga and were all back at base camp, safe and sound. I fell asleep feeling completely relaxed and utterly content.

The next day we took down our camp and walked to Ramche. Ralf, Hiro, and I had another goal in mind: Lhotse. We had planned to take a helicopter from Ramche to Lukla, and then because we were quite late in the season we planned to fly from Lukla directly to base camp.

During our descent, the Swiss expedition had called us on our satellite phone with terrifying news: Norbert had been unconscious at base camp for a while and was apparently temporarily paralyzed on one side. He had probably had a light stroke. Our helicopter was diverted to collect Norbert from as high as possible—this was the first time the pilot had ever flown so high. He found the only suitable landing spot about one hour's walk below base camp, and thankfully Norbert managed to get there with help from a friend. Luckily, visibility was good; otherwise it would have been impossible for the helicopter to land at all in the steep valley. In Ramche we waited for Norbert, who was supposed to be taken all the way to Kathmandu. He was able to walk unsupported, but had a hard time articulating. I was torn between feeling relieved that he was still alive and worried that he would not fully recover from the stroke. We were all the happier when we later found out that Norbert had completely recuperated and was in good health.

We packed our Lhotse gear in separate barrels and flew directly from Lukla to Everest Base Camp, *(Translator's note: This is also the base camp for Lhotse)*, where a new cook was waiting for us. We had not had a break since summiting Kangchenjunga, and after being at base camp for a day we decided on the spur of the moment to walk down to Deboche. Nestled between meadows and trees just below the Tengboche Monastery at an altitude of 3700 meters was the Ama Dablam Garden Lodge—a perfect place to recharge your batteries and get plenty of oxygen. We even had the luxury of a hot shower, which I happily took advantage of.

When on expedition, I usually get a bucket of water from the kitchen boys and have a good wash in our long, tall wash tent, which gives me enough privacy. We also always have a toilet tent. The toilet usually consists of an expedition barrel either sunk into the ground or surrounded by a stone wall. When the barrel is full, it is disposed of. At Everest/Lhotse Base Camp, the barrels are taken down and away from the glacier. Special porters who receive slightly better pay carry the barrels to the landfill in Gorak Shep. Apart from plenty of yak manure, Everest South Base Camp is actually pretty clean. Human waste only becomes an issue higher up on the mountain. The various teams usually agree on where to get their snow for drinking water and where to follow their calls of nature.

In Deboche we spent most of our time eating and sleeping. Hiro, who has not a gram of body fat on him, mastered double portions: two starters, two main courses, and two desserts. I too ate large quantities, at least for me. I usually had Sherpa Stew, a thick vegetable stew, for starters, vege-table fried rice as a main course, and caramel pudding for dessert. The only one who could not satisfy his huge appetite was Ralf. His lips were so badly sunburned that he could hardly eat. As soon as we felt a bit fitter and stronger we went for a walk to the recently reconstructed Tengboche Monastery, where we took part in a two-hour puja. Another highlight was the visit of six nuns who came to see us from the small women's monastery in Deboche.

As it was already late May—the end of the pre-monsoon season—we couldn't afford to stay long at our little holiday resort. After three nights in the lodge we walked back to base camp. Most of the 250 tents, which we had counted on our previous visit, had gone. Hiro, Ralf, and I were the last people on the mountain. We informed the Icefall Doctors—a group of Sherpas employed by the Nepali government to fix the Khumbu Icefall with aluminum ladders and ropes—that we still wanted to attempt Lhotse.

They promised not to remove the ladders and ropes until we came back. The crevasses in the icefall are often very wide, needing as many as five or six ladders tied together to cross them. Without the ladders we would not be able to get through the icefall.

We started on May 24. The icefall didn't pose any problems, even though the ladders were showing some wear and tear, an obvious sign of the long season. With the rising temperatures some of them had lost their grip in the ice and dangled loosely across the crevasses. Though we set off at 4:00 a.m., the heat caught up with us in the Western Cwm, giving Hiro especially a hard time. There was not a breath of air in the bowl-shaped Cwm, and the sun beat down relentlessly. We spent our first night on the mountain at 6400 meters, the site of Camp 2, where we even found running water flowing over a rock into a tiny glacial lake. The following day we climbed to Camp 3 at 7200 meters, which is shared by both Everest and Lhotse climbers. From there, Everest aspirants turn left. We tried to imagine how overcrowded the camps must have been just a few weeks earlier, and felt very privileged that we were alone on the mountain.

We skipped Camp 4 to use the weather window, which was forecast for May 26, and to reach the summit before the weather turned. The last 1300 vertical meters between Camp 3 and the 8516-meter-high summit stretched from the upper part of the Lhotse Face through the prominent couloir on the west face. We started to break trail at 3:00 a.m. The five inches of fresh snow that had fallen during the night made the ascent pretty cumbersome. Hiro lagged behind while Ralf and I broke trail in turns. At 7800 meters, the site for Camp 4, we stopped for a drink and waited for Hiro. Unfortunately, our progress was not as fast as we would have liked. After all, it had only been ten days since we had reached the summit of Kangchenjunga, and we were already on the way to the top of another 8000-meter peak! I guess we must still have been tired.

We had taken a thin 50-meter rope for the long couloir in case we should need to rope up for safety. We knew that the section just below the summit could be precarious depending on conditions and our degree of exhaustion. I continuously looked at my watch. It was just 3:00 p.m., but we were getting closer to the summit and I held onto hope that we would still make it. At 8400 meters, Ralf and I stopped for another drink. I looked at my watch and was shocked when I saw that it was almost 5:00 p.m. It would get dark in two hours.

"Gerlinde, that's it for me. It's getting too late. If we keep climbing we will be caught in darkness. I'm not prepared to take the risk of bivouacking at this altitude."

Ralf said out loud what I had been thinking: We were running out of time. But we only had another 100 meters to go! Should we really give up so close to the summit? The weather was perfect and even though I was not as fresh as a daisy, I still wasn't completely worn out. It was a hard decision for me. I knew that it would get dark, but we had our headlamps.

"Don't you think we could still make it?"

Ralf stuck to his decision, which was a good thing. After our first 8000er together we had had in-depth discussions about what to do if one of us wanted to turn back and the other one didn't. We agreed that we both had to decide for ourselves and would not force each other into something we didn't want to do.

"Would you be upset if I carried on? I don't want to turn back just yet."

"No, it's okay. Give it a go. I am going down."

Ralf accepted my decision even though he was dying of worry, as he later told me. When we said goodbye, his eyes filled with tears. He turned around and started his descent toward Hiro, who was coming up about 50 meters behind us.

I continued to climb up the couloir, carefully putting one foot in front of the other. But I was not concentrating fully and my head was spinning with thoughts. I tried to imagine what it would be like to descend this gully in the dark. The blue ice in the couloir was covered in fresh snow. Would I be able to notice the tricky parts in the dark? I knew that without a rope the tiniest mistake could be fatal up here. Being on my own, I couldn't even secure myself in the rocky section just below the summit. My water bottle was nearly empty, and I didn't have a stove to melt snow. If I bivouacked at this altitude without hydrating, I would almost certainly get altitude sick. I hesitated. Had this been a responsible decision? I was sure that I could reach the summit, but the descent could be life-threatening. The dead

Czech climber who was lying in a bivouac at the foot of the couloir came to my mind. A week and a half ago he and another Czech had been climbing Lhotse without fixed rope, just like us, when he took a fatal tumble down the narrow, icy couloir. He had probably made only a tiny mistake.

I had been climbing for about fifteen minutes when I decided to descend as well. I had come to the same conclusion as Ralf—the risk was too great. I guess I had needed that quarter of an hour to come to the same conclusion. It was good to know, though, that I wasn't going down for Ralf, but because my gut feeling told me to. Even though it was very disappointing, I realized that we had aimed far too high that day. Climbing two high 8000-meter peaks in one season was certainly borderline.

Ralf had been repeatedly turning back to look out for me, and when he saw me coming down he was hugely relieved. He waited for me and hugged me. At Camp 4 the three of us were reunited and descended together to our tent. When we reached the west flank, darkness fell upon us. After about twenty minutes the light of my headlamp started to fade, and shortly afterward it died. In order to save weight we had not brought spare batteries, but we had put new ones in the night before our departure. This could have gone so wrong. I don't even want to think about what would have happened had I been high up in the couloir without a headlamp!

With Ralf lighting the way with his headlamp we got to Camp 3 safely. In the meantime the sky had started to show the first signs of a bad weather front. We had seen the approaching storm for a while, but by now the lightning behind Nuptse was so strong that the southwest face of Mount Everest was completely lit up every time lightning struck. At 7200 meters it was relatively warm—1.4 degrees Fahrenheit—so we decided to spend the night outside under the millions of stars. We put our sleeping bags and mats on the perfectly flattened tent platforms and lay down. It was incredible: Here we were, just the three of us, enjoying the overwhelming beauty of Everest, which is normally inundated by hundreds of people stuck in traffic jams. The strain and exertion of the last few hours had vanished; the disappointment of not reaching the summit had evaporated. Whenever I make a decision, I stick to it without regrets. In this case, my decision was obviously the right one; and the thing I remember most about Lhotse is that wonderful night.

Ralf and I lay awake for quite some time, tightly nestled together, observing the stars. There was no need for words. We had gone through thick and thin; we had made difficult decisions; we had physically reached our limits and experienced extreme emotions. As we were lying there, still feeling the burden of the difficulties of the past few days but knowing that we had mastered them well, there was a deep sense of togetherness.

In this moment, Ralf asked me to marry him.

I said, "Yes."

It was lonely after Lucie had left; only a Spanish team, my cook, and I were left at base camp.

CHAPTER 12
DESPERATION

My knife! It must be somewhere on my harness. It was a small, handy knife Ralf had bought for me when we were climbing in Cortina in the Dolomites. But how could I possibly reach it? I was lying on my left arm and couldn't even move it an inch. I couldn't move my legs, either—they were cemented into the snow. There was less weight on my upper body; the snow was looser there, and I was able to bend my right arm a bit.

Only a few minutes earlier I had been sitting upright in my tent, drinking hot water. I had looked at my watch. It was just before 9:00 a.m. I poured a cup from my flask, drank it, and closed the lid. When I was just about to lie back down on my mat, an incredible force suddenly pulled me off. I couldn't do anything, I couldn't even scream, yet somehow I knew instantly that this was an avalanche. I have no idea what else went through my mind. I cannot remember whether I was ready to die or how long the nightmare lasted. The one thought that did pop into my mind was that an avalanche was pulling me toward the steep precipice just below our camp.

Suddenly it was silent. Where was I? Was my head up or down? I had completely lost my sense of direction, but I knew that I must be somewhere near the precipice. If I moved, I would probably slide further and fall down the abyss. But no—I was buried in the snow and couldn't even move. After some time I could tell that I was lying on my back, with my head down and feet up, and that I was looking upward. There was some hollow space in front of my mouth which allowed me to breathe. I could see the yellow material of the tent directly in front of my eyes. If there had been more snow on top of me or if I had been buried deeper, the tent wall would have pressed against my face. I was unable to move, so how could I get out? My only thought was that I had to slit the material with my knife if I didn't want to suffocate and be trapped forever.

In the morning of May 13, 2007, a snow slab came down the northeast ridge of Dhaulagiri just above Camp 1 at 6800 meters. I had been on the mountain for a month. The weather had proved rather challenging, with clouds building up at noon and snowfall in the afternoons. A huge amount of fresh snow above Camp 1 had significantly increased the avalanche danger. Dhaulagiri, which means "White Mountain" in Sanskrit, was certainly living up to its name. The 8167-meter mountain is infamous for its unpredictable weather and strong storms, making it one of the more challenging 8000-meter peaks.

This time, the Czech female climber Lucie Oršulová and I had formed a women-only team. I had met her on the north face of Everest in 2005, and respected her as an accomplished climber. We had stayed in touch, and when I told her about my plan to climb Dhaulagiri I in spring 2007, Lucie—who is also a competitive skier—decided to join me. Ralf had already climbed Dhaulagiri I, and was leading an expedition to Manaslu with his Alpine school at the time.

Ralf and I were married on March 24, 2007. Before we embarked on our expeditions we went on our honeymoon, a two-week trekking tour in Nepal with our friends and family. Anita and Sonam of Thamserku Trekking threw a wedding party for us at their new lodge in Kongde, which even included a wedding cake and dancing! The group was cheerful and very sociable, and trekking through the Khumbu was fun. My personal highlight was that I could finally show my closest confidante, my sister Brigitte, what Nepal means to me.

After the trek we all went our separate ways. Our wedding guests went back home or, if they were mountaineers, had their own climbing plans. Ralf met his team on Manaslu, and I flew to Dhaulagiri base camp where Lucie was waiting for me. We had initially planned to do a route on the east face, which joins the normal route at 7400 meters, but after a closer look at the face it was obvious that it had become very dry over the years, exacerbating the rockfall danger. So we decided to do the normal route on the northeast ridge instead. The crowd at base camp was international, and it was nice to see familiar faces and old friends. Denis was leading a Russian–Kazakh expedition, and Boris, who gave me a big bear hug when he saw me, was one of its members. Iñaki and his partner Jorge were part of a Spanish team, and there was a big Italian expedition under the leadership of Mario Merelli. We shared our climbing permit with Gianni Goltz, whom I had met in the Alps a few times since our Manaslu expedition, and Cristina Castagna, whom I had met on Gasherbrum II in 2005.

Lucie and I did two acclimatization rotations. On our way to Camp 1 we had to traverse underneath the Eiger, a huge rock face on the north flank of Dhaulagiri. As the face was very exposed to rockfall, we climbed this section early in the morning. On our first acclimatization rotation we stayed two nights at 5750 meters, and on the second we spent two very stormy and cold nights at 6600 meters. I really enjoyed being on expedition with another woman; Lucie spoke fluent German, and we got on very well. As we both wanted to climb light and without fixed ropes, we carried our little tent as well as a thin 50-meter rope up and down with us.

After our first night at 6600 meters, Iñaki barged into our tent. He had just reached the summit with Jorge. He was distraught, telling us that Jorge had taken a tumble just above Camp 2 where they had fixed some rope. He must have missed the end of the fixed rope and fallen for about 800 meters down the east face. We were shocked; it was unlikely that Jorge would have survived such a fall. All the greater was the joy we felt when climbers coming up to Camp 2 told us that he was still alive. Despite his serious injuries, he had dragged himself to Camp 1 and was now being carried down to base camp.

A day later we descended to base camp. We established a deposit camp at 5700 meters where we left the gear we wouldn't need lower down: sleeping bags, tent, sleeping mats, stove, pot, Lucie's big down jacket, and down booties for the night. We dug a hole in the snow, put everything into a big bin bag, tied it up, and covered the hole again. We marked the spot with a little flag and stuck a shovel in the snow in case it snowed heavily. Then we continued our descent.

Jorge's accident had caused great consternation in the various camps, and unfortunately the relief that came with the good news of his survival didn't last long. In the meantime, an Italian group including Gianni and Cristina had climbed to the last high camp. They started their summit attempt on April 29. When they came out of the steep gully, they reached a flat rocky plateau from which they climbed toward the left for another 30 meters to the summit. Sergio, who was in Mario's group, fell to his death in front of his wife, Rosa. His ice ax, which he was holding onto with both hands, broke off. He didn't fall far, but he hit his head badly on a rock and was killed instantly.

With black frostbitten fingers, a completely destroyed Rosa returned to base camp a few days later. The events up there must have been harrowing. I felt the need to visit her in her tent, where she had been cocooned for a while. I asked carefully whether I could come in—I just wanted to give her the feeling that she was not alone. She cried her eyes out, and so did I. I couldn't say much. After a short while she told me about Sergio. They had had a relationship much like Ralf's and mine, and I imagined what it would be like if something happened to Ralf. Rosa asked me to bring Sergio's camera down if I made it to the summit, and I promised that I would. They had left Sergio's body where he had fallen, as there was no crevasse where they could have buried him.

It was very sad to see how someone feels after losing a loved one. Even though I know the dangers and I'm always prepared for disaster to strike, it's tragic when somebody dies. I guess it brings home the reality that it could be me. Lucie was particularly upset by Sergio's fatal accident, as she had never had to deal with death on an expedition before. She almost stopped talking and lost some of her motivation to climb the mountain. I was also affected by these two accidents, but I had seen it before and could probably deal with it a bit better. I tried to make her understand that it was very important to keep concentrating all the time.

While the Italian team was evacuated by helicopter, other climbers started to walk out, leaving our base camp pretty empty. Lucie and I went back up after our rest days and tried for the summit. But when we reached Camp 1, we were greeted by a nasty surprise: All our gear was gone. This was unbelievable—what were we supposed to do? Was this the end of our expedition? Flustered, I phoned our agency and discussed with Lucie whether we could attempt the summit without first going back down to base camp, which would take a lot of time. I could use my down suit as my sleeping bag. I had also packed an extremely light one-man tent, which I had initially planned to use for the night at Camp 3. Fortunately, Lucie had received a down jacket from Gianni's partner. When we met the pair at Camp 1 after their successful summit bid they also gave us their sleeping mats, a stove, and a pot.

We could only explain the missing gear by the fact that after Sergio's accident the Italians had descended rapidly to base camp, and probably asked their high-altitude Sherpas to carry down their equipment. They must have mistaken our deposit for the Italians' equipment, and taken it down to base camp and later to Kathmandu. Had we not been able to borrow some gear, our expedition would have been over. We were very lucky! In hindsight, however, I wonder whether it would have been better to have called it a day there and then.

The weather was good, I was still motivated, and so Lucie and I climbed back up to Camp 2 the following day. On the third day we were in new territory. The 800 vertical meters to Camp 3 were very steep and exhausting, but extremely diverse. We climbed on blue ice and rocky terrain. Belaying each other on the steep icy sections was very time-consuming. The sky clouded over and a storm was brewing in the afternoon. We were both freezing when we pitched our tent and started to melt snow at 7400 meters. We intended to stay there half the night and start our summit bid at midnight. But as we had arrived very late and Lucie was exhausted, we decided to have a rest day and leave the following night. During the course of our rest day, Lucie's condition worsened. She suggested that I go for the summit without her. She became apathetic and refused to drink. Under these circumstances a summit attempt was out of the question. Lucie was suffering from altitude sickness and we had to descend as quickly as possible the following day.

After a restless night during which she repeatedly took medication, we started our descent at 6:00 a.m. It had snowed during the night, leaving a fresh snow cover of about six inches. The start of the climb was not very steep and Lucie was able to get down on her own, even though it was tiring for her. I lowered her down the steeper sections, which slowed our progress. Lucie felt badly about being so weak. She kept on losing her balance and needing to sit down. I also didn't feel comfortable being so pushy, but what other choice did I have? Fortunately, her condition improved the lower we got. When we finally reached base camp after having descended 2700 vertical meters in fourteen hours, she was completely and utterly worn out, saying that this had been the hardest descent of her life. I was simply happy to have gotten her down in one piece.

Lucie didn't want to leave me in the lurch, but it was clear that she would be too exhausted for another attempt. She had to abandon her expedition. I wanted to give it another go after a few days of rest—on my own. The only other expedition left at base camp was the Spanish team. A day before Lucie and our kitchen boy walked out to Marpha, the Spanish invited us for a coffee. Apart from Javier Serrano, whom everyone called Javi, they spoke little English, so it was a very entertaining conversation using hands and feet. They had brought many delicacies from Spain. Ricardo Valencia, who was an excellent chef, wanted to surprise Lucie and me with a Spanish meal, but our cook had already started preparing our dinner and we felt obliged to eat with him. We promised Ricardo that we would stay for dinner next time. Little did I know that there would never be a next time.

After Lucie had bid us goodbye, Bim, our chef, and I were the only ones left at our base camp. The Spanish team was camped about a quarter of an hour farther down. Bim didn't really like being on his own, but I enjoyed the peace and quiet. One day, I sat on a rock gazing into the mysterious mist and wondering whether it was a good idea to continue on my own. I listened to my inner voice, and my gut feeling told me that it was the right time. Ralf gave me Charly's weather report from Manaslu, which I happily shared with the Spanish team. May 14 seemed likely to be a good summit day, but the days leading up to it were supposed to be windy with snowfall. I planned on establishing three camps: one at 5700 meters, one at 6600 meters, and one at 7400 meters.

Javi and two other Spaniards also intended to stay at Camp 1, while Santiago Sagaste (Santi) and Ricardo wanted to start a day later and go directly to Camp 2. It was a relatively warm night, and even though I had set out early a few rocks nearly hit me just below the Eiger, forcing me to hurry up. At the time I didn't see it as a warning, but in hindsight I wonder whether this was yet another sign for me to turn back.

At Camp 1 I had a long chat with Javi. He told me that he had lost a friend on Dhaulagiri a few years earlier. His widow had asked him why they had not chosen a different mountain, but they had simply wanted to climb Dhaulagiri. We had a very deep conversation about mountaineering, life, and death and agreed that the friends we had lost in the mountains wouldn't want us to give up climbing. Life goes on, bad things happen all the time, and we should enjoy every day of our lives; we said what you would always say when you sit together philosophizing. We had no idea how soon our words would come true.

It was snowing during the night. On May 12, Javi, Ricardo, and I were taking turns breaking trail to Camp 3. Santi had a bad cough and fell behind a bit, while the other two Spaniards turned back. About 150 meters below Camp 3 we were caught in a thunderstorm. Clouds rolled in, there was lightning, and it started to sleet. The thunder seemed to be far away, but I suddenly felt an electric shock in my down suit. I had to seek shelter. Digging a snow hole would take too long. I put my backpack with my ice axes on the ground, took off my crampons, and left them there. I walked away, crouched down, and waited for the thunderstorm to abate. Javi, Santi, and Ricardo followed suit. Once the thunderstorm stopped we continued up.

When I checked my watch for the time, the cord of my turquoise bead bracelet broke. A few of the beads fell into the sleeve of my down suit, and more landed on the snow. I couldn't explain why this talisman, which I had taken on many expeditions, broke so suddenly. It was disconcerting. I dug frantically in the snow, looking for the beads. Amazingly I managed to find all twenty-one, and I put them into my down suit. For the first time I wondered, though, whether this climb was just not meant to be. So much had happened and so many stumbling blocks had been put in my way.

I had no choice but to stow away the turquoise beads in my pocket and continue to climb to our camp, however, where I would have to stay the night in any case.

I pitched my tent while the Spanish team were digging out their tents, which had been there for weeks and were covered in the snow that had fallen over the past few days. Santi and Ricardo's tent stood in the middle of the 30-meter-wide ridge, and Javi's was probably 15 meters to their left. I dug my platform to the right of Ricardo and Santi's tent and about 5 meters lower, and used two snow stakes, an ice ax and a ski pole to anchor it. I stuck my shovel in the snow on the right side. Our tents were so close together that we were able to communicate with raised voices. The slope where we had pitched our tents was about 28 degrees and seemed pretty safe to me. There was a steep drop on each side of the ridge with a rocky cliff on the right side. The ridge flattened out farther down, leading to another precipice toward base camp.

A beautiful night was falling, freezing but clear. We agreed to leave together at 6:00 a.m. the following morning and support each other in breaking trail toward Camp 3. Sitting in my tent, I spent a lot of time trying to string the beads back onto the cord of my bracelet. It was extremely important to me to wear it again, which is why I tried tying a knot in the cord and stringing the beads onto it. But no matter how hard I tried, it didn't work. I spent the rest of my time melting snow to hydrate, filling my water bottles, and gazing over to Annapurna I glowing majestically in the evening light.

Early in the morning a storm came up. It didn't snow, but the storm was so strong that it was impossible for us to go out. Around 6:00 a.m. I looked out of my tent. Ricardo had just come back from Javi's tent, and we discussed our plans. We agreed to wait and see whether the storm would abate, but we knew that we would have to set out before 9:00 a.m.—otherwise, we would have to go back down. Apart from my high-altitude boots, I was wearing everything I needed for the climb, including my harness. Every once in a while I looked outside and took a sip from my water bottle. I could no longer sleep and listened to the storm, which was still raging.

TOP: This little knife, which I had on my harness, saved my life after I was hit by an avalanche on my second attempt of Dhaulagiri in 2007. BOTTOM: The lonely Dhaulagiri base camp

And then the avalanche hit.

"I have to cut the tent wall with my knife," I told myself.

"Or else I won't get out.

"Or else I'll suffocate.

"How much time do I have?"

With my right hand, which I could move a bit, I dug through the snow toward my harness, moving along the slings until I felt the cold metal of the knife in my hand. I opened the small carabiner and took the knife, thinking, "I mustn't drop it—that would be a disaster."

I opened the knife with my teeth. The yellow tent wall was still pressed against my face. I had to cut it. I was scared that the snow would come in, cover my face, and suffocate me. But I had no choice.

I cut a hole through the tent. Snow was trickling onto my face, but not much. I needed to clear the snow above the opening before I could get out of the tent. Slowly but surely I shifted the snow with my right hand. It was pretty loose. My air pocket filled with snow but I could tell it wasn't much. Suddenly I could push my hand through the snow into the air. I was buried under about fifteen to twenty inches of snow, which I was able to push away. It took quite a while using only one hand, but I could breathe again, which gave me hope. I tried to rip open the tent wall a bit more to make the hole bigger. As soon as I could sit up a bit, I managed to free my left hand from under my body. My legs were still stuck in the snow, but now I was able to use both hands to dig myself out and push my body through the snow. Thank God, I had not put on my high-altitude boots, as this would have made it much more difficult. And the fact that I had lost my sleeping bag together with the other stuff at our deposit camp actually turned out to be a blessing in disguise.

It took about three-quarters of an hour to fully peel myself out of the tent. I stood in the snow wearing only socks on my feet. Whether or not I would get frostbite didn't matter at the moment; the most important thing was that I was out of the snow. The wind had died down to a complete calm. I looked over to the place where the Spanish tent had been, but couldn't see anything. I looked downward. Had the avalanche dragged them down there?

I was in a weird state of mind. My brain was on autopilot, just as if it didn't belong to me. I needed my boots and sunglasses—without them I would go snow blind, get frostbite, and be unable to help the others. My tent was completely buried in the snow, so I needed a shovel to get to my boots. I turned my gaze to the spot where my tent had been pitched and recognized the handle of my shovel. The anchors of my tent had all been ripped off, but the shovel on the right was still there. I walked over in my socks and then dug out my tent until I found my boots. I couldn't find my sunglasses, but at least I had my gloves and goggles.

The avalanche must have dragged me down about 40 to 50 meters. But where were the Spaniards? Had they too been dragged down, or were their tents still up higher? As I couldn't see anything farther down, I climbed back up. I started digging where I thought Ricardo's and Santi's tent might be. Just before the avalanche had come down, I had seen Javi walk over to Ricardo and Santi, which made me believe that all three must have been in the same tent when the avalanche struck. I was digging frantically, shouting their names: *Ricardo, Santi, Javi!* I couldn't believe that this was actually happening.

I had been shoveling for a long time when I hit something yellow— the skin of their tent, which was covered by six or seven feet of snow. I continued to dig. Suddenly I hit something hard beneath the shovel. A foot. A body. I cut the tent wall and recognized Ricardo's down suit. A little later, I also found Santi. I dug their heads out, but they were both dead, completely embedded in the snow. I had been shoveling for at least an hour, and had I been able to think more clearly, I would have realized that the chance of their being alive was very slim. I guess I just didn't want to believe it.

I couldn't find Javi and figured that he must be in his tent. I walked over and called his name. His tent was covered in snow, but only on the surface. He later told me that he had been sleeping when he heard me call the three names, and he had assumed I was having a nightmare. When he finally replied to my calls, I cleared his tent entrance of snow so he could get out. I told him what had happened and pointed over to his lost friends. He was completely confused and couldn't believe that he hadn't heard a thing.

He desperately shouted out their names, touching them the whole time. He was trying to comprehend what was beyond comprehension.

We had to leave the bodies where they were. We couldn't carry them down and there were no crevasses to put them in. Sobbing, I covered Ricardo and Santi with snow. The snow slab had not been very big, but it had buried the exact spot where our tents had been pitched. Javi and I hurried to get away from this place, worrying about an after-avalanche.

I went back to my tent to look for my equipment and found my crampons and other ice ax. Unfortunately, Javi had left his ice axes and crampons in Santi's and Ricardo's tent, and it was impossible to get them. We descended slowly in a state of shock. The terrain to Camp 1 was relatively easy. When we got to just below the Eiger we had to wait a bit, as the traverse would have been far too dangerous in the heat of the afternoon. From there, Javi would definitely need crampons. He radioed down to base camp, told them what had happened, and asked his mate to bring up some crampons. At 5700 meters I found a satellite signal and phoned Ralf. He had not yet attempted the summit of Manaslu, and even though I felt uncomfortable burdening him with this tragic event, I needed somebody to talk to.

Javi and I got back to base camp at 7:00 p.m. I wanted to get away from that place as soon as possible, so I walked out with the remaining members of the Spanish crew. Via the Dhampus Col, we first walked to Marpha and then to Jomsom, and then flew to Pokhara and finally to Kathmandu. I felt numb. The whole situation seemed like a bad dream. I didn't understand why I was alive while Ricardo and Santi had to die right next to me. While I was digging them out I kept asking myself why my tent had been dragged down and theirs hadn't moved an inch. It was only later that I realized why: Even though my tent was solidly anchored, it had not been frozen to the ground, as I had only pitched it the previous evening. The avalanche was forceful enough to rip out the anchors and drag down the tent. The Spanish tent had been there for weeks; the tent floor must have been frozen to the ground, making it impossible to pull free. Instead the snow piled up on top of it, covering it with a load of compacted snow as heavy as cement.

I also wondered whether Ricardo and Santi had died an instant death. I tried to put myself in their shoes and imagine what it must have felt like. And what would have happened if I had not had the little knife on my harness? I certainly couldn't have ripped the tent with my fingernails. I would never have gotten out of the tent.

In hindsight, there are so many questions and so many different interpretations. Did I want too much? Had I ignored warning signs? Did I not listen to my gut feelings? I usually don't have a do-or-die attitude about summiting. I normally adapt to the conditions of nature and try to recognize and accept them. Why had I insisted on getting to the summit of Dhaulagiri after it had not worked out with my climbing partner? Despite all the incidents that had happened, I had had a good, positive feeling before the last attempt: There was still enough time, and I was feeling strong. After the avalanche came down, I wondered why I hadn't noticed that something was wrong. Could I really trust my gut feeling? This feeling of insecurity was another reason why this incident shook me to the core.

Edurne Pasaban and I pose for a photo after reaching the summit of Broad Peak together on July 12, 2007. *(Photo by Ralf Dujmovits)*

CHAPTER 13

SERENITY

I was aimlessly wandering the streets of Kathmandu. The events on Dhaulagiri had completely thrown me off course. I couldn't imagine going back home; I probably couldn't have coped with the hype surrounding the accident. I didn't want to face all the conversations and interviews. Many people in Jomsom already wanted to know more about it. The only person I wanted to talk to was Ralf. He would be able to understand the fear and desperation I had gone through.

Finally I got myself a trekking permit to meet Ralf somewhere on the trail. He was on his way back after successfully climbing Manaslu. There were hardly any people on the trail and it felt good to walk. Ralf and I met after five days, and finally I could pour my heart out. Ralf had been on Dhaulagiri and knew exactly where the tents had been pitched; he had camped there himself in 1990. Being close and talking to him really helped me.

Back in Germany, I felt very strongly about sticking to our summer plan to attempt K2 after first climbing the main summit of Broad Peak. I would need time to come to terms with the events on Dhaulagiri. It haunted me. Night after night I dreamed about being caught in the avalanche, unable to get out. I knew that getting over this tragedy would be easier if I were in my favorite place: the mountains. The thought of giving up mountaineering because of the accident on Dhaulagiri never crossed my mind.

On the trek to Broad Peak I felt better every day. I was able to switch off; I didn't have to think about anything, I could simply absorb every moment. The weather was gorgeous, and the Karakorum showed itself from its most glorious side. In Urdukas we witnessed an exceptionally beautiful evening.

When I saw the Trango Towers glow majestically in the setting sun, I knew that I belonged there. What could be more beautiful than being there with the man I loved and two good friends, David Göttler and Daniel Bartsch, who were not only extraordinary mountaineers but also accomplished cameramen? Toward the east we could see the very top of Broad Peak, and I spent a lot of time sitting and studying the mountain. Thirteen years earlier I had been there for the first time, reaching the false summit of Broad Peak. Many images went through my mind, and I kept having flashbacks. So much had happened since then. My life had completely changed. But the way I felt when looking at my goal—the mix of joy and awe and the longing to be there—was unchanged.

When we reached Concordia I was taken by the power of the gigantic mountains. No matter where I gazed, I was surrounded by beautiful, imposing peaks: majestic K2, to which I looked up very humbly; Broad Peak in its full enormity; Gasherbrum IV and the very upmost tip of Gasherbrum II, with Chogolisa towering behind us. Would K2 let us climb its flanks and ridges? Would we succeed in reaching its summit in a few weeks' time? I had all of these unanswered questions, but first I wanted to concentrate on Broad Peak. After a two-and-a-half-hour walk from Concordia we reached base camp at 4900 meters, where we pitched our tent in a quiet spot on the moraine. We had a magnificent view of the summit route via the west flank and the west ridge. The mountain had changed significantly over the past thirteen years. The snow and ice gully we climbed in 1994 no longer existed; the snow was completely gone. Given its exposure to rockfall, this route had become far too dangerous. The ascent route was now to the left of a prominent rock pillar.

For acclimatization we spent the first night at 5900 meters and two nights at 6400 meters, a bit higher than the usual Camp 2. Because it was the fiftieth anniversary year of the first ascent of Broad Peak, many expeditions, including Edurne Pasaban with a big Spanish team, were on the mountain. But the various groups spread out very well. We deposited our tents at Camp 2 before we returned to base camp. As we were still acclimatized from our spring expeditions this was all we had to do for acclimatization. The next time we would go up would be our summit attempt.

On July 10, the moment finally came. Charly Gabl had predicted three days of good weather. In order to avoid rockfall—which usually occurred around sunrise—and to be the first ones on the route, we started relatively early at 1:30 a.m. We reached Camp 2 in the wee hours of the morning and had the whole day ahead of us, which meant that we could enjoy the good weather, catch up on sleep, relax, and drink a lot of fluids. Despite having recently spent two nights there, this time I sensed how the events on Dhaulagiri were still haunting me. I kept on analyzing whether the area above us was prone to slab avalanches. Thankfully nothing happened, and I was able to sleep very well that night.

The following day we were the first ones to leave for Camp 3. Just as Charly had forecast, we climbed in beautiful weather even though it was freezing cold in the morning. After having negotiated a short steep face we reached a ledge at 7000 meters where we sat down and allowed the sun to warm us. I just sat there, marveling at my surroundings. The clear air offered an infinite view, and I thought I could actually see the earth's curvature. The neighboring mountaintops were glowing in the first rays of dawn; it was an intense and beautiful moment filled with a lightness that gave me energy. My doubts and insecurities were gone. I knew why I was there: I simply loved being in the mountains, where I could live for the moment and leave everything else behind. Dhaulagiri was far away, and I felt incredibly happy.

After taking some pictures, the four of us continued on our way up. The other expeditions had set up their Camp 3 on a big flat plateau at 7100 meters. We preferred to have a bit more space, and found a safe place about 100 meters farther up, below a vertical ice wall. We felt almost euphoric later on as we were packing our gear for the summit bid. While the sun was setting behind Muztagh Tower, and K2 was still glowing in its most gorgeous light, we were already tucked into our sleeping bags.

That morning we were not the only people going for the summit, which towered 800 meters above us. When we started in the bitter cold at 2:00 a.m., a few people were already ahead of us. After crossing a few wide slopes and a heavily crevassed glacier we had to traverse the headwall gap between the glacier and the bergschrund. From there we followed a wide gully leading to the saddle between the central summit to the left and the false and main summits to the right. David and I started to break trail through deep snow in the 40-degree gully; Ralf took over a bit later. At 8:00 a.m., the first sunlight greeted us at the saddle at 7850 meters. Unfortunately, the wind was too icy so we didn't quite warm up in the sun. While we were waiting for Daniel, the Spanish team of Edurne, Ferrán Latorre, and the Ecuadorian Iván Vallejo, as well as the Italians with Silvio Mondinelli all came up. It was nice to meet good friends up there.

The ridge was windswept from the saddle to the false summit. We climbed across some exposed rocky sections and snow-covered flanks, which were pretty challenging in the strong winds without a fixed rope. Finally we climbed through a chimney which would probably equal a grade V climb. Protected from the wind, it led directly to the relatively flat false summit, where we sat down and rested. Daniel, who couldn't warm up his freezing toes, decided to turn back, as did many other climbers who were happy to have reached the false summit. It was a beautiful day, and I was eager to get to the main summit I had not reached in 1994. Ralf had already stood on Broad Peak's highest point in 1999 and had initially planned to go only as far as the false summit to acclimatize for K2. He changed his mind, though, and decided to come with me, which made me very happy.

We looked across to the main summit, and admittedly I was surprised to see how far away it still was. David, Ralf, and I climbed down into a little notch and then gradually followed the corniced ridge farther up. In the run-up to the climb I had readied myself for coming across the body of Markus Kronthaler, who had died of exhaustion in his bivouac the previous year. Despite having come prepared, I was still shocked when we stopped about 15 meters short of his body. He lay there stretched out as if he were sleeping. His clothes had not even faded. I had known Markus well. We had shared the permit for Shisha Pangma in 2000, and our paths had crossed several times since then. It was painful to see him like this. Had we not known that his brother and a recovery team were on their way from Austria to bring his body home, we would have moved him a bit away from the route and covered him with rocks. I am sure that Markus would have liked to stay up there. We once talked about it, and I remember him saying that he thought it was irresponsible to bring bodies down and put other people at risk. On the other hand, I also understand the parents, who want a place to go and visit their child. But such recovery is often impossible as the terrain can be too difficult and the costs too high.

After I had silently bid goodbye to Markus, we continued on our way to the main summit. The Spanish team with Edurne climbed next to us, and Edurne and I climbed the last 20 to 30 meters together. We get on very well, we know a lot about each other, and it was a good feeling to step onto the summit with her. Silvio also reached the top with us. Broad Peak was his fourteenth 8000-meter summit, and naturally he was over the moon. My own personal highlight was experiencing this moment with Ralf, who had come all the way, just for me. On the way between the false and the main summit, we had literally walked along the border between China and Pakistan. The incredible panorama toward the right, the Pakistani side, featured the countless beautiful mountaintops of the Karakorum. Unfortunately, clouds obscured the view to the left, toward China. The only two peaks higher than us were K2 and Gasherbrum I.

The wind was too cold to stay on the summit for long, so we quickly descended to Camp 3, where Daniel had melted snow for us. We agreed to spend another night at Camp 3 to make the most of our acclimatization for K2. The following day we returned to base camp in very strong winds and heavy snowfall. Once again, Charly's weather forecast was spot on. Our chef, Ghassan Khan, had prepared a special treat for us: Our camp was beautifully lit with kerosene torches, and he had invited other teams to our summit dinner, which was definitely rich in calories.

After recovering and relaxing the next day, we got busy sorting our gear and preparing for the move to K2 base camp, which required another ten porters. While we were organizing our gear, we suddenly heard David shout from the store tent: "Come here, you've got to have a look at this."

A mouse family had moved into his duffel bag, which he had left unzipped in the store tent. Mama Mouse had made a nest of toilet paper and cardboard, which she must have stolen from the kitchen tent. Seven or eight tiny, naked, pink baby mice were cuddled up in it. As David needed his bag, we piled up some stones to build another nest and moved the mice there. After a few hours we noticed that the mice had gone, along with the cardboard and the toilet paper. Shortly afterward, Ghassan Khan called us to the kitchen tent. We must have upset Mama Mouse so much that she had set up a new home in the kitchen tent between the rocks. We lifted the rocks to have a look, but of course she didn't like that, either, and started dismantling her nest again. She scuttled out of the kitchen tent into the store tent, where she built a new nest inside the pole bag. After she had carried all her building materials, she grabbed one baby after another by the neck and lugged them to their new home in the store tent. We watched this amazing scene for a long time. Fortunately she always took the same route, which made it easier for David to film her.

When the time came to take down the store tent, we needed the bag for the tent poles. My suggestion that we take the mouse family to the Slovenians, who had their camp a little bit farther up, was unanimously rejected. So we made another nest for them and moved them a fourth and last time before we finally set off for K2 base camp. I guess Mama Mouse must have come with the food from Askole or Skardu; winter at this altitude is too cold for mice to survive. During a winter expedition to Broad Peak, for example, Simone Moro recorded a temperature of –31 degrees Fahrenheit.

On our approach march toward K2's majestic pyramid, I could feel the excitement growing inside me. My tension had a positive edge. I was so looking forward to climbing this beautiful mountain, but at the same time I felt a sense of reverence toward it. My eyes scanned the face for the route, looking for the best way. There were several options to consider. In 1994 Ralf had climbed K2 via the Abruzzi Spur, which is considered the normal route even though it isn't really an easy way up K2. We intended to climb the Cesen Route, which goes directly to the shoulder and meets the Abruzzi Spur at 7800 meters. Tomo Česen first climbed this ridge in 1986, but he only got to the shoulder. The Basque brothers Alberto and Felix Iñurrategi finished it all the way to the summit in 1994, which is why it is often referred to as the Basque Route. Ralf was absolutely fascinated by the route's clean, steep line, and though he had vowed never to climb K2 again he had decided to join me. Daniel and David were also eager to climb this attractive route and were highly motivated.

We set up our base camp and prepared for our summit attempt so we would be ready once the weather window opened. We talked all day long about our upcoming climb. What tactics would we use? What equipment would we bring? How could we save weight, and where would we pitch our tent?

We planned to skip the traditional Camp 1 and establish three bivouacs on the ascent, the last one being at the shoulder. We wanted to start our summit attempt directly from our last camp, and then ideally descend all the way to base camp, or at least to our Camp 1. No matter how we tried, we could not reduce the weight of our backpacks to less than 45 pounds. We distributed the loads equally between us, but with Daniel and David's film equipment it was pretty difficult. But we had to accept the additional weight if we wanted good footage of K2. Ralf and I had small voice recorders attached to our down suits, as the camera microphones were not sufficient in the fierce winds.

On July 28, Ralf, David, Daniel, and I started climbing the Cesen Route. It starts off in a wide snow gully, moves up to the right toward the rocks, and then follows the edge of the couloir. It finally continues up a pillar until it reaches the shoulder of K2 after about 3000 meters. Five members of an American expedition who had fixed some rope were also on the route. Given the limited space for campsites on the route's steep and exposed terrain, it was actually a good thing that the other teams were on the Abruzzi Spur.

We made good progress on the first day on the face. It was very early in the morning at about 5500 meters when we saw a falling ice serac trigger a huge dust avalanche about 1000 meters above us. David started to film and I had my camera out to take pictures when we suddenly noticed that the colossal white cloud was rolling directly toward us. The avalanche had gained so much momentum and mass that it was thundering down the couloir where we were camped on the right-hand side. As fast as was humanly possible with crampons, we ran right toward the rocks, rammed our axes into the ice—the rock being too crumbly to hold onto—and ducked for cover.

"Be careful Gerlinde—hold on tight!"

I heard Ralf shout, and hoped that our ice axes would hold us. Suddenly the avalanche on Dhaulagiri popped into my mind. I thought about the incredible force that had pulled me down, and how pointless it would have been to fight it. The shock wave as well as the fine particles of the snow masses thundering past us took my breath away. I clenched my ice axes in my hands and prayed that none of us would be pulled down. Our voice recorders were switched on, and we could later hear ourselves shouting and panting.

After a minute or two the avalanche's power had waned, the fine snow particles disappeared, and I was able to breathe again. Ralf, David, and Daniel looked like snowmen but they were still in the same spot, which was a great relief. We were now worried about the Americans, who had been about 100 meters below us where the avalanche would have had greater impact. We called down to them. They had been clipped onto the fixed ropes and were almost unharmed, but one of them had been hit on the arm by a tumbling ice block and eventually had to abandon his summit bid.

We took a deep breath and continued up. We were still shaking, though, and when we found a little rocky ledge farther up we sat down to recover from the shock. Yet none of us wanted to abandon the climb. In front of us was a fissured pillar that would be relatively safe to climb. But the steep and layered rock, mostly covered with snow, also had a few ice sections and was harder than expected. Halfway up to our planned bivouac we gave up the idea to climb K2 alpine style, and happily used the ropes the Americans had fixed on an earlier attempt when they had reached 7200 meters.

After a challenging climb we reached 6400 meters at around lunchtime, and found a perfect bivouac spot. It took a while to stack some rocks to make the ledge bigger, pitch our two tents, and tie them to the rock face behind. Once this task was done we had a splendid viewing platform with magnificent views of the glaciers and peaks of the Karakorum. I examined our camp carefully to see whether it was prone to rockfall and whether the rock around us was solid. That night, whenever I heard a noise I would look out of the tent and try to see where it came from.

The next morning the weather was splendid as we continued up the pillar, which seemed less steep farther up. Depending on finding a good spot for our bivouac, we intended to reach somewhere between 7300 and 7400 meters, but we were very aware that climbing with our heavy packs would get more exhausting the higher we got. At 7200 meters we found a suitable spot to bivouac and, considering the steeper terrain higher up, we decided to pitch our tents there. We had had a perfect day with excellent climbing conditions: partly frozen sugar snow and partly rock that was sometimes covered with ice. There was literally no need to break trail. The route was clear to see, and visibility was good.

But the following day—the day we had intended to climb to the shoulder—was completely different. It was cloudy, we were climbing in thick fog, and the fresh snow was about knee-deep. Breaking trail was strenuous, and we were happy to share the job with the Americans. The biggest difficulty was finding the route in almost zero visibility. As much as I usually curse old fixed ropes—they are particularly dangerous when covered in snow, as you can easily trip over them with your crampons on the descent—on that occasion I was glad they were there. I was particularly happy about a green rope, probably from a Czech expedition from the previous year, which clearly indicated the way. Due to poor visibility and very cold conditions, we hardly took any pictures or shot footage. As we had to store our batteries inside our down suits to keep them warm and prevent them from dying instantly, getting out the camera was a real pain. Every time I wanted to take a picture, I had to insert the battery into the camera and take it out again afterward, an exercise that took quite some time with my big high-altitude gloves. I really admired David and his filming; he even took off his thin inner gloves to adjust the camera settings.

After the strenuous trail-breaking work we were relieved when we finally reached the shoulder at around lunchtime. The shoulder stretches from 7800 to 7900 meters. Constantly exposed to strong winds, it is usually windswept. K2 is notorious for its storms: Climbers have literally been blown off the mountain. We pitched our tents next to each other and anchored them well. This was the point where the Cesen Route and the Abruzzi Spur met, where we would start our summit attempt. The mood in our group was mixed. We were very happy to have reached the shoulder after such a hard day, and felt extremely motivated to go for the summit. But the weather didn't look good, and we were aware that a sudden drop in temperature could result in tragedy. Keeping our bearings in a whiteout would be difficult on or above the shoulder. In order to find our way back to camp on the descent, we put in markers every 25 meters or so from the end of the Cesen route.

Ralf talked to Charly on the satellite phone. He forecast wind, but said the weather should hold for another day before turning.

The skies cleared in the evening. K2 towered above us in its full beauty, and we could clearly see the route all the way to the summit through the Bottleneck. At the very top of this narrow couloir we would have to traverse underneath a huge hanging serac toward the left. Feeling optimistic, we crawled into our sleeping bags early and agreed to set out at midnight. Sleeping was out of the question as the wind, which soon turned into an outright storm, was rattling against our tent. When we looked out of our tents at midnight, the soft light of the full moon was illuminating the mountains, and we could see a huge cloud angrily covering the top of K2—not a good sign at all. The gale-force wind was so loud that we had to use radios to communicate between our two tents. We postponed our departure first to 2:00 a.m., then to 4:00 a.m. When the weather had still not improved by 5:00 a.m., we made the tough decision to descend. By now, K2 was covered in thick cloud all the way to the top of the Bottleneck and we were no longer able to see across to Broad Peak from the saddle to the summit. The blizzard blew a lot of snow into our tent vestibule, and it was bitterly cold; the temperature must have dropped below −4 degrees Fahrenheit. No matter how disappointed we were, we had no other choice: We had to go down.

We dismantled our tents in the storm and descended, carrying all of our gear on our backs. Climbing down and rappeling about 3000 vertical meters in ten hours, we arrived at base camp safely. Ralf decided that climbing the Cesen Route all the way to the shoulder was enough for him and called it a day. He would wait for us at base camp in case we had another go at the summit. The news that there had been an avalanche accident on his AMICAL alpin expedition to Gasherbrum II also affected his motivation. Daniel, David, and I hoped for another weather window to try again.

The weather was particularly bad over the following days, and our patience was put to the test. At base camp the wind, snow, and rain were tolerable, but higher up the mountain was completely obscured for two weeks, and it was clear that the weather up there was very windy and snowy. Our chef, Ghassan Khan, who had worked in a five-star hotel in

On the ascent to our last camp for the attempts on the main summits of Broad Peak and K2, we warmed up in the first sun rays of the day at about 7000 meters (from left: David Göttler, Ralf, and Daniel Bartsch).

Karachi but had opted for a more adventurous life as an expedition cook, tried everything he could to cheer us up. With his assistant cook, Jacoob, he barbecued kebabs and baked the most delicious cakes.

Charly's weather reports forecast bad weather for a prolonged period, and it started to look as if the weather just wouldn't improve. But finally there was good news: Between Friday, August 10, and Saturday, August 11, he forecast a weather window of one and a half days—not a lot, considering we would have to climb 3600 meters all the way from base camp to the summit. The four of us discussed whether David, Daniel, and I would stand a chance of getting to the summit on Saturday, as Charly also predicted the weather would deteriorate again at 8000 meters on Saturday evening. David and I were confident that we could make it to the summit and back if we climbed nonstop, carried a very light pack, and didn't sleep. We knew there would be a lot of fresh snow up there, requiring a lot of trail breaking. We also knew that we could only do it if we used the fixed ropes. What we didn't know was whether we would be able to go without sleep. In the end, this was our only chance, and even though everyone thought we were completely and utterly mad at first we decided to give it a shot. But we agreed that we would only continue to climb if we were absolutely sure that we had enough energy left to descend safely.

Despite the time pressure, I gave myself a few hours on Thursday to mentally prepare for our summit attempt. As always, I withdrew to my tent to gear myself up for the coming days. I mentally climbed the whole route and familiarized myself with the cruxes, which I knew all the way up to the shoulder. I tried to imagine everything that I might face up there: steep terrain, freezing cold, storms. I laid in my tent imagining myself breaking trail, inching up slowly, and dealing with utter exhaustion. I always envision every step in detail, which helps me accept and cope with whatever situations develop. Once I set out, I channel my energy and concentrate only on what is in front of me.

When we were ready to go, a Slovak and his two Polish teammates joined us—they had initially attempted a new route on K2's west face—along with one member of the American expedition. The seven of us embarked on this exciting challenge on Friday at 2:00 a.m. This time I carried only 16.5

pounds in my pack instead of 45. I didn't even take my toothbrush, which is rather unusual for me. We stayed in constant radio contact with Ralf at base camp.

At 8:00 a.m., we reached the site of our first bivouac at 6400 meters, where we rested, melted snow, and hydrated. At 2:30 p.m. we got to 7200 meters. The weather was still gorgeous with a light breeze. We got into a tent of the American team to melt snow and hydrate. I needed to warm my cold toes. We had climbed about 2000 vertical meters, and we definitely needed a rest.

After three hours we set off again toward the shoulder. I struggled with the cold and prayed that my feet would warm up once I was on the move again. The day was waning; while the mountaintops still glowed in the evening light, the valleys were already engulfed in darkness which was slowly creeping up toward us. The whole atmosphere of the scene was very special, beautiful and eerie at the same time. Would we be able to climb through the night? What would we face beyond the shoulder? The weather still looked good, but would it really hold until Saturday evening? There were many uncertainties. The most important thing was to keep a level head, remain concentrated, and not overestimate our abilities.

During the night I suffered from debilitating fatigue; I could barely keep my eyes open, and every single step was a huge effort. David and Daniel were also dead tired. We stopped for a drink. I nearly emptied my flask and felt a lot better for it. Breaking trail was becoming more arduous farther up.

At 2:30 a.m., Daniel, David, the American, and I finally reached the shoulder. The Polish team had fallen behind. David and I tried to pitch one of the tents we had left up there, but it was almost impossible in the strong wind. I nodded off for about an hour underneath the flysheet, which we simply propped up with a couple of walking poles. The others didn't manage to use their tent for protection and on top of that, they had also lost their cooking pot. They spent the night outside and went down the following morning.

David had already set off at 5:30 a.m. to warm up in the first sunlight. I followed about half an hour later. It seemed as if the Polish–Slovak team wouldn't come, which meant that we had no help breaking trail. The two of us made very slow progress, exhausted from the previous 3000 meters. We knew that we had to turn back at 3:00 p.m. at the latest—with or without the summit.

At 9:00 a.m. David and I reached the point where the slope steepens just below the Bottleneck at 8200 meters. I had the impression that there was a lot of fresh snow on the slope and that it was dangerous to climb. We checked the time and calculated whether we would have enough time to make it to the top and, more importantly, back down. We were only 400 meters below the summit, which only seemed an arm's length away, but 400 meters is a long way at that altitude. The Bottleneck is steep and the terrain is challenging all the way to the top.

I called Ralf, who had been observing our moving headlamps all night long, and asked him about the latest weather report. If the storm would only come up at midnight and not 7:00 p.m. as previously predicted, we would be able to make it. But Ralf couldn't tell us what we wanted to hear. He could already see the first cirrus clouds form behind Chogolisa in the south, closely followed by huge cumulus clouds. Ralf didn't want to influence our decision, but he urged me to consider the dangers and be careful: "I love you, with or without the summit of K2."

David and I mulled it over. Even though we were very tired, the weather was still good and we were tempted to carry on. But we couldn't risk getting caught in a storm. Too many climbers had lost their lives on the shoulder of K2. I thought about the 1986 disaster, when many people had died. The wind was howling on the shoulder below us. It was simply a white surface with no sign of life and you would never know that tents or people had ever been there. Here, the storm swallowed everything.

We had no other choice but to turn back.

Staying focused during the many rappels was a huge challenge, given how exhausted we were. Having been on the go for thirty-nine hours, David and I reached the bottom of the face at five o'clock in the afternoon. Ralf, who had been tense for the same period of time, climbed up to meet us. We were both overjoyed when we fell into each other's arms.

Even though we didn't reach the summit, I felt a heartfelt satisfaction. Climbing without sleep in very difficult conditions had been a new, enriching experience for all of us. Abandoning our summit attempt had been extremely hard, but we were able to make the right decision in time. I didn't quite exceed my personal limit, but I was very close. From base camp we looked up to K2 and knew that we would come back: The mountain would always be there. When we looked back up two hours later, at 7:00 p.m., we could see that the storm was raging higher up, blowing huge snow drifts off the shoulder.

For dessert, Ghassan Khan made a six-foot-high cake with the inscription: "K2—Try Again!"

Leaving for the summit in freezing cold temperatures at 7800 meters *(Photo by David Göttler)*

CHAPTER 14
JOY

R alf, I've got to go back to Dhaulagiri."
In the fall of 2007, I was convinced that I wanted to attempt Dhaulagiri again in the spring of 2008, a year after the avalanche disaster. I felt the urgency to return, but didn't really know why. My inner voice just told me to go back. Maybe it was because I had run away from base camp in May 2007? Also, I wanted to attempt the same route. I knew it was going to be hard, but I no longer wanted to put it off.

Ralf considered joining me, but he had already made plans to go to Makalu in the spring, and as he had already been to the summit of Dhaulagiri I encouraged him to stick to his plans. Of course I would have loved to have a trusted person with me, but I didn't want him to come just for me.

On our mutual expeditions to Broad Peak and K2, David and I had talked a lot about the avalanche disaster, and as he also wanted to climb Dhaulagiri we decided to go together. I was sure that David would understand the emotional stress this expedition would have on me and would have sympathy if it became mentally too difficult. After this idea was born we organized the climbing permit, which we shared with the Spanish climber, Carlos Pauner, and his two teammates.

The closer we came to leaving, the more I thought about what to expect on Dhaulagiri. Some of Ricardo and Santi's friends and family had contacted me in the summer of 2007, when they were planning a recovery expedition for the fall, and wanted to know more details of where the bodies might be. But the masses of snow on the mountain made it impossible to find them. Now, a year after the tragedy, I had no idea what we would find up there. Would the tent still be buried under the snow? Would I be able to see bits of it? Would the ridge be windswept, and would the two bodies be uncovered? I had to be prepared for anything.

Ralf and I traveled to Kathmandu together. The evening before he left for Makalu, we hardly talked but felt very close. We just hoped that we would come back safely from our expeditions. I remembered my own Makalu expedition seven years earlier and tried to imagine what Ralf could expect. Saying goodbye before a Himalayan expedition is always tough, given the potential danger.

Two of our friends, Kathrin and Andrea, trekked with us to base camp at 4700 meters. When we caught the first glimpse of the Dhaulagiri range, my eyes filled with tears. The events I had been longing to deal with were getting closer. I was happy to approach the mountain slowly; it gave me time to get used to the idea that I was actually going back to the place that had caused me so much pain. When we arrived at base camp it was snowing heavily. I was unexpectedly overcome by sadness and broke down in tears. When Janak, our cook, stepped out of the kitchen tent to welcome us, David told him that I needed a few minutes alone. I was getting drenched by the thick snowflakes falling from the sky, but I just stood there sobbing.

At base camp the nightmare about the avalanche, which had haunted me for a long time right after the accident, came back. The first few days were a struggle. I doubted whether returning there had been the right decision. I spoke a couple of times to Ralf, who had reached Makalu base camp in the meantime. He reinforced my decision, but told me to stay at base camp a bit longer if I wasn't ready to climb just yet. Being able to tell Ralf that I was not coping well was already a great help.

In order to acclimatize, David, Andrea, Kathrin, and I climbed to 5300 meters up the French Col, which was opposite Dhaulagiri. Just outside base camp we came across the plaque for Ricardo and Santi. A few of their friends had mounted it on a big rock last fall. From the pass we had a tremendous view of Dhaulagiri and were able to see the whole route to the summit. How would it feel to stand up there? Would Santi and Ricardo still be there? The events of the previous year just wouldn't stop haunting me.

Two days after our return to base camp we said goodbye to Kathrin and Andrea, who then trekked to Marpha via Dhampus Col. On April 19, David and I climbed up for the first time and spent one night at 5850 meters. In order to optimize our acclimatization we stayed there for the day, drank a lot, and continued heading up in the night. When I climb with David, we often move during the night when it is coldest and spend our days in the tents where it's warm and sunny. During the day I recover and sleep better than during the night, when I am usually freezing cold. This approach works well for both David and me, while Ralf prefers to sleep at night. Of course we can only do this in stages, and when navigation is relatively easy. Climbing during a full moon when you no longer need your headlamp is particularly beautiful. The moonlit mountains and the millions of stars, which still shine through the moon's intense light, create a unique mood.

David and I left Camp 1 at 3:00 a.m. We started out early not only because of the moonlight, but also because the wind usually picked up in the mornings. We were the only climbers on the route at this early hour, and we walked at a steady pace in the bright moonlight. As our visual perception was limited, the sound of our breathing and the crunching of our crampons in the frozen snow seemed even louder than usual. Gradually the sun came up in the east. Experiencing sunrise in the Himalaya will never cease to fill me with joy.

At about 6550 meters, David suddenly called out, "Gerlinde, can you see the remains of a tent up there?"

I did see the tattered pieces of a tent, but this was not the place where the avalanche had come down.

"Yes, David, but this is too far to the left. We didn't have our tents there. These must be the remains of some tents from the fall, or an earlier expedition."

We continued going up. A few minutes later, I stopped. In front of us was a perfectly even platform—white and untouched.

"It was here."

I clearly remembered the rock on the right, underneath which we had pitched our tents. Apart from a slight breeze, it was completely calm. The level snow platform gave the impression that nothing had ever happened here. It was perfectly flat without the slightest unevenness.

There was a long, pondering silence. And then, God knows why, I told David every single detail of the whole story again, even though he must have known it inside out by then. I had the urge to talk and babbled on and on. David listened politely, asking an occasional question. Finally, he said, "Gerlinde, I can't believe it was here. If I didn't know different, I would pitch my tent exactly here. This seems like the perfect place."

We climbed for another 150 meters and established our camp right underneath a high, steep ice wall, slightly overhanging at the top. We could pitch our tent easily and felt safe. The Ecuadoran climber, Iván Vallejo, and the Spanish group had also pitched their tents here. So had Valery Babanov from Russia and his mate Nickolay Totmyanin, who had switched over to the normal route after they had tried to tackle the unclimbed west face. David and I had no problems with the altitude, and I felt relieved that we had already passed the site of the accident. It was good for me to talk about the events again; I felt great, and was finally able to let go of the demons from the past.

We were the only climbers who spent this freezing night at camp; everyone else had gone down. David woke me at 4:00 a.m. We didn't want to miss sunrise, but it was still too cold to head out, so we waited for the sun to hit our tent. This particular morning at 6750 meters was one of the most magnificent I have ever experienced in the Himalaya. I'll never forget it: I felt incredibly happy to exist; happy about this wonderful world opening up just in front of me; happy for being allowed to be part of it and being alive. On the same mountain, within a distance of about 150 meters, I had experienced the most wonderful as well as the most horrible moments. . . .

We descended to base camp, and by 8.30 a.m. we were already having a cup of coffee prepared by Janak. After a few rest days we were ready for our summit bid, but as so often happens, our patience was put to the test. The winds were very strong higher up, and it snowed most afternoons. Due to the big difference in temperature between the Kali Gandaki Valley, which lies at an altitude of 1000 meters, and Dhaulagiri, as well as the resulting convection flow, clouds rolled in every afternoon. We visited Edurne and her team, who were camped a little farther up the hill; I emailed and talked to Ralf; and we kept in shape using our pull-up bar, which we had brought to base camp. David had had a locksmith construct a metal frame with two diagonal bars on the left and right as well as a cross bar for stabilization—it was a bit of a luxury, but we allowed ourselves the extra 15 pounds. When we first started doing our pull-ups at base camp we were completely out of breath, but we improved by the day. Some of the other teams also came down to train, and at the end of the expedition both our cook and the kitchen boy were in great shape!

Getting ready for the summit also involved washing my clothes, which I did in a large bowl of boiling water, rinsing in the freezing glacial water. I had to do this well in advance as my clothes took ages to dry. My washing line was a piece of thin cord which I tied to the poles inside the mess tent; had I hung up my clothes outside, they would have frozen rock solid.

May 1 turned out to be a possible summit day. David and I had initially planned to push to 6750 meters in one day, but we were so fed up with sitting around at base camp that we started a day earlier and spent a night at 6200 meters. When we passed the spot of the fatal avalanche on our way to our initial Camp 1, we saw some tents that belonged among others to a Polish expedition led by Arthur Hajzer, whom I knew from earlier expeditions. I told him that this was the place where the avalanche had come down a year earlier, but he only responded, "No Gerlinde, that's impossible." Though I assured him that this was exactly the spot of the accident, he didn't believe me, and reassured me that nothing would come down this year. They stayed there. I wonder whether they were aware that Ricardo and Santi's tent was probably right underneath them.

We intended to try for the summit from Camp 3 at 7350 meters. The temperatures for May 1 were forecast to be very low, around –22 degrees Fahrenheit, and the winds very high, around 40 miles per hour. This was a bit worrisome, but with precipitation forecast for the following days we felt encouraged at least to give it a try. The other expeditions had obviously made the same decision. Edurne and her team of ten as well as Iván and the two Russians joined us on our summit bid.

Over the years, I have developed my own personal strategy for the cold nights at the high camps. While I use a thick and very warm sleeping bag weighing 5.7 pounds at base camp, at the higher camps I sleep in my down suit and a very thin, lightweight sleeping bag weighing 2.2 pounds. For extra warmth, I fill my Nalgene bottle with hot water. It keeps me hydrated during the night, and serves as a wonderful hot water bottle. I usually start off by putting it on my feet and later move it closer to my body to keep the water warm.

The night at 7350 meters was severely cold and very windy. We chose to set off between 2:00 and 3:00 a.m., while Edurne and her team decided to wait out the storm for a while.

When we finally departed I could see the two headlamps belonging to Iván and his mate, who must have left earlier. David left twenty minutes ahead of me, as our tent was only big enough for one person to get ready at a time, and it would have been impossible for him to wait around at these cold temperatures. It didn't take long for me to catch up with him. For the first 300 meters we climbed on blue ice and mixed rocky ground. We only had to break trail between the rocky sections and the traverse, which was filled with drift snow and hence fairly avalanche-prone. For this, the 7mm 50-meter rope I always carry in my pack came in handy. When we reached the edge of the rocks David put me on belay while I inched my way through knee-deep snow to the other side. I climbed facing into the slope, using both my ice axes. This was the trickiest section of the climb, not necessarily because of its steepness but because of the avalanche danger. Once on the other side I belayed David across. Iván, Valery, Nickolay, and a Czech climber were right behind us, and thanks to our tracks they were able to traverse the slope without setting up a belay. A little later, Edurne and her team followed us.

Farther up the mountain the wind was so strong that the fresh snow was swept away and we climbed on frozen sugar snow. The exposed terrain was challenging, with sections of blue ice and snow-covered rock slabs. Some parts were extremely delicate and we had to be careful not to lose our concentration. We were all fighting against the cold. The wind was so cold that my fingertips would not get warm even with hand warmers inside my gloves. After the long traverse between 7700 and 7800 meters we negotiated blue ice all the way up to the summit couloir. I knew that

TOP: On May 1, 2008, we reached the summit of Dhaulagiri around midday. We shared Iván Vallejo's joy in having reached his fourteenth 8000-meter peak. BOTTOM: David Göttler climbing to our last camp on Dhaulagiri

we had climbed well into the morning, but I couldn't check the time as my watch was buried underneath my down suit and I didn't want to take off my gloves. Taking photos demanded a lot of effort, and every once in a while I would step behind a rock, where I was safe and protected from the wind, and wiggle my fingers and toes to warm my still-icy feet and hands. My down suit's hood was tightly closed around my head, completely iced up by the moisture of my breath. I wore my skiing goggles as they fit tighter around my face than my sunglasses. The only body parts exposed to the wind were my nose and chin, which I had generously covered with sunscreen and cold-protection cream.

Finally we reached the bottom of the summit couloir, which led to the rocky plateau just below the highest point. Halfway up the couloir, we let Iván go ahead. It was his last 8000-meter peak and we felt he should be the first to reach the summit this season. When we got out of the gully and covered the last few feet to the summit, I could hardly believe it. Unlike the previous year, when everything had gone wrong, everything had gone so smoothly this time—and now David and I were standing on top of Dhaulagiri. I felt extremely humble and grateful that I was finally allowed to stand on this summit. It was a very moving moment, and I burst into tears. Iván also cried, shouting and cheering, and it was a real pleasure to share his joy. Like many Latin Americans, Iván is a very emotional person who is able to express his sincere and unconditional happiness.

With taking pictures and filming, twenty minutes passed quickly. Everything takes a bit longer at those altitudes, even the simplest movements. It was bitterly cold and we could already see clouds swirling up in the sky. I didn't even think about eating or drinking. In the meantime, Narcio, Ferrán, Radek, and Fernando of the Spanish team had arrived on the summit. We congratulated each other and were immensely happy to have mastered the first half of our goal. Apart from these very emotional and bonding moments, I always need a few silent minutes to look around, absorb, and succumb to the feeling of having made it, simply savoring my happiness.

Soon, worries about the descent started to creep into my thoughts. David and I had agreed to go down all the way to base camp. Descending 3000 vertical meters would be most exhausting, but spending another night at this altitude would also be very tough on the body, so it was better for us to keep moving and descend in one go. At base camp we would recover faster with our good sleeping bags and enough to eat and drink. We knew that we would climb into the night, but we had our headlamps and spare batteries and we certainly felt strong enough to make it. We were both still able to concentrate, which was a good thing given that we had never used the fixed lines on this climb. Now, after our summit success, we had no allowance to make even a single mistake. When we left the summit I thought about the upcoming descent covering 3000 meters. I imagined every step: First I would have to get down the couloir safely, and then I could worry about the next step. I tried not to think about base camp, but concentrated on the moment, with a heightened awareness of every move. Losing one's balance can happen so quickly.

As forecast, the weather closed in. At the start of the traverse we hunkered down for almost an hour and waited for visibility to improve. The strong winds had already covered our tracks with snow, but when the clouds lifted for a moment we were able to traverse the slope unroped. We reached our last camp at 7350 meters, packed it up, and continued down. On this challenging terrain the descent took a long time. On the steepest sections we used our own rope for rappeling, but for the most part David and I downclimbed on the frontpoints of our crampons, sometimes facing the wall, sometimes facing downhill. At the beautiful camp at 6750 meters we took a long break, melted snow, drank a lot of water, and ate a little bit to gain strength for the remaining 2000 meters. Darkness fell when we set off again. From there the terrain was easier and we stopped only occasionally for a well-deserved rest, as fatigue was slowly getting the better of us. It was a beautiful starry night and not as cold as it was higher up. Having mastered the most difficult sections, we now had time to marvel at the sky and philosophize about the beauty of life. We were tired, but exuberantly happy.

At three o'clock in the morning we walked into base camp. Finally I could feel my body and mind relax. Now we had really made it. Janak made us some soup and a hot drink, and after I crawled into my sleeping bag at 5:00 a.m. for a long while I couldn't fall asleep. Only just starting to warm up, I realized how cold I must have been all day. Even though I was extremely tired, I felt quite energized by the events of the past few days. Tucked into my sleeping bag with my eyes closed, my mind was still somewhere up there.

On our way back to Kathmandu I began gradually to focus on my new goal. Ralf, David, and I wanted to go back to Lhotse, where we had turned back two years earlier. The plan was to meet Ralf somewhere in the Khumbu after his Makalu climb. David and I organized supplies and food in Kathmandu, flew to Lukla, and trekked to Namche Bazaar, where we waited for Ralf. He had put off his summit bid. First of all his climbing gear had arrived late at base camp due to a helicopter crash, and then birds had ransacked his deposit at Camp 2, where he had lost his tent and food. As if that were not enough, he had also contracted acute bronchitis, probably because he had been stranded at base camp without his warm down gear.

Ralf aimed to summit on May 11. After our phone call the night before, I felt worried; he had sounded hoarse and was coughing a lot. He said he would start at 2:00 a.m. and would call me once he was back at the high camp. David and I arrived in Namche Bazaar exactly on his summit day. My thoughts were with Ralf. I tried to imagine where he would be at every moment: at the bottom of the French Couloir, on the plateau, on the traverse to the false summit. . . . We had lunch in a small lodge, and when my watch said 12:15 p.m. I said to David, "He could be on the summit now." I expected him to phone me at around 7:00 p.m. at the latest.

Seven o'clock came and went, and still no word at 8:00 p.m. I was edgy. When he still had not called by 9:00 p.m., I tried to convince myself that there were more important things to do, such as melting snow and hydrating. Then it was past 10:00 p.m. Nothing. I got increasingly agitated. Maybe he had run out of batteries. Ralf didn't call the whole night. I lay awake in my room, beside myself with worry. For the first time I understood what Ralf must have gone through every time I went on expedition without him. Up until then we had either climbed together or I was on expedition and busy with my own plans. I knew that he was physically not in top form, and I tried desperately not to imagine the worst.

He didn't even send a text message during the night. When David saw me at breakfast, it only took a quick glance at me for him to notice.

"I guess I don't even have to ask whether you've heard from Ralf," he said.

I cringed. It couldn't be true—what had happened? I tried to call him again. Up until then his phone had been switched off, but this time it was ringing. It cracked and someone answered. I was very nervous: "Ralf, is that you?" It sounded as if somebody wanted to say something but was unable to utter a word.

I cried out anxiously, "Ralf, what's happening? Say something, please!" At that moment I imagined the worst. Maybe he was lying somewhere, seriously injured and unable to speak.

On the approach to the French Col you get a stunning view of Dhaulagiri and its ascent route.

I could hear someone pant on the other end of the line. It took me a while to realize that he must have been so weakened by his bronchitis that he had lost his voice. Reception was good and he was trying to talk to me, but I couldn't understand a word.

"Ralf, where are you? Are you okay?"

He attempted to make an affirmative sound. I figured out that I had to ask questions, which he could answer with yes or no. From the little I understood, I could make out that he was at the Makalu La at 7400 meters and had been to the summit.

"Ralf, please come down as fast as you can and be careful! And call me when you get to base camp. If you can't talk, just give the phone to the cook or anyone else I can talk to."

I phoned AMICAL alpin and Ralf's parents to tell them that everything was okay. In the evening I waited again for his call, but as before, he didn't ring. I was at my wit's end.

After another sleepless night, I received a text from Ralf's phone. My hands were shaking when I opened it. He apologized profusely. When he had reached base camp the cook had given him a glass of red wine, and after only a few sips the alcohol had completely wiped him out. He had gone to his tent and immediately fallen asleep. He was very sorry to have caused me such agony. I didn't feel angry, but was extremely happy and grateful that he was safely back at base camp.

When we met at the Ama Dablam Garden Lodge in Deboche a few days later, Ralf was still hoarse. I had just come out of the shower—I wanted to look good for him—when I heard the roaring noise of a helicopter. David and I ran down to the helipad. Ralf climbed out of the helicopter clad in down jacket, scarf, and hat, carrying his backpack and wearing a full beard. I flung my arms around his neck: an emotional reunion after all the tension on Dhaulagiri and the worry about Ralf. Even though I had sometimes wished he were on Dhaulagiri with me, it is a great asset in our relationship that we can let go of each other. We both follow our own plans and are confident that the other person will do the right thing and know when to turn back. And on top of that, meeting up afterward is always wonderful. Nevertheless, we have both been in situations where we were extremely lucky, and this is why we will probably always worry about each other.

After a few rest days we trekked to base camp. David and I spent one night at 6400 meters, as we thought that we might have lost some of our acclimatization. When we came back I was also coughing, but felt sure that this was the typical "Khumbu Cough," which is often contracted at high altitudes. It didn't even cross my mind that I could have picked up Ralf's bronchitis. My mind was more occupied with the news that our friend Gianni Goltz, who had reached the summit of Mount Everest without bottled oxygen on May 21, had died on the descent. And a day later we found out that our friend Iñaki was altitude sick on Annapurna I and was fighting for his life at a high camp on the east ridge. Our mood was subdued. How could this have happened? We prayed that Iñaki would pull through and get down as fast as possible.

Having learned from our experience in 2006, we planned to spend a night at 7800 meters to shorten the summit day. Even though Ralf had taken antibiotics and had recovered from his bronchitis, he told David and me that we should not worry about him if he went slower. We left base camp on May 24 and reached the last camp at noon on May 26. Ralf's condition had deteriorated again, and he coughed a lot during the night. The three of us left camp for our summit attempt at 3:00 a.m., but Ralf turned back after about 100 meters. His physical condition simply didn't allow him to continue.

David and I climbed to the bottom of the long couloir at 8150 meters. It was a very chilly morning and neither of us managed to get warm. We could only expect the sun to reach Lhotse's west face at around 10:00 a.m. David couldn't feel his toes, and his nose was showing the first signs of frostbite. After we had exchanged a few words we decided to go down. Other than the cold, which also started affecting my toes, there were a few other factors contributing to our decision. I couldn't stop thinking about Gianni and Iñaki, and I realized how badly I wanted to reach the top of Lhotse together with Ralf. It would be his fourteenth 8000-meter peak and most probably the last one we would do together. The reason David and I had waited for Ralf in the Khumbu was that I wanted very badly to reach the summit with him. And now I was here, 350 meters short of the summit, while Ralf was down at Camp 2 at 6400 meters. No, I wanted to be with him on his way to the summit of his last 8000-meter peak.

In the evening all three of us made it back to base camp. Ralf's condition had gotten worse during the descent through the treacherous Khumbu Icefall. He now had a temperature, and a doctor from the Philippines who was at base camp diagnosed him with the early stages of pneumonia. I was glad that David and I had abandoned our climb and supported Ralf on his descent. At the same time, I questioned our agreement that the one who wants to continue climbing should do so, as long as the other one is well. We had no idea that Ralf's illness would worsen. I didn't want to imagine what could have happened if he had descended on his own.

That night I crawled into my sleeping bag with mixed feelings; I must have been anticipating the bad news we received the following morning. The Swiss climbers Ueli Steck and Simon Anthamatten, who were attempting the south face of Annapurna I, had tried to rescue Iñaki, but unfortunately their help came too late and Iñaki died of pulmonary edema at noon on May 23. This was truly beyond belief. It was the second time in two days that we had lost a good friend in the mountains. Ralf and I just didn't want to believe it. Once again it proved that even the most experienced high-altitude mountaineers are not immune to altitude sickness.

On our way back to Lukla, the three of us sounded like an orchestra. Ralf was hacking away, David had a very dry and painful chest cough, and my wheezing was getting worse. Strangely enough, I felt worse the lower down we got. In Namche Bazaar I developed a fever, and when we got home my doctor diagnosed me with bacterial pneumonia in both lungs. I must have caught it from Ralf. Back home, I was barely able to walk up and down the stairs. Could I really go on another expedition in this state? I had planned a second attempt of K2 for the summer of 2008, but I would have had to be in top form for that undertaking. As hard as it was to admit it, I was simply not. With a heavy heart I cancelled my K2 expedition.

Maybe it was a blessing in disguise. Had I gone to K2 I probably would have taken advantage of the first weather window around August 1. On that and the following day eleven climbers lost their lives as a result of a huge ice avalanche that came down from the hanging glacier just above the Bottleneck. Among them was the Norwegian climber Rolf Bae, whom we had met during our first attempt of Shisha Pangma's south face in 2004. He was hit by the ice avalanche and tumbled down right in front of his wife, Cecilie Skog. Unfortunately, there is no way around the hanging seracs, and mountaineers have to climb right underneath. It is an objective danger that could happen to everyone. This horrible accident was not caused by the inexperience of the climbers as reported by many media outlets. Being quick is the only way to mitigate this hazard.

Turning back on Lhotse in May 2008 didn't seem like a failure at all. In my view, failing means not coming back from the mountain. When I abandon a climb because I have the feeling that it is too risky, as I did on Lhotse in 2006 or on K2 in 2007, it is always the best possible decision at that moment. I never regret it afterward or wonder whether my decision was the right one. I am still very ambitious; otherwise, I would not return to a mountain two or three times. If an ascent doesn't work out, I don't despair but I do give it another go. I don't want to conquer a mountain; I want to climb it humbly and gratefully. In the high mountains I have learned that I can only reach my goals with patience, restraint, and enthusiasm. Even though I am tiny and fragile compared to the majestic peaks, they still allow me to come back feeling incredibly strong and happy.

In May 2009, I finally succeeded in summiting Lhotse—together with Ralf, just as I had longed for. Sharing the moment of him reaching his fourteenth 8000-meter peak was a very deep and indescribable feeling. *(Photo by Ralf Dujmovits)*

CHAPTER 15
PERSEVERANCE

Nestled in a magnificent spot between Mount Everest and Nuptse, Lhotse, at 8516 meters, remained our main objective. Once you leave the southern route, which teems with people trudging up toward the summit of Mount Everest—as far up as 7600 meters the routes are the same—the crowd thins out significantly. For our expedition in 2009, though, we changed our strategy. In both 2006 and 2008 we climbed and acclimatized on another 8000-meter peak before attempting the world's fourth-highest mountain. This time around, we wanted to fully concentrate on Lhotse. With Lhotse being high on their wish list, our friends David Göttler and Hirotaka Takeuchi came with us.

We acclimatized on Island Peak, which at 6189 meters is a popular, technically easy trekking peak in Nepal. I had never climbed it before. It was well worth it: the views of Makalu, Ama Dablam, Lhotse, and Nuptse were breathtaking. We had initially planned to climb the north ridge, but it was so dry and prone to rock- and icefall that we chose to stick to the normal route. After spending one night 150 meters below the summit we climbed to the top the following day and then stayed another night about 30 meters short of the summit. Spending two nights right opposite the gigantic Lhotse south face was very impressive, and definitely increased my excitement about our upcoming expedition. There weren't many people on the mountain, and I enjoyed the relative solitude, which I knew would be gone once we reached the base camp shared by both Mount Everest and Lhotse climbers.

Once we were back in the small settlement of Chukhung, which lies at an altitude of 4750 meters, we packed up and left for base camp. We opted to go via the Kongma La, a pass of 5500 meters, which took us past picturesque turquoise-colored lakes and offered magnificent views of the surrounding giants. We also got a good glimpse of our intended route on Lhotse's west face. After one night in Lobuje we finally reached base camp on April 23, and were surprised to find it a lot less busy than expected. Even though we were right in the middle of climbing season, there were significantly fewer trekkers and mountaineers than in the previous year, which we thought could be attributed to the global financial crisis. The tents were not pitched as closely together, the mood was friendly, and I felt positive and motivated. It snowed during our first few days at base camp, but the strong winds higher up immediately blew it off and conditions were looking pretty promising.

Another reason for acclimatizing on Island Peak was to minimize our trips through the treacherous Khumbu Icefall. We saw several ice avalanches come down the west shoulder of Everest, which towers above the left-hand side of the icefall. Nevertheless, we still had to face it once before our summit bid to spend a few nights higher up. We climbed through the icefall in the coolness of the night, which was safer than day, pitched our two small tents at Camp 1, and continued up to Camp 2 through the Western Cwm, the glacial valley between Everest, Lhotse, and Nuptse. We stayed two nights at 6400 meters, where we enjoyed the glorious surroundings and spent our days chatting in stunning weather. Ralf told us about his adventures on Nuptse's northwest ridge in 1989, and we analyzed our previous attempts on Lhotse, considering what we could do better this time.

On April 29 we climbed up the Lhotse Face, which was partly covered in frozen sugar snow and partly in blue ice, and spent another two very cold nights at 7300 meters. From there we had a glorious view of Pumori and could see as far as the south face of Cho Oyu, where Denis Urubko was attempting a new route; our thoughts were with him. His first ascent of this particular route turned out to be successful, and we later congratulated him on his fourteenth 8000-meter peak. I wondered whether I would also get to congratulate Ralf on the same achievement in a few days' time. I really hoped so!

The four of us rappeled down the Lhotse Face and returned to base camp, where we rested, ate and drank a lot, and got our gear ready for our summit bid. We were well acclimatized, but our intention to go for the summit as soon as possible was thwarted by the weather, as so often happens in the mountains. Strong winds and snowfall tried our patience for the next sixteen days. We kept checking with our weather expert in Innsbruck, Charly Gabl. Every time we talked with him we hoped for a better forecast, but the storms remained too fierce. Up high, wind speeds were reaching around 35 miles per hour, and with temperatures dropping to –31 to –36 degrees Fahrenheit, it was simply too cold. In those freezing conditions, climbing a relatively high 8000-meter peak without supplemental oxygen was impossible, given that the body loses too much heat through heavy, rapid breathing. In my experience, –22 degrees Fahrenheit and wind speeds of 25 miles per hour is the absolute maximum a body can sustain for a reasonable amount of time without bottled oxygen. We also closely watched the avalanche situation on the Lhotse Face, which was rather dangerous after the constant snowfall over the previous few days.

In order to pass the time and exercise at least a bit, I walked down to Gorak Shep and climbed up to Pumori's Camp 1, which was an easy climb even in bad weather. I also hiked up to Kala Patar, a 5675-meter peak just outside Gorak Shep, enjoying the breathtaking view of the surrounding mountains. We also visited our friends at base camp, read a lot, and listened to music. But even though we tried hard to divert our minds, after about two weeks of this we got quite edgy.

Finally, Charly forecast better weather and warmer temperatures for May 21: "only" –16 degrees Fahrenheit at 7800 meters, and a maximum wind speed of 25 miles per hour on the summit. This was definitely our day! We were very excited—would our third attempt of Lhotse be successful? Fortunately, the strong winds had blown off the fresh snow, which would save our having to break trail. The conditions were perfect. As we had done previously, David, Hiro, Ralf, and I spent one night at 6400 meters and another at 7300 meters. While climbers were queuing at the fixed lines on the turn-off to Everest just above the Yellow Band, we were almost alone. We dug out a platform for our two tents at 7850 meters, the camp from which we intended to climb directly to the summit. But we didn't want to leave before 5:00 a.m. as the sun only reached the Lhotse Couloir in the late mornings, and we knew that we would certainly need the warmth of the sun higher up.

As Ralf and I were getting ready in our tent, I was bursting with excitement. I so wanted Ralf to reach his fourteenth 8000-meter peak, and his chances actually looked good. Excitedly I checked to see that my crampons were fixed properly, I had packed my spare gloves and sunglasses, and I had everything I needed in the breast pockets of my down suit: camera battery on the right side, water bottle and dried fruit—five dried figs and a few apples—on the left side. I then followed Ralf into the night.

Shortly after we set off, the sun's first rays touched the surrounding mountaintops and I could sense the positive energy of the breaking day. I felt invigorated and happy that we were making such good progress. We started off on frozen sugar snow, but we were surprised to find a lot of rock higher up. In 2006, the couloir had been one icy gully with a bit of snow, but now the ice had vanished and the couloir was now very prone to rockfall during the day—which was why we had to move quickly. When we reached the point where first Ralf and then I had turned back, I realized how close we had been to the summit.

The last 80 vertical meters led over broken rock to the highest point of Lhotse. When I noticed that Ralf was behind me, I stopped in a protected spot about 10 meters below the summit and waited for him. When he finally reached me I was shivering with cold, but I had set my mind on being with him when he took his final steps to his last 8000-meter summit. It was a wonderful moment when we reached it at around 11:00 a.m. Finally, our long-cherished dream had come true: Ralf had reached his life's goal. We were so moved and exhausted that neither of us could say a word. Deep down inside, Ralf was overjoyed; tears were running down his cheeks, while I felt extremely privileged to be able to share this moment with him. Together we marveled at the surrounding giants, such as Makalu and Everest, but we also took a good look at the corniced ridge between Lhotse and Nuptse, which seemed impossible to climb.

In the meantime I had gotten so cold that I wanted to go down even though David and Hiro had not arrived yet. We met them on our descent and waited in our last camp for their return. From there we all climbed down to 7200 meters in semi-darkness. When we reached base camp the following day we all felt drained, but extremely happy.

Ralf, unusually relaxed, didn't feel like packing up immediately and leaving. I don't think I had ever seen him so laid-back. He sat at his laptop all day reading the emails he had received for finishing all fourteen 8000-meter peaks.

"Oh, this is so sweet. Gerlinde. You have to look at this. Can you read this email. . . ."

He did that for hours on end; I simply didn't recognize my husband. We also spent a lot of time hosting the friends who popped in to congratulate him. For the first time it was me who urged that we leave: "Ralf, I think we should slowly start to pack up!"

We had planned to be back in Kathmandu in time to join the opening ceremony of the Thulo Sirubari School, which we financially support together with the charity Nepalhilfe Beilngries. In the end, the only remaining tent was the mess tent where Ralf, still totally engrossed in his email, sat on the last remaining chair.

But finally we left. In Thulo Sirubari, we were met by a brass band that accompanied us on our walk to the school, which was a bit farther up the hill. Around five hundred pupils who could now enjoy a better education welcomed us with bouquets and flower garlands. The opening ceremony was very meaningful for everyone involved, and Ralf and I felt like we had reached yet another summit, albeit a more social one. After this moving event we took a plane home, where I spent only ten days before setting off again—once more for Islamabad.

I would trek to K2 with David Göttler, while Ralf would come a little later leading a team of Austrian television reporters to base camp. His plan was to stay at base camp and not climb the mountain, as he had already reached the summit of K2 in 1994. The weather was good enough for David and me to take a plane from Islamabad to Skardu, where we caught a jeep for the adventurous and bumpy road to Askole. I had been on this road many times and felt sure that this was actually the most dangerous part of the expedition. Little did I know how true this would soon prove to be. When we reached a place where the road narrowed on a slight rise, our driver stopped to have a closer look at a waterfall that had swamped the road with a lot of mud and rocks. Before he left the jeep, he pulled the handbrake and placed a huge rock behind the rear wheel to stop it from rolling backward. Our liaison officer Fazeel also got out of the car, closely followed by David, who wanted to film the raging water on the road. I stayed in the car and waited, but as they took such a long time to come back I also got out to take a few photos.

Once I stepped out, the car started to move. Rolling backwards, it somersaulted twice and tumbled down a precipice of about fifty feet. Slack-jawed and with shaking knees, David and I gazed at the car, unable to fathom what had just happened. We immediately followed the driver, who was clambering down the slope to the car.

I yelled, "David, can you switch off the engine? It's leaking petrol."

"I'll try, but the key is broken," David answered.

The Pakistanis, who were in the car behind ours, rushed down to our jeep and switched off the engine. Now it was safe to get our daypacks out of the wreck as well as David's hardcover suitcase, which had been catapulted between some big boulders. Fortunately, our climbing gear was in a separate vehicle. I was lucky: Even my laptop, which was behind the back seat, had survived the fall. But the jeep was a complete write-off, beyond repair.

We were all pretty shaken after the accident. I couldn't stop thinking about what would have happened if I had stayed in the car. The Pakistanis patted me on the shoulder, saying, "You are lucky; you are very lucky!" God, were they right! And fortunately, luck stayed on our side! Across the waterfall, the owner of the agency was also stuck, and in his extreme relief that nothing had happened to us he gave us a ride to Askole. The Pakistanis were convinced that Allah must have saved us. Whatever had, it made me lie awake for a long time that night, wondering whether I would have been quick enough to jump out of the side window of the plummeting jeep. David and I talked about it for quite some time until we finally agreed that after surviving this accident, nothing could go wrong on our expedition.

From Askole it took us about a week to reach base camp with our twenty-five Balti porters in tow. After we had paid them off they formed a big circle around us, wishing us good luck on K2. In their broken English they asked us to show them the route, but they clearly could not understand why anyone would want to go up there.

We arrived on June 22, which was still early in the season. There were only two other teams at base camp, an American expedition and a pair of extreme skiers, a Swede called Fredrik Ericsson, and an Italian named Michele Fait. They intended to climb the Cesen Route and do a ski descent. When we reached base camp, they had already established their Camp 2 and were spending a night up there to acclimatize. The following morning they climbed up a little higher and started to ski down. David and I watched them through our binoculars. The slope was very steep, often only allowing them to slide down horizontally. When they had mastered the steepest part, with a slope of about 45 degrees, we breathed a sigh of relief. But suddenly we saw one of them gain too much speed after a turn.

"David, he is falling!" I shouted.

Unable to break his fall, he plunged all the way down, about 600 meters to the bottom of the face. David and I wanted to sprint across to him, but we ran out of steam very soon as we were not properly acclimatized. We saw the other skier, who turned out to be Fredrik Ericsson, swiftly ski down to his mate and drag him to the foot of the wall. Michele was no longer alive. We covered him with snow and left his body at the bottom of the face until it was later recovered. Fredrik and I walked back to base camp together, talking about friendship, dreams, living life to the fullest, and death. No matter how sad the situation was, we had to decide what to do next. As I speak Italian, I took over the difficult task of ringing Michele's father and telling him about the accident. We stayed in touch until it was decided that Michele's body would be transported to Italy. When the helicopter arrived a few days later, Fredrik also jumped in and left.

With this difficult start to our expedition, we postponed our first acclimatization rotation by a few days in order to come to terms with the tragic accident. We never really managed to get over Michele's death during the course of the expedition. On our first acclimatization rotation, which we did in bad weather with little visibility and heavy snowfall, we spent one night at 5850 meters and two nights at 6350 meters, in exactly the same spot where we had camped in 2007. Then a weather front moved in, forcing us to stay at base camp. During that time my friend Cristina Castagna occasionally popped in for a visit. She was climbing Broad Peak, and we had bumped into each other on the walk in. Ralf had already started trekking toward base camp, and every day I grew more excited to see him. Before his arrival, though, David and I went on our second acclimatization rotation to get ready for the summit. We had to break trail through fresh knee-deep snow and spent an impressive night on a bivouac ledge at 7100 meters. Our tent was snug against the rock wall like an eagle's nest, from which we had a clear view of base camp. It was great that we were the only people on the Cesen Route, and we felt very content when we climbed back down to base camp. With our pre-acclimatization from our Lhotse climb we felt well prepared for our summit attempt.

But first we had to wait for a weather window. On July 11, Ralf, Franz Fuchs, the producer, and Andreas Gradl, the cameraman for Austrian television ORF, all arrived at base camp. We spent the following days talking and working on the documentary about our K2 attempt.

But a week later, bad news overshadowed our happiness at base camp: Cristina had fallen to her death during her summit attempt on Broad Peak. We had been so close during the previous weeks, and now she was dead at the young age of 31. She was such a positive, cheerful woman and a fellow nurse. My first reaction was to pull the plug on our expedition, but the more I thought about it, the more I saw that it had not been an evil force of nature that had caused both accidents, but the climbers' own actions. Canceling our expedition would have brought neither Cristina nor Michele back to life.

After about ten days the snow stopped. At one point a big avalanche thundered down the Cesen Route. David and I set out for our summit attempt on July 22. Fabrizio Zangrilli, an American climber who had pitched his high camp independently, accompanied us to just below the shoulder. David and I also put our tent there, as the spot was better protected than the shoulder, which was very exposed to the wind. Charly Gabl had forecast perfect weather for July 26, and the gorgeous sunset boded well for a good day. We felt very excited as we crawled into our sleeping bags that night.

It was freezing cold but the sky was blanketed with stars when we set out between 3:00 and 3:30 a.m. to tackle the mixed terrain. When we reached the shoulder, we could see huge chunks of ice that must have been left from the previous year's ice avalanche, which killed 11 people. Mindful of that terrible accident, on our trek to Concordia David and I had already checked out the conditions of the icefall. From that distance we could see a V-shaped gash in the ice that looked as if a huge ice block was just about to crash down. At base camp we had analyzed how we would climb this dangerous passage. Studying photos, we agreed that we would climb along the rocky wall on the left to circumvent the narrow part of the Bottleneck.

Day was breaking around us, and we could see all the way into China in the dawn light. The valleys were covered in clouds and the mountaintops were glowing violet-yellow, making me stop and look around in amazement. This exceptional light changed my inner perception; I felt completely detached from everything, as if I were at a different level of awareness. At that very moment I was so close to realizing my big dream, and all signs pointed to a successful summit.

As agreed, David and I traversed toward the left below the Bottleneck. Unfortunately, the snow was pretty deep, and breaking trail slowed us down considerably. We also roped up in the steep section, from which we could clearly see the gash of about 25 meters in the ice; the broken piece was tilting dangerously toward us. It was only a matter of time before the ice block would detach and come thundering down. Circumventing the block was definitely the right thing to do.

The rock turned out to be very crumbly. Placing an ice ax was tricky, and it was almost impossible to put in protection. We had not brought any nuts

TOP: The gigantic pyramid of K2— a majestic view of a daunting mountain *(Photo by Ralf Dujmovits)* BOTTOM: After I had to turn back twice at 8300 meters in 2009, I went back to K2 a year later. Ralf and I attempted the Cesen Route, where we spent two nights at an exposed camp. *(Photo by Ralf Dujmovits)*

or bolts, and setting up a belay point proved difficult. We had expected to be climbing in low grade V, but we found ourselves in precarious broken terrain in high grade V. Knowing that our belay points were weak, and that under no circumstances were we allowed to make a mistake, was mentally exhausting. We were holding our breath. But we were obviously not the first climbers who had come up with this strategy of traversing to the left to avoid the narrow part of the Bottleneck: On a little ledge, I saw a tattered yellow tent and one of the simple carrying frames the porters had used in the old days. At the time, I was so focused on my own climbing that I had no inclination to look more closely at this old equipment, but I guess it must have been from Fritz Wiessner's 1939 expedition.

We were aware that our progress was dangerously slow. We tried to reach better rock by traversing to the right and climbing another two pitches. Once we reached the top of the second pitch we faced another rock wall, which David thought might be about grade VI. We knew that it would be impossible to climb such a high grade with no belay points at this altitude—we were above 8000 meters. It was probably more dangerous than climbing the Bottleneck. We had no choice but to turn back.

Anyone who has ever wasted a perfect day by misjudging the situation will understand what this decision, which we made at 2:00 p.m. in perfect conditions, meant for David and me. We now knew that the rocks on the right side were no alternative. Subdued, we traversed further to the right, rappeled one pitch on an ice screw, and descended to base camp. On the way down I looked for other alternatives, in case we decided to go for another summit attempt. But at the end of the day, there were only two options: either climb the Bottleneck or abandon the climb.

Around 11:00 p.m. Ralf picked us up from the bottom of route. As he was due to go back with the film team the following morning, we had a very intense discussion. Ralf, who had observed our every step on the mountain, had been extremely worried when he saw us crossing the precarious rocky ground. He thought that it would have been safer to go through the Bottleneck as quickly as possible. His disappointment about my not going back with him after summiting and my regret at disappointing him didn't make our farewell easy.

Two days after Ralf left, David did too; he was not interested in another summit attempt. Fortunately, I soon got over my gloomy mood. The thought of trying again was actually quite motivating. I didn't get involved in the discussions of the other teams who were on the Abruzzi Spur, and only arranged with my Kazakh friends to meet me on the shoulder, take turns at breaking trail, and get through the treacherous Bottleneck as quickly as possible.

I climbed up the Cesen Route for a third time, but now it was different: I was alone. Climbing such a route on this mountain on my own, left to my own devices without consulting other climbers, was a very special feeling. At 7900 meters I phoned Ralf, who had already arrived in Islamabad. Hearing his familiar voice and telling him where and how I was really helped.

When I reached the shoulder I was engulfed by thick fog. I felt incredibly lonely—neither sad nor scared, simply alone. Thinking about all the crevasses higher up, I sat down and waited. Continuing up in zero visibility would have been too dangerous; I had to wait for the weather to clear. I hoped that the Kazakhs would be there too, somewhere in the fog. Deep down I felt the urge to see and hear other people, but the thick fog seemed to swallow every sound. There was no sign of life. After half an hour, the weather finally cleared, and I could see that the Kazakhs' tent was only about 15 meters away. Maxut, Vassiliy, and Sergey had arrived two hours before me, and we were all very happy to see each other!

Shortly after we left our camp on the shoulder we realized that the wind had blown a lot of snow onto the slopes, so breaking trail would be hard work. We fixed the icy sections on the Bottleneck as well as the immediate traverse on the left. On less steep terrain the snow was hip-deep. Trying to get through took digging. I couldn't get my leg up high enough to take a step. We had to dig deep just to move a single step, and it took about an hour to cover a few feet. Up until the very last minute before we turned back I lived in the hope that we could make it. But it became clear that once again, K2 was denying me its summit. We were running out of time. The snow was getting deeper until in the end it reached up to my belly. Apart from me, only one Kazakh and an American helped break trail, and we didn't make much progress.

This was the second time that year on K2 that I had had to abandon an attempt in perfect weather. We were only about 300 meters below the summit on pretty easy ground. I had never before gotten so far on K2. We have to accept nature for what it is—that's actually what makes high-altitude mountaineering so fascinating. I decided against the Kazakhs' suggestion that we spend another night on the shoulder and try for the summit again the next day. My body felt tired after Lhotse and two attempts on K2. I didn't want to run the risk of getting thrombosis, which happens easily at high altitude as the blood gets thicker. And so I went back down to base camp the same day.

The expedition was over. Though I went home without the summit, I had learned a lot. During those two months I had experienced many beautiful as well as difficult moments. It was not only the two fatal accidents, but also the difficult interpersonal relationships with other expeditions; the selfishness of some mountaineers at the expense of others; and the envy I experienced. The exceptional situation of an expedition doesn't make it easier to deal with such feelings. I was looking forward to going home to normal life; the mountain would still be there.

After a busy but also very enriching period of giving presentations, Ralf and I went to Sicily, where we enjoyed unspoiled rock and Italian cuisine for two weeks before winter set in. Once the ski mountaineering season had started, we began to prepare our expedition for the following spring. Our goal for spring 2010 was clear: Mount Everest—the only 8000-meter peak in the western Himalaya I had not yet climbed, and the only 8000-meter peak Ralf had climbed using supplemental oxygen. His dream was to reach the summit without "the bottle." I was still focused on the north face, wanting very badly to try it again even though we knew that the conditions on the face would be better in the post-monsoon season than in the spring, when the gullies are often covered in blue ice. But fall was out of the question—we had already planned to go back to the Karakorum in summer.

We made a conscious decision to climb as a team of two. On the north face, it would be difficult enough to find good bivouac spots for our small tent. Just as in 2005, we set up our base camp on the remote central

Rongbuk Glacier. Once our three yak herders and their seven yaks had left, our cook Sitaram, Ralf, and I were more or less alone. Only blue sheep and snow grouse walked leisurely through our camp; we could see their tracks in the snow in the mornings. Sitaram fed the snow grouse, and over time they got pretty chubby and cheeky, too. They even began to stick their heads into our mess tent, wondering whether there was any food left over for them.

From our Advanced Base Camp (ABC) at 5550 meters we established our path to the bottom of the face. In order not to get lost in poor visibility, we built around 150 cairns. They proved to be crucial, especially when we started our second attempt on the face after three weeks of bad weather. The first time we climbed on the face was not only to acclimatize—we spent two nights at the bottom of the face at 6200 meters—but also to do route reconnaissance and look at the current conditions. The bergschrund was definitely the biggest obstacle. After climbing one pitch we constructed a V-thread and rappeled down. We had seen enough, and it was not particularly encouraging. There was enough blue ice on the face that we would have to frontpoint most of the route, put each other on belay, and dig out platforms with our ice axes, all of which would take us far too long to do. Retreating would be almost impossible. We both knew that if the conditions didn't change, attempting the north face would be hopeless.

We had to adopt a wait-and-see approach. We were still not well enough acclimatized and needed to sleep high, so we climbed up to the North Col via the Odell Route, which we had done before, and spent two nights well above the col at about 7650 meters. After six days on the mountain we went back to our ABC, but instead of tackling the north face we had to sit out more bad weather—for another twenty-one days! Even though we kept busy, doing the twenty-minute walk down the glacier to collect water, reading, and listening to music, we both experienced serious lows. Fortunately they occurred on different days, so we were able to cheer each other up. Our power supply was also suffering, as our solar panels could not get enough sun in this bad weather. It was already mid-May, and we were running out of time.

When we climbed back to the north face on May 16, we were hoping that the blue ice would be covered by fresh snow. It was. The bergschrund was now filled with broken seracs and blanketed in snow, and getting across was no longer a problem. There was also compressed snow on top of the ice on the face. The beginning of the slope was about 70 degrees. We climbed up slowly, using two ice axes, until we reached the Japanese Couloir where the slope flattened out to about 55 degrees. In the couloir it was obvious that the fresh snow had not really bonded with the ice. The Hornbein Couloir right above the Japanese Couloir was full of fresh snow, which came down in loose powder-snow avalanches. The couloir was constantly hit by the spindrift and we were in the direct line of fire. The snow was quite powerful and once almost pushed Ralf off the wall. In these conditions, we couldn't possibly continue on that route.

After climbing seven pitches, we retreated and rappeled off V-threads. Back at base camp, Ralf told me explicitly that climbing the north face in these conditions was out of the question for him as it was too time-consuming and dangerous. I felt reluctant to abandon the north face project, as I had completely identified with it. I was still hoping for the spindrift to stop once the winds abated. But when Charly's forecast gave us only one single day of good weather to climb without supplemental oxygen, I came to the same conclusion: The risk of getting stuck on the face would be too high.

We had no choice then but to follow the Odell Route up to the North Col and then take the normal route to the summit. The forecast for the coming days didn't look good: The winds were to remain fierce. Finally, Charly forecast less wind for May 23 and 24. We immediately set out for the North Col even though the weather was still stormy. We decided to stay there for two nights; the weather forecast predicted snowfall, but with higher temperatures, May 24 looked better as a possible summit day. The following day we climbed up to Camp 2 at 7650 meters, where Ralf spent a pretty bad night; he was coughing and hardly got any sleep. The next night at Camp 3—at 8300 meters, the starting point for the summit—he still couldn't sleep or recover. When we were having breakfast at 2:00 a.m., he was too tired to hold his cup. I looked at him, worried.

"Gerlinde, I can't go," he said. "I am too tired. You'll have to go without me."

He was right. It would be disastrous if he nodded off on the summit ridge. It was too dangerous for him to go on, and even though I knew it I was full of questions. Should I really go without Ralf? He so wanted to climb Everest without supplemental oxygen! Was he really just tired, or was he struggling with the altitude? Could I leave him on his own?

Ralf calmed me down, saying that he was simply too tired and that I should go for it. He would sleep a bit longer and then descend to the North Col and wait for me there. And so it happened that I set off on my own just before 4:00 a.m. It was still snowing heavily. At that point, I had no idea that there were other climbers in front of me, the first group having left at 9:00 p.m. In the light of my headlamp it was hard to make out their tracks, which were already covered by the fresh snow. It continued to snow, but the temperature of about –11 degrees Fahrenheit was quite comfortable. Though the sun began to rise when I reached the northeast ridge, visibility didn't improve much. But with the fixed rope it was almost impossible to get lost on the partially rocky ridge.

At the First Step, a 30-meter high rock wall, I met the Italian climbers Abele Blanc and Marco Camandona. Just above the Second Step, which would be a lot more difficult without the ladder installed by the Chinese, I bumped into Michele Enzio and Silvio Mondinelli. I had known Silvio for a long time, and we continued up together. At this point the first summiters were already on their way down, but thanks to the bad weather the route was not very busy, which meant we could easily give way to each other without getting caught in traffic jams. After a relatively flat section on the ridge we reached the Third Step. At 15 to 20 meters, it's shorter and technically easier than the other two steps, but it still takes both hands to climb it, which is very tiring at an altitude of 8650 meters.

Even though the summit no longer seemed far, it still took me another two hours before I finally put my foot on the highest point on Earth. At 12:30 p.m. I stood on the summit of Mount Everest with four Italian climbers. It was just the five of us; nobody had come up from the south side.

It was completely silent. Pure white snowflakes were softly spiraling down on us. A blanket of fog covered us, and visibility was down to about 20 meters. There was a light breeze in the air. It was a moment I cannot describe with words and I would have so loved to share it with Ralf. I didn't expect to feel so uplifted just by reaching the summit of Everest; my dream had always been to climb the north face, and not to the summit itself. I looked toward the top end of the north face but couldn't see much. Good thing we didn't do it! Our situation would have been epic in these weather conditions.

I thought about all the people who were close to me, and thanked them in silence: Ralf, my family and friends, everyone who had kept their fingers crossed for me, Mother Goddess of the World, and creation. Even though I felt good, I wanted to know how clearly I was thinking at 8848 meters. I gave myself three mathematical problems. I multiplied eight by seven, and then two- and three-digit numbers, and was actually happy with the outcome—though nobody checked it. But while my mind seemed clear, I definitely felt the altitude affecting my body. I was breathing heavily and my pulse was racing. My lungs and heart were working at high speed as I had never felt before.

I was happy not to be completely on my own, that I could share this wonderful moment with four friends. Despite our puffy down suits we hugged each other, took each other's pictures, and agreed to stay together on the descent. I dug around in the snow for a while and chose two rocks from the summit of Everest, one of which Ralf later had made into a beautiful pendant for me as a present. When we climbed down the Third Step it was still snowing, but when we reached the Second Step the storm had broken through the cloud cover, and suddenly the breathtaking view I had been so longing to see opened up before my eyes.

We could also see toward Camp 3, and I was surprised to spot our tent there. Did Ralf leave it there for me to warm up on my way down? I was very cold, probably because of the storm. It was 3:30 p.m., and I had been going for almost twelve hours; I was exhausted and my legs were shaky. When I was about 30 meters away from the tent, I saw Ralf walking toward me. He had waited the whole day at this altitude to welcome me, give me a hot drink, and celebrate my summit success with me. Sharing this intense moment with him, even though he had not been there all the way, made me happier than anything else.

I crawled into the tent to rest but my heavy breathing made it difficult. I was still panting, and didn't stop until we reached ABC of the normal route in the middle of the night. The effects of Mount Everest's extreme high altitude were setting in; on my way to the summit, the air felt even thinner at 8700 meters than I had ever experienced on other 8000-meter peaks. When I woke up the following day, my face and fingers were swollen and my whole body felt tense. I felt dehydrated and worn out. I had never been so exhausted after climbing an 8000-meter peak. I think climbing

On May 24, 2010, I reached the summit of Mount Everest. I held the flag of *wir sind eins*, an aid organization I have supported for many years. Even though my dream of climbing via the north face had not come true, it was an incredibly exhilarating moment. *(Photo by Silvio Mondinelli)*

Everest without supplemental oxygen is the absolute limit a human body can reach.

From the ABC of the normal route, it was still an eight-hour walk to our ABC below the north face. We arrived in the dark, and I could already hear the yak bells from afar. I asked Ralf whether he could hear the same thing; I was not sure whether I was imagining it, but he too could make out the tinkling of the bells. The yak herders and their animals had arrived two days too early! And so we spent half the night packing to go down to Chinese Base Camp the following day. Forty-eight hours after standing on the top of Everest, I was physically down from the mountain, but mentally I was still somewhere up there. It was all happening far too fast for me.

I started feeling euphoric about my summit success when we were on our way back to Kathmandu, and then again at home once I had regained my strength. We postponed our flight to Islamabad—we were getting ready for another attempt of K2—by one week to give me more time to digest the events of the past few weeks. On my trek to K2 base camp, I finally allowed myself to focus on my new goal. What was I to expect? I could already tell from our campsite at Concordia that the upper part of the Bottleneck didn't look as daunting as it had in 2009; the big serac David and I had been so worried about had come down. I looked across to Broad Peak and thought about Cristina. I though about the many intense and enriching conversations and all the fun we had had together. I deeply hoped that we and all the other mountaineers would be spared any accidents this year.

As we had on Everest, Ralf and I climbed in our small team of two. After the experience in 2009, Ralf didn't want to worry about me at home or at base camp. Another reason he decided to accompany me was that he had become an enthusiastic filmmaker, and he wanted to make videos of our expeditions. At base camp we had found a nice spot with comfortable rocks to sit on, and we often had visitors join us there. Compared to the previous year, the mood was friendlier, which I attributed to the fact that 2010 saw quite a lot of women at K2 base camp.

For our acclimatization we spent two nights at 6300 meters and two nights at 7100 meters on the Cesen Route and felt great. We were confident that in combination with our acclimatization from Everest, we were in top form. The Swede Fredrik Ericsson, whom we had met the previous year, was also back with his teammate Trey Cook to realize his dream of doing a ski descent on K2. They joined us on our first acclimatization climb.

On July 23, a huge avalanche thundered down the entry couloir on the Cesen Route, which meant that the path was clear for our first summit attempt. On July 26, six people, namely Fredrik, Trey, Fabrizio Zangrilli, the Polish climber Kinga Baranowska, as well as Ralf and I, reached the last bivouac just underneath the shoulder. We arrived there pretty late and were not sure whether we would have enough time to rest sufficiently for a summit push. But the weather turned during the night and then we had no choice but to descend. While we climbed down, Fredrik put on his skis and set off. The slope was very steep and I didn't even dare look at him, as it brought back the memories of his friend Michele's fatal accident the year before.

After a few rest days, we set out again on August 3. We made better progress than we had before; there was less drift snow. But we were faced with a new problem. Due to the relatively warm weather there was a lot of rockfall lower down the face. At our second bivouac at 7200 meters, rocks were literally plummeting down onto our tents. One rock hit the tent of the two Poles, Tamara Stys and Darek Zaluski. It went straight through the tent wall, continued behind Darek through his sleeping mat, and finally made its way through the tent floor. Ralf and I wore our helmets inside the tent, and I didn't want to think about what would happen if such a rock came flying down onto our tent. To be on the safe side, I even slept in my helmet!

The following day, when we continued up toward the camp underneath the shoulder, Ralf decided to turn back. He deemed the rockfall too dangerous. The rock, which is usually kept in place by permafrost, was so loose that it was almost impossible not to kick any debris down, putting other climbers at risk. On top of that, rocks were tumbling down from above. Ralf was no longer willing to take the risk, even though he would also be faced with rockfall on the descent. Having already stood on the summit of K2, he was less motivated.

Fredrik, Trey, Fabrizio, Kinga, and I reached the shoulder in the afternoon. Darek and Tamara came up a bit later, and another Pole and a Russian arrived in the evening. The skies were completely clear and we could see for miles, which definitely boded for good weather the following day.

According to Charly's forecast, it would be windy during the first part of the night. Fredrik, Trey, and I started our summit bid at 1:00 a.m. Trey turned back after a short while. Like the others who had stayed at camp, he didn't trust the weather, and his fingers were just too cold. He had to be careful, as he had gotten frostnip a few weeks earlier. Just as Charly had forecast, the wind abated after a while and the cloud cover on top of K2 started to lift, leaving only a bit of haze around the Bottleneck. Ralf told me over the radio that apart from the summit, the skies were clear all around. I passed this information on to Fredrik.

"Today is our day," he responded. I agreed, and we smiled at each other. This time the snow was only calf-deep, which was rather pleasant compared to the previous times when I had had to break trail through hip-deep snow. Not only did we have perfect conditions, we also worked well together. After about 50 meters, the person in front would step aside and let the other one take over for the next 50 meters. At about 7:00 a.m., we reached the Bottleneck. Its gradient was about 70 degrees, with one section reaching 75 degrees. On this mixed ground we wanted to put each other on belay. I took my 50-meter rope out of my pack and gave it to Fredrik; it was his turn to lead. His skis were strapped to the sides of his pack. I heard him hammering a piton into the ice to make a belay. Suddenly the banging stopped, and within a moment Fredrik was cascading down past me, dragging a few rocks with him. I heard a loud scream, and then he was gone.

I was petrified. Leaning on my ice ax, I could neither move nor comprehend what I'd just seen. Fredrik had fallen. It was exactly what everyone hopes will never happen.

Despite this horrible situation I stayed calm and thought about the next steps. I wanted to climb down to have a look whether I could see him anywhere. I was very much aware that I had to be extremely careful and couldn't make a single mistake. Continuing my climb was completely out of the question.

I descended for a bit and found one of Fredrik's skis. It was wedged in the snow; I guess he must have lost it during his fall. I couldn't find anything else.

I radioed Ralf. He didn't answer immediately, and I feared that he couldn't hear me.

"Ralf, Ralf. Please, do you copy?"

Finally he answered.

"Ralf," I told him, "Fredrik fell!"

Ralf tried to calm me down, but was so shocked himself that he was barely able to speak. I couldn't even explain how it had happened—I hadn't seen whether Fredrik had lost his footing in the snow, or whether a piece of rock had come loose when he was placing the piton.

I started to descend slowly. Ralf stayed in touch with me by radio to keep track of where I was and to encourage me. I couldn't really reply on the radio, but I could tell that he was very worried about me. He had informed the other climbers who were still on the shoulder, and Darek and Fabrizio came down to meet me. After a long rest in my tent on the shoulder, I descended to base camp. It's difficult to describe how I felt. I was simply functioning on autopilot.

In the meantime, Ralf had scanned the mountain with his binoculars and discovered a black dot to the left of Camp 3, which he thought might be Fredrik. He must have fallen about 1000 meters. The Russian climber, Juri Jermatschek, climbed down from their Camp 3 toward the left and tried to get as close to the body as possible. He didn't get all the way there as the avalanche danger was too high. Fredrik's father in Sweden decided that no further risks should be taken, and now Fredrik is resting at a spot with a view of his two favorite mountains: Chogolisa and Laila Peak.

Leaving K2 was painful. But how much more painful must Fredrik's death have been for his family and his girlfriend?

Between 2007 and 2010, I had reached K2's shoulder six times and had made it as far as 8300 meters four times. For a long time, I was not sure whether I would ever go back to that mountain and try for a seventh time. K2 and I had shared a lot of good but also a lot of sad memories. But despite the tragic events, I still felt positively drawn toward K2. It was so imposing and majestic.

The mountain stood there as it had always stood. We are the ones who move, climbing up its flanks to test our abilities. The reason why I still pursue high-altitude mountaineering, even after such tragic events, is it's my way of living a fulfilling life; it would be hard for me to live without it. On the other hand, I know I can minimize the risk by being as realistic as possible on my climbs. Not that I am overly confident and think that nothing could ever happen to me—quite the opposite. I believe that the risk is partly fate, which you can also face in everyday life whenever you happen to be at the wrong place at the wrong time.

After so many attempts, I was thrilled to stand on the summit of K2 at last; my final 8000-meter peak! (*Photo by Maxut Zhumayev*)

CHAPTER 16

FULFILLMENT

The base of the North Pillar is in the shade. A little farther up, indirect sunlight gently touches the slopes on the right side of the ridge. In a few weeks we should be pitching our tents just below the first steep section, which marks the beginning of the beautiful north ridge of K2. Effortlessly—if a bit clumsily—I fly along the mountain's snow-covered flanks. Through my 3D glasses I can see every detail of our ascent route. The rock walls on this 3000-meter-long ridge stand out in three dimensions.

What sounds like a dream became reality in June 2011. Stefan Dech, the director of the Remote Sensing Data Center of the German Aerospace Center, took Ralf and me on a virtual flight over K2. Nine months earlier he had been to one of my presentations. As he told me later, he could sense that I would go back to this mountain. In order to support me, he launched an elaborate project with the help of the latest satellite data, creating a three-dimensional map of K2. By using aerial pictures of the mountain taken from different angles, animation experts were able to model the data spatially. And so it happened that just before our departure on my fourth expedition to K2, we ended up in the Earth Observation Center in Oberpfaffenhofen near Munich, looking at our goal through the eyes of a satellite.

We were completely stunned by the result. Neither Ralf nor I had expected to lay our eyes on such detailed photographs of the North Pillar. The quality of the pictures was incredible, and they would be of great help once we were there. Some sections turned out to be a lot flatter than we had anticipated. Others were a lot steeper; and some which we had intended to climb turned out to be almost impossible, as they were too icy and avalanche-prone. These pictures enabled us to look for alternatives and identify possible sites for our bivouacs. We were especially interested in the upper part of the mountain, as we had hardly seen any pictures of it. After traversing the Japanese Couloir we would only have to negotiate the summit pyramid to reach the highest point. The summit pyramid was much less steep than we had thought, though it seemed a lot longer. Still, it looked like it wouldn't be too difficult to climb. With the animation laboratory's staff, we analyzed the cruxes; we could sense their enthusiasm for the project and their joy to be able to assist us. Armed with many excellent printouts and maps, we left the Earth Observation Center with the feeling that Stefan Dech and his team would be with us on our expedition to K2. Having seen these impressive pictures I was even more motivated: Getting a good look of the route had given me a better idea of what to expect.

I actually only decided at the beginning of 2011 to dare another attempt of K2. Up until then, I could not quite figure out whether or not I wanted to go back. After having climbed Carstensz Pyramid in the western central highlands of Papua province in Indonesia in autumn 2010 and spending my climbing vacations in Thailand at Christmas, my positive feeling for K2 returned and I knew that I wanted to give it another go. This time, though, I wanted to attempt it via its northern route from China. I was simply drawn to this mountain, but I couldn't possibly go back to the south side after what had happened the previous year.

For quite some time Ralf and I had been toying with the idea of going to the Chinese side. We were particularly excited about the approach march through the Shaksgam Valley. Kurt Diemberger, who had been there several times, told us about it and showed us some pictures—a spectacular and completely deserted landscape shaped by arid mountain slopes and the Shaksgam River, whose water level rises so high with the snowmelt that crossing the valley becomes impossible. We knew we wanted to go there one day even if only to trek and see the valley. Of course, we had also been tempted by the North Pillar of K2, but up to that point it had always seemed too steep and tough for us.

Given the technical difficulties of the route, this option also meant that Ralf and I would not be able to go in our team of two. Climbing alpine style would be out of the question. We would have to fix long sections of the route and would need to be with a bigger team to get our gear from base camp to Advanced Base Camp (ABC). Getting this team together turned out to be quite easy in the end. I had kept in regular and very close contact with Maxut Zhumayev and Vassiliy Pivtsov, the two Kazakh climbers I had met on Nanga Parbat in 2003, when they gave me the nickname, "Cinderella Caterpillar." We had also been on several expeditions on the south side of K2 at the same time, and we had gotten to know and appreciate each other very well over the years. It did not take a lot of effort to get them excited about an expedition to the North Pillar. We also managed to bring on board the Polish climber Darek Zaluski, whom we had met during our previous attempts of K2. Ralf's longtime friend and photographer from Argentina, Tommy Heinrich, who also had K2 experience, joined us as the sixth member of our team.

I was especially happy that Ralf was going to join me. When we left base camp after Fredrik's fatal accident in 2010, he said, "If you ever go back to K2, I will certainly not join you." At that time, I couldn't even imagine that I would ever go back to that mountain. So it meant even more to me that Ralf was keen to go to the Shaksgam Valley without me trying to push him.

The only way to get to base camp on the north side of K2 is with camel support. They are the only pack animals able to cross the torrential rivers. The camel herders charge a lot of money for the transport, and as the climbing permit in China is also a lot more expensive than in Pakistan, it turned out to be one of our most expensive expeditions ever. For this reason, it was a blessing when the American National Geographic Society offered to financially support our undertaking. After having meticulously examined our project, they agreed to fund us with their highest contribution ever. Even though it covered only a fraction of our costs, the boost to our budget was very welcome.

When we finally set off at the end of June I was full of anticipation and particularly excited about our trek with the camels. For Vassiliy and Maxut it was easy to get to Bishkek. They didn't even have to take a plane: From Almaty it was a three-hour bus ride to get to the Kyrgyz capital, and from there we took a car to Kashgar. Once in Kashgar the Kazakhs simply went to the supermarket to get their supplies for the next two months. Ralf and I, on the other hand, had spent a few weeks meticulously calculating how much food we would need for the approach march and our time on the mountain and sorting out what we could send by cargo in advance. This is how differently you can organize an expedition to an 8000-meter peak!

I almost didn't recognize Kashgar, the provincial capital; the mainly Uyghur population had risen to four million since I had passed through on my way to Mustagh Ata sixteen years earlier. From Kashgar we went overland to the starting point of our trek, the village of Illik, where all of us were invited to sleep in the mayor's living room. The next morning, the families of the village gathered in front of the house and laboriously started packing. Once all the loads were distributed, eight Kyrgyz camel herders got on their donkeys and led thirty-five camels carrying our gear. The two cooks, a translator, the National Geographic journalist Chip Brown, and the six of us followed them on foot. Curious, I watched these strange animals. I was fascinated by how elegantly and rhythmically they strode for hours on end without having to stop once.

After our seven-hour days, they truly deserved to shed their loads and walk around freely in the evenings. We had to choose our camps according to the availability of grass for the camels to eat and water to drink. On the third day we crossed the 4800-meter Aghil Pass. After a long descent, the beautiful valley Ralf and I had dreamed of for a long time suddenly opened up in front of us. On the right side, the Shaksgam Dolomites rose into the air; on the left, the scree of the steep, eroded slopes rolled down to the bottom of the valley, where a brownish river meandered through. We gazed at a rough, almost surreal landscape dipped in beautiful sunlight, with not another soul around. Apart from the sound of the river whose course we followed, there was complete and utter silence.

TOP: Camels made crossing the Kulquin River in the Shaksgam Valley en route to K2 possible. *(Photo by Ralf Dujmovits)* BOTTOM: Fixing rope in the storm on K2 at about 7000 meters *(Photo by Ralf Dujmovits)*

All of this peace and quiet fled when we embarked on our first river crossing. I had never sat on a camel before, and I have to admit that I was a little apprehensive, even though the procedure was actually quite easy: The camel squatted down, you sat on it, and then it got up again. The problem was that the hind legs went up first. Though I had known this would happen, the first time I tried it my camel rose so abruptly and unexpectedly that I nearly fell off. But then it moved very gracefully toward the riverbank. I was mesmerized by how safely it waded through the deep and raging water, quickly reaching the other side. Without the camels, we would not have stood a chance of crossing the rivers. At the wider sections it almost felt as if I was swimming with the camel. We depended on them; they always took us safely to the other side. But we were not the only ones making use of their amazing river-crossing skills. A few sheep and calves, which were going to graze near base camp during the summer, were tied onto the pack animals and taken to the other side. Despite my absolute fascination, I was relieved every time I felt solid ground beneath my feet again.

After five of the most beautiful and impressive days Ralf and I had ever experienced, we reached base camp at 3900 meters. It was nestled in an idyllic spot: We had clean water, lush greenery, and small hares hopping happily around; once we even saw a herd of wild donkeys. As expected, we were the only expedition on the mountain. On the day we arrived we got a glimpse of the upper 1000 meters of K2, which seemed alien and inaccessible from this side. We could not see the mountain from base camp, as we were still a long way away: It was about 9.7 kilometers to ABC at 4650 meters, and the same distance again to the start of the climb. Due to scree and the trail's steepness, it was too arduous for the camels to go on with us. The camel herders and their donkeys helped us get the first loads to our intermediate deposit camp, but left us shortly afterward.

After some tough price negotiations, the head herder said, "Next time we will give you a better price." We laughed out loud, as we were all hoping that there wouldn't be a next time!

From this point on we had to fend for ourselves. The only other person to join our group was our Uyghur cook, Abdul, who came to ABC with us and returned down to base camp every once in a while to get more supplies. In six weeks the herders would be back to pick us up, which meant that in the meantime we couldn't count on any help if something went wrong. We were aware that helicopter rescue operations were not allowed in China, and an overland rescue would be more or less impossible, due to the rising water level.

This was an exciting moment: Had we brought enough supplies? It had been hard to calculate how much food we would need for such a long period of time. We had 100 kilos of potatoes, which would be gone by the end of the expedition. At the beginning Abdul was surprised by how much we could eat when we came back from the mountain ravenously hungry. But he quickly got used to our appetites and prepared hundreds of the little traditional dumplings called "momos" whenever we returned to camp.

Time seemed to fly during the following days as we carried our climbing gear to ABC and then to a deposit camp at 5050 meters. Moving up and down between camps proved helpful for our acclimatization. Though our packs were heavy, I felt elated—a feeling that had accompanied me since the beginning of the expedition. I was confident about climbing the route, which had first been scaled by a Japanese team in 1982. I enjoyed its beautiful landscape and its solitude, and I was happy to be far away from the hustle and bustle on the south side of K2, and my sad memories.

On July 5, when we set up our first camp at 5300 meters about five minutes away from the bottom of the North Pillar, I set my eyes on the aesthetic line of the ridge and was awestruck. Even though we would have to climb at grade V up there, and none of us really knew what to expect over the next few weeks, my positive feeling never faded.

Once on the pillar, we found the terrain a lot steeper and more demanding than we had anticipated, which meant that we had to fix a lot of rope and set protection gear to secure the mixed sections adequately. As we climbed up and down the route repeatedly, we had to re-fix gear that had been damaged by falling rocks. We even thought it necessary to fix rope on sugary slopes that didn't exceed 40 degrees but were very avalanche-prone. We actually preferred climbing on the ridge. It seemed safer than the flanks, where some mountaineers had been caught before in slab avalanches. Heavy snowfall rapidly increased the avalanche risk, and huge amounts of new snow made load-carrying to the higher camps even more exhausting.

On July 14, Ralf and I spent the first night at Camp 2 at 6600 meters. Together with the others, we had already set up an intermediate camp at 5950 meters and a deposit camp on the rocky shoulder at 6250 meters. Starting from Camp 2, which was on the first flat ledge of the pillar, we no longer left the tents but carried them in our backpacks and pitched them at our next bivouac. On this day we had been climbing for fourteen and a half hours and were completely worn out. I had a hard time melting snow and getting some fluid down, but the evening sky compensated for all the hard work. We had seen many impressive sunsets before, but this one filled me with an extraordinary, deep joy. The surrounding mountaintops were glowing in the most magnificent evening light. After enduring a very strenuous day, it felt as if nature was emanating enormous power and energy at that moment. Among those mighty mountains, I felt small and insignificant. For a while, both of us just stood there, almost petrified, without saying a word. I was in awe and eternally grateful to be in that place.

After returning to ABC to spend a few rest days there, we headed out again. On July 22, Vassiliy and I reached Camp 3 at 7300 meters while Maxut, Ralf, and Darek deposited our ropes at about 7000 meters. As a bad weather forecast had thwarted our plans to reach Camp 4—the last camp before the summit—we descended to ABC the following day.

In the weeks during which we fixed the route and set up camps, I greatly appreciated the harmonious way our team worked together. Even though we were six climbers from six different countries—Vassiliy is a native Russian—we had no problems communicating. Each one of us was sensitive enough to step forward or back off when needed; each of us contributed to the expedition and showed consideration for the others. I wouldn't think twice about going on another expedition with every single member of that team again.

As the weather didn't improve, we decided to go down to base camp for three days to get some more oxygen and enjoy the lush green of the meadows and bushes—a welcome change after weeks of being surrounded by scree, snow, and rocks. Not even this period of bad weather diminished my enthusiasm. I remained motivated, feeling confident that this time everything would be all right.

When the weather improved at the beginning of August, we waited for another day for the snow to settle and for the steeper slopes to unload. Then we set off for a second attempt and reached a small rocky ledge at 7900 meters which was just big enough for our two tents. A blizzard kept us there for a whole day and another night. But when we opened the iced-up zipper of our tent the next morning, we could not believe our eyes: Snow-covered peaks rose above thick cloud cover that reflected the shadow of K2. The sky above was clear, though freezing cold—it was a view with a grandeur I had never experienced before. Captivated by this natural spectacle, we climbed for another 100 vertical meters, discovered a good site for a possible bivouac, and had a closer look at the Japanese Couloir. This is the point where the North Pillar of K2 becomes so difficult that the route veers to the left into the steep snow gully, which eventually leads to the summit pyramid.

After this trip to above 8000 meters, we tackled the 3000 vertical meters back to our camp, downclimbing, rappeling, and wading through deep snow. Then we continued to walk another 10 kilometers across the moraine, which is partly covered in boulders, all the way to our ABC. After a very exhausting week on the mountain we were in desperate need of a good rest.

We had initially planned to recover, eating and drinking a lot, and relaxing for a few days, before finally tackling the summit. But as so often happens, the weather was not on our side. It snowed for days on end, K2 was mostly hiding in the clouds, and the mood within our team became increasingly quiet and serious. One morning, we could not believe our eyes when we looked out of our small tent across to the kitchen: Our mess tent had completely collapsed under the weight of the heavy, wet snow, with only a few tent poles sticking into the air. On that day the mood in our team hit rock bottom. We even contemplated abandoning the expedition as, on top of it all, we had also exceeded our planned climbing period.

"You know that our expedition permit has expired, and so have our visas for China," Ralf emphasized.

"Nobody will check on us back here." I tried to calm him down. "Nobody will find us here; we'll sort it out later." I was not yet prepared to give up my hope of summiting.

We spent the whole day fixing our tent. In the evening, we sat together and tried hard to rebuild our confidence as much as we could. But the bad weather continued.

I used this downtime to prepare mentally for summit day. As I always do before a summit attempt, I withdrew to my tent, put on my headphones, and listened to relaxing music as I went through every little detail of the climb. It took me a whole afternoon to mentally ascend and descend the mountain. I imagined how I would wade through belly-deep snow; I envisioned the many steep sections on mixed ground; I felt my cold hands and the extreme exhaustion that we would have to endure over many hours and days. I tried to feel the cramped conditions in the tiny bivouac tent, the freezing cold up there, and the storm rattling on the tent walls. Envisioning a climb beforehand always helps me cope better with the difficult conditions on the actual climb and stay calm. Of course, when I do this I also think about the beautiful moments that give me strength: The colorful sunrises and sunsets, the breathtaking views, and the deeply moving starry nights. I see myself taking the final steps to the highest point. It's only when my mind wanders back to base camp and sees our cook that I open my eyes and feel ready to start my summit attempt.

After a long, trying period, Charly Gabl finally provided us with good news: August 21 would be the perfect summit day. In order to get there on time, though, we would have to leave ABC in bad weather. The six of us set out for the summit on Tuesday, August 16. It was still snowing, but Charly had forecast dry and stable weather for the end of the week. In view of the huge amounts of fresh snow, we spent August 17 at Camp 1. We wanted the avalanche-prone slopes on the way to Camp 2 to unload. Fortunately, we had a few hours of sunshine on this impromptu rest day. Massive avalanches came down on the surrounding steep slopes around us, which boosted our confidence.

In order to catch the good weather window for the summit day, we were very keen to reach our bivouac at 6600 meters the following day. Unfortunately, it started snowing again at midnight and it was still snowing when we left at 5:00 a.m. Breaking trail through the deep snow slowed us down significantly.

It was difficult to judge the avalanche danger, but it was certainly precarious, which was reason enough for Ralf to turn back after two hours. His gut feeling told him to go down. I appreciated that it was too big of a risk for him, and I also understood that he was probably less motivated than the rest of us, as he had already been to the summit of K2. I still considered the situation reasonable enough for me to carry on, though; I could tell that my gut feeling was right. Ralf and I had agreed beforehand to let the other one go in case such a situation occurred, as long as the other person was well and could safely descend alone. Nevertheless, I felt extremely tempted to convince him to carry on with us. Likewise, he was so worried—as he later told me—that he would have loved for me to go down with him. Letting each other go despite the strong bond between us was extremely hard in that situation.

The same afternoon, Tommy decided to turn back and join Ralf at ABC, leaving the remaining four of us to go on slowly digging our way through hip-deep snow up the gradient slope. At that point it was clear that we wouldn't make it to Camp 2 before dark, and so we decided to sleep at our deposit on the rocky shoulder instead. In wise foresight I had packed a very light bivouac tent for emergencies. The biggest challenge was for the four of us to somehow squeeze into this small two-man-tent. After a few attempts, we finally managed to huddle up to each other inside, and even melt enough snow for all of us to drink.

After a night that was anything but restful, we climbed in stormy conditions over ice and rock that was very steep in places to Camp 2, where we arrived at 3:30 p.m. I had left my radio up there and was happy to be able to contact Ralf again after one and a half days. He was very relieved to find out that we had arrived safely at 6600 meters. While we were talking, he received Charly's latest weather forecast and then his tension turned all at once into absolute euphoria: The weather situation had changed, and

August 22 had now become our perfect summit day. This was good news, putting us back on schedule. Charly also said that the jet stream would subside and we could look forward to a calm night.

This time, unfortunately, Charly was not right. Our tent rattled in the storm the whole night, depriving us of our much-needed sleep; and the following day showed no sign of improvement, either. Despite the hostile conditions, we packed our gear, put on our heavy packs, and started to break trail up the pillar. The strong wind was extremely tiring. At about 6900 meters, Vassiliy suddenly stopped and said to me, "Gerlinde, what is happening to your Charly? He has predicted better weather for days! Where on Earth is it?"

Somehow I felt responsible, as I was the one who knew Charly the best. I trusted his judgment, and I was convinced that he would be right in the end. After all, it does happen that the jet stream moves slowly and takes longer to subside. In some sections on the pillar the wind had blown off the fresh snow, which made our progress easier at times. Finally, at about 7:00 p.m., the wind abated completely.

I felt extremely relieved about the prospect of a quiet night at 7250 meters. Our food rations had dwindled significantly. Inside the tent, we put out the remaining provisions and diligently rationed what we were allowed to eat in order not to run out. Considering how little was left, there was no more room to maneuver.

The next day went very smoothly. Conditions on the mixed terrain were perfect, and we reached our designated bivouac spot at 8000 meters in the early afternoon. That left us with enough time to prepare for summit day. We sharpened our crampons and ice axes and spent hours melting snow. We had a marvelous view of the Kunlun Mountains and the Japanese Couloir. It was only another 600 vertical meters from there to the summit. We were all pretty confident that the following day would be the day for which we had been longing for such a long time.

Half-sitting, I spent the night next to Darek. Every one of us tried to relax in our own ways. I wanted to let go of my thoughts and be free of all worries, but one question kept creeping up: "Will tomorrow be the day when we will reach the summit of K2? Will we be allowed to step onto the top after six attempts and three expeditions on the south side?"

I was still unable to find an answer. I couldn't wait for 5:00 a.m.—the time when we planned to set off. We were standing in front of the tent, ready to go, when suddenly I had a flash of intuition: "Gerlinde, take the small emergency bivouac tent." I also packed a stove and a light titanium pot. Just to be on the safe side, Vassiliy and Darek took a gas cylinder each. Each of us also put 50 meters of rope into our packs. Now we were finally ready to go.

The route across to the couloir turned out to be very iffy, and we made slow progress. From where we were it was hard to identify the safest way to cross the steep slope. Several attempts to cross the gully failed as we sank up to our bellies into the snow. At this point, Ralf's retreat turned out to be a blessing in disguise, as he followed us through his binoculars. From ABC he could see a big crevasse running from the right side of the couloir to the rocky edge on the left. He told us to move directly underneath the crevasse, as it would protect us in case of an avalanche. We followed his advice and safely crossed the couloir. It would have been impossible for us to see the crevasse from where we were, as a few steep, icy sections lower down blocked the view. I'm not sure whether we would have dared to cross the couloir without Ralf's guidance. Feeling relieved, we carried on even though it was already pretty late in the day. We had to continuously dodge or withstand spindrift, which was very time-consuming. Soon it was obvious that we would be denied the summit again. With a heavy heart I radioed Ralf to tell him what was going on, but when I got through to him I didn't get a word in edgeways. Ralf was babbling on excitedly: "Gerlinde, great that you're getting in touch. I have a new weather forecast."

Could that be it? Would August 23 really be the perfect day? We had a second chance! We briefly discussed whether to go back to our tents, but then decided to bivouac at 8300 meters. On a 50-degree slope just below an ice wall we found a safe spot that was protected from the powder avalanches and started digging out a platform just big enough for our small tent. It took us about an hour and a half to set up our bivouac, which we would only use for a few hours as we intended to set off again at midnight. We were now in our down suits, making it even more cramped than the night we had spent on the rocky shoulder. But in those freezing temperatures, sleeping was out of the question, anyway. As the piercing cold crept through my body, I concentrated on every single body part to keep the feeling under control. We regularly sipped hot water and shared half a cup of tomato soup between the four of us. Apart from some dried fruit and muesli bars we had saved for summit day, this was the last of our food.

Even though the constricted space in the tent was almost impossible to bear, we treated each other with care and respect. I particularly felt sorry for Darek: At 6 foot 5 inches tall, he had to twist his body into a weird shape to fit in. As I had done so often, I reflected that people from the former Eastern Bloc were much better at suffering than we from the West.

We all had a common goal that we wanted to reach together—in fact, the goal was only possible to reach together. Even when I had to wiggle my stiff body out of the tent to relieve my bladder, nobody got annoyed. On the contrary, the others actually reminded me to clip into the ice screw for safety, as the slope dropped down steeply below the tent. I had envisioned this situation during my mental preparation and stuck to my resolution to drink as much as possible, even though taking my clothes off and putting them back on when I went to the toilet was a real drag.

And there I was, sitting in front of our tent at 8300 meters, staring into a clear night underneath a sky with more stars than I had ever seen before. My eyes wandered down to the glacier and up toward the stars, and I felt completely protected and secure. I sensed an overwhelming strength inside me, as well as the feeling that something, or someone, was looking after us. I wasn't afraid of the following day, which would determine whether or not we would reach the top.

When we left at 1:30 a.m., Darek decided to stay in the tent a little longer to use the space to stretch and warm up a bit. After the three of us had climbed for about 50 vertical meters we turned back. It was simply too cold, −18 degrees Fahrenheit inside the tent. We could no longer feel our fingers and toes and were running too much of a risk of getting frost-bite on our extremities. We went back to our tent and decided to wait until the morning, so that we would only have to climb in the shade for a short while.

We set out again at 7:30 a.m. longing for the first rays of the sun to warm up our bones. We kept to the outer left edge of the Japanese Couloir, but due to the deep snow we gained scarcely any ground. The gully was also full of snow, posing a substantial avalanche danger—another reason why we kept so close to the rocky edge. Vassiliy, Maxut, and I took turns at breaking trail. Darek lagged behind a bit; despite the bitter cold, he was still filming. The snow was hip-deep and covered by a hard crust. We had to change lead every ten to fifteen steps. First we shoveled the snow with our hands, then we put a knee on top of it and pressed the snow down far enough to step on it. Then we straightened the leg. Despite this laborious process we ended up in almost the same spot as before. We did this ten times in a row, left and right. It took ages, and we didn't make any real progress. Once we took three hours to climb 30 vertical meters in snow that reached up to our bellies.

We had been on the go without a rest for eight consecutive days, and the enormous strain had taken its toll on our bodies and minds. At one point even I started to doubt whether we could actually make it to the top—and, more importantly, back down again. I thought to myself, "Is it really possible that after almost ten weeks of complete exertion and deprivation, we have to turn back again, so close to our goal. Will we really be denied the summit of K2 again?"

I didn't say a thing, though. I looked first at Vassiliy and then at Maxut. We kept on working in silence. Everyone knew what the others were thinking. But we kept up our unspoken agreement: "We'll give it a go and won't give up."

Time flew until we finally reached the rocky terrain above the gully, where we could move a bit faster. The ridge came closer, and I felt so motivated by the prospect of maybe reaching the summit, after all, that I felt a huge boost of energy. When I stepped onto the broad summit ridge, I checked my watch: It was already 4:30 p.m. Vassiliy and I sat down and waited for Maxut and Darek. I switched on the radio to talk to Ralf, but I was unable to speak.

"Gerlinde, I can see you and I think you guys have a good chance to make it!" I could hear the excitement in his voice, and I could tell how anxious he was. "A lot of people are with you right now."

Looking up towards the summit ridge, I listened to Ralf. His words, and the thought of my friends and other like-minded people being with us in their thoughts at exactly that moment, gave me new impetus and motivated me to go on, endure, and draw new hope and faith. It may sound strange, but for the final 100 meters I almost felt as if I were being carried.

I only found out later that my website crashed that day because so many people were trying to log on. After Ralf had descended to ABC he had provided our office back home with regular updates, which were published on my home page. On August 23, the website saw seventeen million clicks.

The summit ridge was flatter and completely windswept. Only the edges of our boots broke through the snow. I thought about Stefan Dech and the time we had spent in the animation laboratory of the Earth Observation Center. It was thanks to him that I knew how much farther I would have to go to the summit. Would the satellite be taking photos at this very moment? Would it be possible for them to see us?

Vassiliy and I climbed together. We discussed whether we should wait for Maxut and Darek, who had fallen behind. Vassiliy told me to go ahead; he would wait for Maxut and step onto the summit with him. The two of them had climbed all of their 8000-meter peaks together and wanted to do the same on K2. Just as for me, it was the last peak on their list of the fourteen highest mountains in the world.

I consider it a gift from Vassiliy that I was allowed to step onto the summit by myself. The slope in front of me became increasingly flat. During my last steps to the top of K2 an incredible calm spread through my body. Those few minutes were among the most awe-inspiring moments in my life—and the most difficult to describe. "Coming home" is probably the most apt description. It really felt like coming home.

The sun was already low when I placed my foot on the highest point of K2 at 6:18 p.m. The mountains around me were bathed in a beautiful glow all the way to Nanga Parbat. It was completely calm. I dropped down to my knees and couldn't hold back my tears. "Thank you!" I said out loud. This "thank you" was directed to the universe, to creation, to Ralf, who lent us his tireless support, and to all the people who were keeping us in their thoughts.

Wanting to share the moment with Ralf, I called him on the radio. "Ralf, Ralf, I have arrived," was the only thing I could say before I broke out in tears again. At first, he couldn't speak either as he was crying too, but once we both recovered I described to him the incredible panorama of the Karakorum that was touching my soul. I was particularly taken by the view toward the northeast, where the setting sun projected the pyramid-shaped shadow of K2 against the Kunlun Mountains, which were gently touched by the fading daylight. The view straight down was also pretty overwhelming, with gigantic glaciers merging from all sides: the Baltoro and Godwin-Austen Glaciers; the glaciers from Broad Peak and Gasherbrum II; and last, but not least, the Shaksgam Glacier on the Chinese side.

Then I switched off the radio and just sat there. The quarter of an hour I spent alone on the summit of K2 happened on a different level of awareness—it felt further, higher, deeper. I became one with everything around me, with myself, and with the world. My sense of being part of nature and the universe was extremely strong; I can still feel it today when I meditate. It's one of my power sources.

Up there, I also remembered my friends who are no longer among us: It felt as if Cristina and Fredrik were with me. After Vassiliy arrived with Maxut, we talked about Fredrik. We looked down toward the Bottleneck, where Fredrik had fallen to his death the year before. I could really feel his presence. And then we just embraced each other; the moment didn't need any words. We had all tried to reach the top of K2 before and were denied the summit many times. Finally we had made it, despite the difficult terrain and the almost superhuman effort it had taken—or maybe because of it. For so long I had wanted this mountain to accept me, and this time it did.

I became aware that many people who meant well also wanted the same thing for us. Feeling incredibly grateful, we stood there: Four insignificant people on the summit of that magnificent mountain. We were the first climbers in three years to reach the summit of K2.

When Darek reached the summit at 7:00 p.m. we took a few photos before we quickly started our descent. The setting sun had already dipped the sky in dark orange, and darkness would soon fall upon us. I felt confident, as I was used to descending to base camp at night as well as finding my way down steep terrain by the small beam of my headlamp. This was certainly a huge advantage. When we left the summit, we consciously reminded each other to stay focused all the way and not to make the slightest mistake. To be on the safe side, we had changed the batteries of our headlamps. Slowly the horizon turned to a glowing red, and then the light was gone. On the way down, we waited for each other, checked each other's gear, and made sure that we were all okay. We were constantly watchful to see whether any of us at any time needed help. We knew that by no means would we be allowed to miss that moment.

While Maxut and Vassiliy spent the night in the small bivouac tent at 8300 meters, Darek and I carried on to Camp 4. I had planned to melt some snow before Darek arrived, but I was pretty confused when I only saw the Kazakhs' tent and not ours. The storm had blown it away and it was dangling over the abyss, still attached to a rope. Full of sleeping bags, mats, stove, and other equipment, the tent was too heavy for me to pull it up as a whole, and so I had to retrieve every piece individually—and of course I wasn't clipped into anything. It took me the better part of two hours to get everything out of the dangling tent, pitch it again, put every-thing back inside, and set up the stove.

Darek and I slept well that night, our third night at almost 8000 meters or higher. Fortunately, we had acclimatized well during our gear carries. When I woke up the next morning, I felt nice and warm. The sun hit the camp very early and there was nothing better and more pleasant than basking in its warmth. When I talked to Ralf on the radio I described our ascent route in every single detail. But he urged me to get down as quickly as possible, as the camel herders refused to wait any longer. If we didn't show up at base camp on the evening of the following day, they would leave without us. Ralf didn't want to imagine what it would be like to spend the winter there, at the foot of K2. . . .

That was the end of relaxing in the sunshine. There was no way we could let the camels leave without us. While Vassiliy and Maxut made their way down toward us, Darek and I packed up. The four of us descended as quickly as our exhausted and starved bodies would allow. Not only did we have to take down the ropes and protection gear—we simply dragged the ropes behind us—but getting through the deep snow and breaking through the crust lower down was a huge struggle, even on the descent.

We were completely shattered when we reached Camp 1 at 3:00 a.m., but we didn't get much time to recover. We had to set off again at 7:00 a.m. Ralf and Tommy were going to meet us at our deposit camp at 10:00 a.m. to take some of our load. When I crawled into my tent with my last strength, I found a plastic bag with two chocolate bars on my sleeping mat, along with a note Ralf had written to me on a piece of toilet paper, the only thing that must have been available for him to write on. My hands were shaking when I read it. His words were words of despair; he had obviously entertained the idea that the four of us might not come back. He had let me go, but in his heart of hearts he felt very differently. I was deeply touched by his concern about me. He wrote that he only had one wish, which was that we would come back somehow.

When he put his arms around me at the deposit camp a few hours later, the tension of the past weeks fell off me like a gigantic mountain range. Joy and incredible relief overwhelmed me. The feeling from the summit came back, and it slowly dawned on me: Now that we were all back down safe and sound, we really had made it to the summit of K2. I had felt deep joy and gratitude on the summits of all my other 8000-meter peaks, but on all levels this feeling had never been as strong as on K2. I had never been so moved as I was on the North Pillar of K2. For me, everything fit together wonderfully: The therapeutic isolation from our hectic world; the extremely challenging and difficult route; the perfect team; and, ultimately, the immensely moving mental experience.

By reaching the summit of K2, my life's dream had come true. Even before arriving home from my previous expeditions to 8000 meters, I used to feel the urge to immediately set off again in search of a new adventure, a new mountain. This was certainly not because of my alleged pursuit to become the first woman to reach the top of all fourteen 8000-meter peaks. This was never my motivation. I love the world of the high mountains because of their purity and clarity as well as the unique opportunity they offer to experience nature in its most unspoiled form. These mountains clearly present beauty as well as danger; they demand precise decisions, careful handling, and respect.

I no longer have to set off immediately in search of something new. My many years of going on expedition, especially to K2, have changed me on many levels. I'm no longer the same woman who joined an expedition and reached the false summit of Broad Peak seventeen years ago, nor am I the same woman who stood on the summit of Nanga Parbat in 2003. K2 was a touching spiritual experience, so deep and beautiful that it will stay in my heart for the rest of my life.

EXPEDITION TIMELINE

1994 June/July	Broad Peak, Pakistan (false summit, 8027m)
1995 May	Mustagh Ata, China (reached 6600m)
1997 October	Ama Dablam, Nepal (6814m, Southwest Ridge)
1998 April/May	Cho Oyu, Nepal/Tibet (8188m)
1999 June	Alpamayo, Peru (5947m, Ferrari Route)
2000 April/May	Shisha Pangma, Tibet (Central Summit, 8008m)
2001 April/May	Makalu, Nepal (8485m)
2002 April/May	Manaslu, Nepal (8163m)
2003 April/May	Kangchenjunga, Nepal (reached 7200m, North Ridge)
2003 June	Nanga Parbat, Pakistan (8125m, Diamir Route)
2004 April	Xifeng Peak, Tibet (7221m)
2004 May	Annapurna I, Nepal (8091m, French Route)
2004 July	Gasherbrum I, Pakistan (8080m, Japanese Couloir)
2005 May	Shisha Pangma, Tibet (8027m, South Face and traverse)
2005 May/June	Everest, Tibet (climb abandoned due to rescue)
2005 June/July	Gasherbrum II, Pakistan (8034m, Southwest Ridge)
2006 May	Kangchenjunga, Nepal (8586m, South Side)
2006 May	Lhotse, Nepal (climb abandoned at 8400m)
2007 April/May	Dhaulagiri I, Nepal (reached 7400m)
2007 June/July	Broad Peak, Pakistan (main summit, 8051m)
2007 July/August	K2, Pakistan (reached 8200m, Cesen Route)
2008 May	Dhaulagiri I, Nepal (8167m)
2009 May	Lhotse, Nepal (8516m)
2009 July/August	K2, Pakistan (reached 8300m, Cesen Route)
2010 April/May	Everest, Tibet (8848m, Odell Route, North and Northeast Ridge)
2010 July/August	K2, Pakistan (reached 8300m Cesen Route)
2011 June/July/August	K2, Pakistan/China (8611m, North Pillar)
2012 April/May	Nuptse, Nepal (7861m, East Ridge)
2013 April/May	Denali/Mount McKinley, Alaska (6168m, West Rib)

CO-AUTHOR'S NOTE

Gerlinde looks up. She studies the route, analyzing its steepness and the distances between the bolts. The top rope still dangles down; as she does so often, she is contemplating whether to lead the route or climb it on a top rope. As always, she pulls the rope down and starts to lead. Apart from her strength and elegance, I admire her strong will, which is also noticeable on a rock climb. Combined with her stamina, it must be this strong will that gets her up those 8000-meter peaks. When I lower her down, her eyes sparkle with happiness.

This book is based on more than seventy hours of interviews, recorded mainly on a mutual climbing holiday on the Greek island of Kalymnos. I would like to thank Gerlinde and Ralf as well as the publishing house for allowing me to combine work with fun. Gerlinde let me read her expedition diaries, and for their mutual expeditions I used Ralf's electronic diaries, which were extremely useful.

During long and intense conversations, Gerlinde told me about her life and expeditions. I will never forget one evening, though, when we reversed our roles of me being the interviewer, and Gerlinde being the storyteller. We had been climbing in the Iliada sector until late afternoon. Ralf was already on his way back to our holiday office, when Gerlinde and I decided on the spur of the moment to go up to the Jurassic Park sector to climb the Themelis route, which a few British climbers had recommended to us. When Gerlinde started the climb, the setting sun illuminated the route on the pillar between the two grottos. The rock was glowing in warm shades of orange, and despite the noise of the wind, I could hear Gerlinde squeal with happiness about the beautiful climb. By the time I had reached the top of the 30-meter climb, driven by Gerlinde's encouraging cheers, it was dark. Exhilarated about our achievement, we walked down through the thorny bushes, and when we got to the path I felt close enough to Gerlinde to start talking about myself.

Gerlinde hardly ever spoke about the hardships of her expeditions; she concentrated more on the beauty of the Himalaya and the joy she felt when she was up there. However, I never failed to notice how much the deaths of other high-altitude mountaineers affected her—no matter whether they died in accidents which happened right in front of her, or whether the deaths occurred within her family or circle of friends. Only when I wrote these horrifying stories down did I realize how much Gerlinde must focus on a goal not to lose direction. Controlling her emotions is probably yet another prerequisite for her success.

K2 was certainly an 8000-meter peak that posed a particular challenge for Gerlinde. On one hand, she repeatedly had to endure disappointing setbacks and shattering moments; on the other hand, she bore the unquenchable desire to reach the summit—a fascination that made her go back to the Karakorum again and again.

After she had finally reached her goal in 2011, we conducted several interviews, doing the first one on the phone just before she returned to Germany. The last interview took place in an Alpine hut in Graubünden in Switzerland in the summer of 2013. After we had roamed the forest collecting mushrooms for a few hours, we sat down at the kitchen table to clean our booty and talk about K2. I was sitting opposite a woman who had matured through her many experiences and now emanates a peace of mind. A woman who, despite having stood atop the highest mountains in the world, could get very excited about every single mushroom she found underneath a tussock. A woman who, despite having risked her life so many times, has remained incredibly humane, and who had told me so much about herself over the last six years that my connection with her goes far beyond a book project.

Thank you so much for your trust, Gerlinde.

St Gallen, Switzerland, in the autumn of 2013
Karin Steinbach Tarnutzer

TRANSLATOR'S NOTE

I met Gerlinde in the spring of 2007, when she came back from the ill-fated expedition to Dhaulagiri I, where she was caught in an avalanche and lost two friends. I remember sitting with her in the gardens of the Shangri La Hotel—at first in my capacity as the assistant of Miss Elizabeth Hawley, the Himalayan archivist, and later as a journalist—listening to her story. The German climbing magazine *Alpin* had asked me to write an article about it, and I remember feeling uncomfortable asking her for an interview, as she was still grieving over the loss of her friends. She agreed to talk to me even though she told me that she dreaded the media back home. Maybe she was willing to meet me because I was the assistant of Miss Hawley, who has kept the records of Himalayan expeditions in Nepal since 1963 and who Gerlinde respected very much; or maybe because we have had a good rapport since our very first meeting. When she told me about the incident, she said, "It feels so good to talk to someone about it." I was touched by her trust and felt incredibly drawn to this warm-hearted woman who, despite the horrific events she had just experienced, had not lost the sparkle in her eyes.

Over the years, we occasionally met in Kathmandu—either for the Himalayan Database or on social occasions. I later started translating her newsletter, and over the past two years we have become good friends. In 2012, when I was blogging for Russell Brice and Gerlinde was climbing Nuptse with David Göttler, we spent quite a bit of time together at Everest Base Camp. We talked about the translation of her book, and Gerlinde indicated that she would love for me to do it. I was very moved, but also realized that I would be just the right person for the job: I know Gerlinde and Ralf and the world she loves so much; and I have met many of the people she talks about in her book. And so it happened that Mountaineers Books chose me to put Gerlinde's words into English, which is a great honor for me.

With this translation, I have tried my best to keep Gerlinde's voice and not lose any of the heartfelt emotions she describes—be they for the mountains, for nature, or for the people around her. The book reflects why Gerlinde climbs mountains, which is certainly not to break records, but purely for the love and affection she has for them.

Describing the harsh environment of the Himalaya came almost naturally to me, as I did a large part of the translation at Everest Base Camp in the spring of 2013, while attempting Nuptse. Once at Camp 2, I was tucked up in my sleeping bag in a snowstorm, happily typing away with freezing fingers. It was indeed the perfect environment for a perfect mountaineering story.

I would like to thank Gerlinde for allowing me to tell her story to an English-speaking audience; Mountaineers Books for giving me the chance to do this work; my friends Ralph Schweizer and Monica Piris, for proofreading and improving my English in places; and my friends and family for bearing with me over the last six months and understanding that I was completely engrossed in this translation. I hope you will enjoy reading this book as much as I enjoyed translating it.

Kathmandu, September 2013
Billi Bierling

MOUNTAINEERS BOOKS is a leading publisher of mountaineering literature and guides—including our flagship title, *Mountaineering: The Freedom of the Hills*—as well as adventure narratives, natural history, and general outdoor recreation. Through our two imprints, Skipstone and Braided River, we also publish titles on sustainability and conservation. We are committed to supporting the environmental and educational goals of our organization by providing expert information on human-powered adventure, sustainable practices at home and on the trail, and preservation of wilderness.

The Mountaineers, founded in 1906, is a 501(c)(3) nonprofit outdoor activity and conservation organization whose mission is "to explore, study, preserve, and enjoy the natural beauty of the outdoors." One of the largest such organizations in the United States, it sponsors classes and year-round outdoor activities throughout the Pacific Northwest, including climbing, hiking, backcountry skiing, snowshoeing, bicycling, camping, paddling, and more. The Mountaineers also supports its mission through its publishing division, Mountaineers Books, and promotes environmental education and citizen engagement. For more information, visit The Mountaineers Program Center, 7700 Sand Point Way NE, Seattle, WA 98115-3996; phone 206-521-6001; www.mountaineers .org; or email info@mountaineers.org.

Our publications are made possible through the generosity of donors and through sales of more than 500 titles on outdoor recreation, sustainable lifestyle, and conservation. To donate, purchase books, or learn more, visit us online.

**MOUNTAINEERS
BOOKS**

1001 SW Klickitat Way, Suite 201
Seattle, WA 98134
800-553-4453
mbooks@mountaineersbooks.org
www.mountaineersbooks.org